HORIZONS IN THEORY AND AMERICAN CULTURE
Bainard Cowan and Joseph G. Kronick, Editors

Purloined Letters

PURLOINED LETTERS

ORIGINALITY AND REPETITION IN AMERICAN LITERATURE

Joseph N. Riddel

EDITED BY

Mark Bauerlein

LOUISIANA STATE UNIVERSITY PRESS
BATON ROUGE AND LONDON

Copyright © 1995 by Louisiana State University Press
All rights reserved
Manufactured in the United States of America
First printing
04 03 02 01 00 99 98 97 96 95   5 4 3 2 1

Designer: Amanda McDonald Key
Typeface: Sabon
Typesetter: Moran Printing, Inc.
Printer and binder: Thomson-Shore, Inc.

Library of Congress Cataloging-in-Publication data

Riddel, Joseph N.
    Purloined letters: originality and repetition in American
literature / Joseph N. Riddel ; edited by Mark Bauerlein.
      p.   cm.
    Includes bibliographical references (p.) and index.
    ISBN 0-8071-1872-9 (cl)
      1. American literature—History and criticism—Theory, etc.
    2. Emerson, Ralph Waldo, 1803–1882—Criticism and interpretation.
    3. Poe, Edgar Allan, 1809–1849—Criticism and interpretation.
    4. Influence (Literary, artistic, etc.) 5. Originality in
literature. 6. Repetition (Rhetoric) I. Title.
    PS25.R53 1995
    810.9—dc20   94–30483
                                               CIP

"Reading America" first appeared in *MLN*, XCIX (1984) under the title "Reading Ameri-can / American Readers." "The 'Crypt' of Edgar Poe" first appeared in *boundary 2*, VII (Spring, 1979), and "The Hermeneutical Self: Notes Toward an 'American' Practice" was first published in *boundary 2*, XII–XIII (Spring/Fall, 1984). The volume editor offers grate-ful acknowledgment to the editors of these publications. Excerpts from Gertrude Stein's *Four in America*, *The Making of Americans*, and *Lectures in America* used with permission of the Estate of Gertrude Stein. Excerpts from *Lectures in America* (copyright 1985) also used with permission of Random House, Inc. Grateful acknowledgment is also given to New Directions Publishing Corporation for permission to quote from the following copyrighted works of William Carlos Williams: *Imaginations*, copyright © 1970 by Florence H. Williams; *In the American Grain*, copyright 1925 by James Laughlin, copyright 1933 by William Carlos Williams; *Paterson*, copyright © 1946, 1948, 1949, 1958 by William Carlos Williams. Ex-cerpts from "From Poe to Valéry" from *To Criticize the Critic* by T. S. Eliot. Copyright © 1948 by Thomas Stearns Eliot and copyright renewed © 1976 by Valerie Eliot. Reprinted by permission of Farrar, Straus & Giroux, Inc., and Faber and Faber Ltd.

The paper in the book meets the guidelines for permanence and durability of the Committee on Production Guidelines for Book Longevity of the Council on Library Resources. ⊚

CONTENTS

Abbreviations

CW *The Collected Works of Ralph Waldo Emerson.* Cambridge, 1971–.
4 vols. to date.

> Vol. I: *"Nature," Addresses, and Lectures.* Edited by Robert
> E. Spiller and Alfred R. Ferguson.

> Vol. II: *Essays: First Series.* Edited by Alfred R. Ferguson, Jean
> Ferguson Carr, and Joseph Slater.

> Vol. III: *Essays: Second Series.* Edited by Alfred R. Ferguson,
> Jean Ferguson Carr, and Joseph Slater.

> Vol. IV: *Representative Men: Seven Lectures.* Edited by Walter E. Williams and Douglas Emory Wilson.

J *The Journals and Miscellaneous Notebooks of Ralph Waldo Emerson.*
Edited by William H. Gilman *et al.* Cambridge, Mass., 1960–82.
16 vols.

W *The Complete Works of Ralph Waldo Emerson.*
Edited by Edward Waldo Emerson. Boston 1903–1904.

Purloined Letters

INTRODUCTION

JOSEPH G. KRONICK AND MARK BAUERLEIN

In the course of writing *The Inverted Bell,* his exemplary theoretical study of American modernism, Joseph N. Riddel had begun to isolate what he considered the fundamental dilemma of the "American" writer. There, extrapolating his formula from William Carlos Williams' own eccentric "history" of American writing, Riddel posits, *"American* is synonymous with *beginner,* and a beginner is one who, if he is not to be condemned to repeat the past, is bound to reinterpret it and thus to create his own time. . . . He is committed, that is, to the paradoxical role of depriving himself of all his myths in his effort to discover a primary myth—an idea coincident with things, where his new beginning will not be repetition." To enact that "coincidence," to reinstate an "original relation to the universe," as Emerson says, so that *writing* will be neither a simple "repetition" nor derivation of the past becomes the peculiarly "American" problem. The problem is doubly complicated by the realization that not only must the myth itself be "primary," but the enactment of it must also be primary. If the reinstatement of an originary power is itself customary, then no genuine origination can follow. Hence the "American" problem is a problem of "beginnings" that must be begun over and over again, never in quite the same way. This is why, Riddel says, "it would be possible to write a 'history' of American poetics in terms of 'beginnings,' or better, in terms of the changing sense of beginning."[1]

From the mid-seventies until his untimely death, Riddel did just that, composed his expanding ruminations upon American beginnings, his "history" of American problematics of origination. In between organizing conferences, running a critical studies program at UCLA, reviewing countless manuscripts for presses, and producing a steady stream of student-scholars, Riddel launched a sequence of essays exploring his cardinal "American"

---

1. Joseph N. Riddel, *The Inverted Bell: Modernism and the Counterpoetics of William Carlos Williams* (1974; rpr. Baton Rouge, 1991), 44.

oppositions—creation vs. representation, poetry vs. criticism (or the "preface"), geography vs. "ego-graphy" (to borrow Stein's phrase). Many of those essays focused upon American modernism and postmodernism (Stein, H. D., Stevens, Pound, Olson, and so on), particularly upon the putative difference between the two. Other essays treated the question of origination philosophically in readings of poststructuralism and its discontents. Still another grouping carried the question of modernism—which is, to Riddel, a question of beginnings and repetitions—back into classic nineteenth-century American literature (Emerson, Poe, Hawthorne, Melville, William James, and so on).

This volume brings together the latter series of readings, half of which have never before been published. Readers of this book may at first be disoriented by Riddel's assertion that "American" literature is an oxymoron. They may even find his insistence that "America(n)" appear within quotation marks, particularly when coupled with such incompatible concepts as "literature," "poetry," "tradition"—but not "writing"—to be eccentric or inexplicable. But if we remember that "American" literature belongs to a conceptual order that correlates periodization with national boundaries, and that it is the order itself, not the historicity or nationalism, of "American" literature that Riddel wishes to interrogate, his quotation marks assume essential importance. Puritanism, federalism, transcendentalism, and modernism readily correspond to their European, particularly British, counterparts, above all with the Enlightenment and romanticism. But "American" (again, a concept, not a reality) is somehow uncanny or ambiguous. But despite its complexity, the linking of literary forms to historical consciousness has produced, despite variations, a fairly consistent, if contradictory, legacy for those texts we call "American." This legacy assumes a certain destiny, a transference and a correspondence, that sends the letter(s) from Europe to America and, in our post(modern)age, beyond. The system of what Jacques Derrida calls postal discourse presupposes a certain concept of Being that aligns the letter and nature, or so a more traditional Americanist/historicist would have it. But as Riddel's readings persistently reveal, the letter is always already overtaken by the relays and delays that divert it from its destination, that cast the "beyond" as an uncertain future.

For, indeed, it is a question of "American" letters—the tradition American writers receive and the transmission, the sendings, that situates "American" literature in the postal age. This belatedness or errancy that postpones any arrival of "American" letters cannot be reduced to a narrative of self-origination, with all the duplicity and blindness that such a dream entails, nor to a dialectic of revisionism, with the hope of a transumptive deliverance from the anxiety of influence. Finally, the belatedness of "American" literature cannot itself serve as the unreflective definition of a writing that has its origins elsewhere, say, in a European ancestry, that it can never overcome but only transcribe onto new soil.

"The scandal of 'American' thought"—yet another phrase that may disturb readers—lies as much in its "poetic," that is, unsystematic, character as in its "notoriously limited canon." The "scandal" is not merely the nonsystematic character of thought, nor even simply the tendency to regard this eccentric writing as a national literature. Rather, it is the transposition of a univocal history with its teleological order and hierarchical structure onto a writing that resists such onto-theologic conceptualizations. For Riddel, "American" texts tell a different story or stage a different scene, one of "destruction" (Williams' word) and "re-naming" (his word again). So, against the tendency of Americanist criticism to reproduce genealogies that anchor the dualisms of "American" thought in an "unequivocal history,"[2] Riddel proposes that "American" literature is already a "'critical' or self-critical literature . . . addressed to a certain degree to the problematics of clearing the ground for something 'new' which has not as yet appeared, and perhaps cannot ever appear as such, that is, *the new*" (21). Contrary to our histories, this "new" literature has not yet appeared. Indeed, it may be that the nonappearance or futural aspect denotes the self-critical and self-reflexive character of "American" literature, attributing to it a temporality that resembles irony more than it does cause and effect, origin and destiny, past and future.

To identify this history as ironic, therefore, is not to invoke a historical order that incorporates reversals and negation within a cause-effect relationship, a tropological genealogy that either begins with the recuperation of the word that is "one with the thing," as F. O. Matthiessen reads Emerson, or ends in the poet purged of "irony along with the nostalgia for origins in order to arrive at an American lineage of prophecy and power," as Harold Bloom reads Emerson (44). In his reading of American criticism, Riddel notes that most efforts to define American literature invariably have "re-

2. See pp. 42–43, below. Subsequent references to later pages in this book are given parenthetically in the text.

course only to the most ordinary notions of literary history" (43). These histories stage "American" literature as a repetition of Western tradition and as a radical overthrowing of that tradition. As in T. S. Eliot, self-reflection is elevated as the originary force in "American" literature. What result are not only narratives that place American literature inside and outside history, as the titles of our most familiar critical histories contradictorily suggest, and not only the conflict—both ideological and logical—between the individual and tradition, but also mytho-poetic readings of American history as the renewal in "thought" of the "unmediated 'vista'" that once opened upon a new world that, as for *Gatsby*'s sailors, receded from view.

For Riddel, "American" thought has always been inscribed within a tropic economy that both undoes myths of origins and frontiers and prevents any dialectical sublations of this thought's contradictions. The contradictory saying of "American" thought that Emerson named "self-reliance" begins as a rejection of "American" thought and literature. Hence Riddel's epigraph to the second chapter: "Pray don't read American. Thought is of no country" (*J*, XII, 40). The poetic "origin" of "American" thought consists, then, in the transgression of origins, a transgression that reinscribes "the poetic within pure thought"; that is, it begins in criticism (59). "American" literature is nothing, if not critical, which is to say that what "'American' literature represents, in the very figure of 'Man Thinking' or the 'central man,' is critical thought itself" (44). This origin is not, therefore, the self-reflexive and self-engendering origin that stages American literature within a nativist genealogy, a world enacted through style, as in Richard Poirier, nor in an Adamic self, as in R. W. B. Lewis. These efforts to construct an American tradition according to formalist categories or by thematics of discontinuity or the repudiation of the past have proven to be far more harmonious than past and recent debates over formalism and historicism would lead us to believe. The portrayal of American literary history within a tradition, even as the end of an exhausted history, and as an exception to tradition indicates the recuperative power of self-reflexive poetic language. For Riddel's Emerson, however, "the 'eternal procession' of cause and effect outruns the grammar that would close it or return it to the center" (50). In Emerson's tropological economy, there is no closure, "no circumference to us," around which a new circle, another eye/I cannot be drawn (*CW*, II, 181). This new circle, this quotation—"all minds quote"—is what Riddel calls the "American signature."

In "Purloined Letters," the first chapter, Riddel invokes Emerson and argues, as already noted, that "American" literature is "a 'critical' or self-critical literature, and addressed to a certain degree to the problematics of clearing the ground for something 'new' which has not yet appeared, and perhaps cannot ever appear as such, that is, *the new*." The desire for originality is, by now, an all-too-familiar theme in American literature, and Emerson's desire for an "original relation to the universe" is but one such example of an argument that may be called an "American" genre. This "original relation," this "first" union between America and the universe, is a repetition, but not a copy. In calling for "a poetry and philosophy of insight and not of tradition," Emerson calls for a new revelation, but this new revelation will come by a *critical* reading. The "original relation" will make use of the old words. Nature, after all, is a metaphor of the human mind, and it is only by reading it aright that any relation will appear. But this would only be a tropological displacement, since mind, too, is a metaphor insofar as it belongs to the circuit of language as described in *Nature*. The recuperation of the original or primary meaning of words will be a critical reading, a *"transgression,* the crossing of a line," to use Riddel's citation of Emerson's example of the natural origin of words. As transgressive, this original relation between mind and nature is already a trope, a crossing or chiasmus, that prevents any return to primary/primal speech. The sign, like the metaphors that we call "nature," is "originally" doubled, "folded upon itself originally," Riddel says, "so that any lines (or reflection) that project from it also recross it" (65). In other words, the path of thought leading from words to natural facts, which are themselves already metaphors, as Emerson states, does not turn back upon itself tying end to beginning but always exceeds the mark, projecting another circle or figure.

The "original" crossing or troping that stands as a first language or American idiom is already doubled so that it can never be first or original but a repetition with a difference, what Emerson calls "quotation." In "Quotation and Originality," an essay that has only recently been read with any scrutiny, Emerson suggests even "the originals are not original. There is imitation, model and suggestion, to the very archangels, if we knew their history" (W, VIII, 180). This lament for the limited store of original thought argues for the belatedness of American literature. Indeed, the name for this condition of belatedness is "America," a misappellation, having been taken from one who followed Columbus. We are, as Charles Olson wrote, the "last first people." Repetition is projective, but not proleptic. The "new yet unapproachable America" of which Emerson spoke would not be reached by an anticipatory promise nor would it be discovered in a hermeneutical act of self-finding. Riddel asks, Is it "to be 'America's' fate and history to be beyond History, that is, to fulfill the ultimate goal of Spirit, Freedom, working out the idea of Democracy" (27)? If America is beyond History, it is, as Olson said in his Mayan Letters, "the *second time*," which isn't history at all.[3] America, then, is a repetition, an echo, as Hegel would have it, of the Old World, at once fated to be the end of history and not yet historical.

Emerson's essay on quotation provides Riddel with what might be called a critical model, if he were not so suspicious and cautious of assuming that reading could be adapted to a model and remain reading, that is, both theoretical and critical. The reader's work, however, consists of quotation, not merely quotations that serve as citations and examples, but quotation conceived in a sense much like Emerson thought it, as creative reading. When confronted with a text as exuberant as Riddel's, we may think this "creative reading" is a "wild" one that fails to adhere to the authority of the text. Such a misplaced respect for the text—for canonicity, to be more precise—betrays a certain resistance to the most salient features of American literature. Riddel may be said to agree with Williams' reply to H. D.'s censure of his mocking tone in "March": "There is nothing sacred about literature, it is damned from one end to the other."[4] Following Williams, Riddel locates in "America"—more word than name—the literary questioning of nationality and canonicity. He writes, "A national literature, after all, is definable only after the moment in which its masterpieces are recognized, when the history of its literature has closed, or it is in decline" (120). If there were such a thing as "American" literature, it would need to resolve the contradictions of belatedness that Emerson acknowledged in "Quotation and Originality" and, as Harold Bloom has said, in all his works. But whereas Bloom resolved this dilemma by reading Emerson's essays as metaleptic utterances, Riddel's argument for the "horizonal" character of the American poem emphasizes "its critical, transformative, translative, disseminative effect" rather than "its affiliation with truth and meaning." Hence, "'America' is not discovered, but invented, and by 'reading'; that is, by translation" (100). As the very concept of literature is entangled in

3. Charles Olson, *Selected Writings*, ed. Robert Creeley (New York, 1966), 113.
4. William Carlos Williams, *Imaginations*, ed. Webster Schott (New York, 1970), 13.

canonicity, the writing that is "American" cannot be "literature," since it is already a translation without an ur-text or original. There has not yet been an "American" literature. It has always already been something to come, "a letter never yet written, a metaleptic letter" (21). The figure of metalepsis recurs throughout the book and is one worth pausing over. As the attribution of a present effect to a remote cause, the metaleptic letter is one that "invents" its origin as futural, not as a recuperable past. This invention, moreover, is a troping and en-troping, a metonymic substitution of one trope for another without center, limitation, or closure, only equivocal action and reaction, quotation.

If all "American" texts are written before the letter, they are "notes toward" or "prefaces," as Emerson's "The Poet" is a letter to Whitman, and Whitman's *Leaves of Grass* is a prolegomena to some future democratic poetry, and Adams' *Education* is an "avowedly incomplete" "working model for high education" for the coming century. American letters posit not only an audience to come, as in Whitman's "Crossing Brooklyn Ferry," but also a literature to come, as Emerson's "The Poet" anticipates an American poet and Hawthorne's prefaces seem to promise an art, perhaps the novel, that will replace his romances. In Wallace Stevens' words, the American writer cannot repeat "what was in the script"; he must invent it instead. This invention is self–reflexive, for if "American thought seems to originate in the need to think our own originality," it also must describe itself—inscribe itself—as the end or "beyond" of history in order to cover over the belatedness that haunts it (79). This gesture is marked by Williams' repeated call to "begin again" and Pound's "make it new." American literature, as Riddel says, "repeatedly begins again by staging its own origin as an exception, as a reflection on its unique difference; yet, even this very difference is a projection of what American thought and literature would be if they could but realize themselves" (79). America writes itself as both the end of history and beyond history; yet this script was written before America was "discovered," at least according to Williams' *In the American Grain,* and has been repeatedly echoed by such philosophers as Hegel, Heidegger, and Kojève. The "American" difference, its self-representation as exception, rests in its first needing to clear the ground before it can invent itself. Therefore, American letters are always, for Riddel, prefaces, and critical ones at that.

Riddel suggests that the allegorizing of American thought as self-engendering always begins in a critical doubling that undoes the ideal of the transparency of thought and its object, that is, the very identity that an American "origin" both depends upon and predicates. American literature, lacking "a proper parent," never conforms to the old genres. As "orphans of the west," American writers must invent their origins in an anticipatory gesture of fulfillment, a gesture that never resolves itself, since it originates in a critical doubling of the self-identical being of self-reflexive consciousness.

What Riddel calls the "doubling of the ideal of self-reflexiveness" might be termed a hyperreflexivity were it not that this doubling is an "intervention." "American" literature's need to invent the conditions of its own being has meant that the ground must be cleared to make way for the new in a gesture that is at once destructive and constructive. That is, "American" literature insists upon its originality in its transumptive—and critical—act of turning itself from an effect into a cause. Readings of American literature as original and self-reflexive/reflective must presuppose the unity or identity of subject and object. According to this reading, American literature invents itself in reflecting upon its own condition for being. Rather than reproduce European models and genres in a new setting, American writers must find a new expression to embody the conditions of a self-engendering nation. Williams, in an essay crucial to Riddel's reading of "American" literature, argues that unlike Hawthorne, whose mimetic narratives merely reproduce in a New England locale "what everyone else in France, England, Germany was doing *for his own milieu,*" Poe had to invent the "ORIGINAL TERMS," invent an American writing.[5] But American invention is perverse, a turning of quotation into a "new" beginning: "Every word we get must be broken off from the European mass. . . . I am a beginner. I am an American. A United Stateser." This from *The Great American Novel,* itself a plagiarism and parody of Joyce, where Williams also writes, "Everything that is done in Europe is a repetition of the past with a difference. Everything we do must be a repetition of the past with a difference."[6]

Defining itself in its difference from the Old World, American literature must mediate from its position of belatedness, that is, write from its post-position in history. This postal character of American letters is most fa-

5. William Carlos Williams, *In the American Grain* (1925; rpr. New York, 1956), 229, 226.

6. Williams, *Imaginations,* 175, 211.

mously evident in the first sentence in *Nature:* "Our age is retrospective." An acknowledgment of America's belatedness, *Nature* also presents itself as a prospective origin for a future literature, but it does so in the curious fashion of a quotation from an "orphic" poet, whose tales of fall and redemption are themselves instructions in origination as repetition. Emerson characterized American literature as a continuous process of quotation, self-quotation, a prospective art we learn from the horizon: "Men seem to have learned of the horizon the art of perpetual retreating and reference. . . . I quote another man's saying; unluckily that other withdraws himself in the same way, and quotes me" (*CW,* III, 28). As a consequence of belatedness, quotation, for Emerson, cannot be limited to the repetition of the past and certainly not elevated to a recuperation of it either. It is, rather, an agon, an effacement of an "original" that is nothing but another quotation or "circle," as he calls it in the essay with that figure as its title. Just as there is no fixture in nature, no circle around which another circle cannot be drawn, so there is no original or first text. Let one man speak, another will speak and draw a circle around him: "Then already is our first speaker, not man, but only a first speaker" (*CW,* II, 181). Quotation, then, is part of a strategical war of retreat and reference. This figure or trope is without reference; it has no fixed object and is not a thing-in-itself. It is what Emerson calls "literature," as Riddel rightly says: "Literature is the horizon, a 'point outside of our hodiernal circle through which a new one may be described'" (50). This new circle will be a quotation, and as such, the point outside the circle is inscribed within it. It is divided within itself or a present not present to itself.

Self-reflection necessarily presupposes a split or doubling that permits thought to regard itself as from a distance. Most theories of self-reflexivity thematize the text's capacity to turn upon itself and refer to itself in its totality. Meaning, therefore, rests upon the identity of the text's self-cognition with its referential function. In this critical "consciousness"—for theories of self-reflexivity presuppose a consciousness in the text—the text knows itself to be its proper content. A certain Kantianism underlies this notion of the "critical" insofar as it presupposes a formal unity in transcendental consciousness, that is, in the unity of consciousness that grounds the text's self-identity. Upon this self-reflexive totality rests the claim for the autonomy of literature. Historicists of various stripes object to this argument for its ignoring the material conditions of the production of the text, but in doing so, the historicist ignores the linguistic grounds of representation. Rather than address the problem of the epistemological reliability of language, the historicist avoids reading, the very activity that undoes the illusion, the mystification, that language is a vehicle for phenomenal cognition or a medium for conveying empirical knowledge. Self-reflexive theories of literature do not necessarily ignore content or representation but are concerned with the conditions that make content or representation subject to cognition, thereby transforming textual signification into thematic material.

Critiques of deconstructive criticism often turn upon its supposed ignoring of history and such culturally determinative conditions as gender and class. These critiques frequently reflect a confusion of thematic material and representation with the condition of textuality. They tend to ignore textuality altogether for the sake of less complicated issues of "subject matter." What distinguishes Riddel's reading of "American" literature is his questioning whether literature can be adequately described by such categories as thought, canonicity, nationality, or authority. In raising the question of originality in American literature, Riddel seeks not to refashion yet another historicism but to deconstruct the very concepts of originality and "American." Unfortunately, if read carelessly, Riddel may be taken to be arguing that "American" literature is but a repetition of Old World writing, a quotation. But this would presuppose that what precedes quotation is itself an "original" or that quotation is something extraneous to a text rather than a condition for any text's readability, for an absolutely original or unique work would be absolutely unreadable. Moreover, such a reading leaves untouched Riddel's challenge to historicist and formalist concepts of a national literature and language. Riddel does not simply reject the mythologies that have constituted "American" thought nor does he replace nonreflexivity with a self-reflexive thought that defines itself by dialectical negation. Riddel formulates an "origin" of "American" thought in what may be taken as a reflexive movement of effacement and projection. He defines critical thought as that which "mythologizes itself in the very gesture of disguising and effacing its 'poetic' nature and its mimetic link to all the old myths of origin it has rejected" (44).

This reflexive moment, however, does not resolve itself as a self-reflexive totality wherein "American" thought emerges from the self-canceling of the old myths it rejects. The condition for the effacement of its links to the old myths precludes any such resolution because "American" thought can only become "present" by virtue of an irreducible other that resists the ideality of a self-reflexive totality. Riddel locates this otherness in quotation. In distinguishing literature written in America from "American" literature, he writes that as a "'critical'" literature addressed to the problem of overcoming belatedness, "the 'American' literature I am talking about is no more than a vaguely apprehended 'other,' but a futural other, to which the actual literary texts we have and study are kinds of prefaces or notes toward; prologues written both after and before the fact, before the letter. They are necessarily written, then, in the old received letter, in the old words and forms, and are in a sense quotations of them. . . . But they are no less, by a kind of ironic reinscription, quotations of the future, of their own potential otherness" (21). Written in the old letter and before the letter, "American" literature is not simply belated nor is it metaleptic, reversing early and late, but is more radically futural by its very constitution as quotations.

Quotation not only invokes repetition but also signifies a certain excess, a "primary" doubling that effaces any pure origin or *archê*. Quotation possesses a self-reflexive structure, or what Riddel calls an "ironic reinscription," that does not produce a repetition that would be the coincidence of self and other or of speech and its object but reinscribes the self in a parabola, which does not close upon itself. We mark at this point the limiting condition of self-reflexivity and must either erase this limit or designate it not as a mirroring structure, wherein the subject returns to itself, but as a figure for the always already divided or doubled source. Quotation is what Derrida would call the invention of oneself as other.[7] Emerson gives a name to this originary invention: it is Genius, the reply to the "preponderance of the past." "The divine resides in the new. The divine never quotes, but is, and acts. The profound apprehension of the Present is Genius, which makes the Past forgotten" (*W*, VIII, 201). If the divine never quotes, the new or original can be recognized only in proleptic fashion, by a certain positing of the divine that "makes the Past forgotten." The purely original does not exist. In Nietzschean fashion, Emerson elevates the present moment by pleading for the necessity of an active forgetting. The Genius is he who forgets he is quoting. The original, by definition, cannot be repeated—it would be a self-quotation—but is the product of active forgetting, the loss of our "sempiternal memory." Therefore, there is no "first man," only a "first

7. Jacques Derrida, *Psyche: Inventions de l'autre* (Paris, 1987), 19.

speaker," a "crescive self" who quotes and in drawing a new circle retreats beyond the horizon. "It is the eye which makes the horizon," but this eye is also "the highest emblem in the cipher of the world," an empty sign, an "I" whose only force lies in its being quoted (*W*, III, 44; II, 179).

Riddel addresses these issues at length in "Purloined Letters" and "The Hermeneutical Self." Emerson's "crescive self" is a stolen letter that signifies only in its being displaced and therein denying "its representative function" (30). The scandal of "America" is that it "was an old name for a new world that had no history." As a repetition of old myths, America is quotation. Consequently, its history, as Riddel says, "would be its language," a language that is not a hermeneutical circle, one that resolves itself in understanding, but a simulacrum or quotation that displaces in repeating. Riddel calls this performative rather than hermeneutic.

As performances, American writers' claims of originality constitute a quotation, the opposite of their ostensible purpose. This reversal undoes the genealogical and metaphysical orders that try to give a home to America and ground American life in the closed structure of a unique self's past, present, and future. That is, these self-addressed self-inventions are subject to effects of repetition and displacement that break up hermeneutical circularity.

As the missives of orphans of the West, American letters are like those dead letters that make all American writers Bartlebys. If these letters always may not arrive at their destination, they survive their deaths as a testamentary document, a legacy that would beat death by virtue of its being a testament to come. Riddel locates in Derrida's "Envois" such a fable for American letters, a "scene of entropic crossing" that dislocates or decenters the itinerary that would translate something called "Western thought" to America. In this fable for criticism, "Poe is evoked as a metonymic figure for a certain notion of 'literature,' and one of the names, but not the only one, for 'America'" (19). Poe's position as the most American of writers and as most other would give him a certain claim to exemplarity were it not that exemplarity implies a canon against which he can be measured. Poe's singularity may be, as Riddel suggests, his greatest claim to be American were it not again a matter of elevating singularity or heterogeneity into a canonic principle. If Poe is a figure for "America," he is also a disfiguring of the linear narrative that goes under the name "American" literature. In "The 'Crypt' of Edgar Poe," Riddel reminds us that for Eliot, Poe was a "French creation" (121). For William Carlos Williams, Poe was misread by the French and was the most American of writers. That is, he possessed the "genius of *place*," which for Williams is a clearing of the ground, itself another name for writing. The poetic line traced out of Poe is more a chiasmus, a crossing, than a linear descent—indeed, the "House of Usher" denies the very possibility of linear descent.

So Poe is the metonym for a notion of literature that Riddel calls "criticism," a text produced by the entropic crossings, the passages from text to text, that make up the hybrid work called "America." It is what Emerson named "creative quotation." Criticism is Riddel's name for the "deformities"—his word—that constitute those texts called "American" literature. In describing American literature as criticism, he means more than to evoke Eliot's complaint over the "'penetration of poetic by the introspective critical activity'" (122). Criticism is what makes American literature an original repetition of not European literature exactly, but we can say of writing. It is not unusual to describe American literature as a self-invention, a literature that must define itself in its difference from the European tradition—*vide* the special attention given to romance as the paradigmatic American genre. But to characterize American literature as a self-invention is to presuppose more than the self-reflexive closure of the text that restricts the disseminative force of writing. Whereas self-reflexivity implies that the text constitutes itself in such a fashion that the external meaning coincides with the internal operation or performance of the text, Riddel's concept of broken reflection points toward an otherness, an outside, that makes the performative reflexion possible but prevents any closure. If American literature has always insisted upon its originality as the condition for its identity, it can do so only "by breaking the order of self-reflexive thought that defined the western family of nations" (32). The breaking of the European order comes by way of supplementation, an invention of the "American" genre by way of quotation. The American writer is an orphan, as Riddel says, because he exposes the genealogical order of history to the logic of the supplement—that is, repetition as invention. Therefore, he subtitles his first essay "Some Notes on the 'Future' of 'American' Literature" because American literature is "a poetic idea before the letter" (31)—that is, it comes into being not as anticipation of the future, but as a sending that crosses, a reflexive doubling that detours the letter from its destination. This is what makes American literature outstanding, or to use Emerson's figure, a circle that cannot close but must always be repeated.

Poe and Emerson serve as metonymic figures for American literature, a literature that does not designate a national boundary or historical identity. "American" literature is a critical name for writing, even criticism itself, or as Riddel would say, a critical "po-em," a name designating the double and contradictory tradition that never can quite distinguish the ratiocinative tintinnabulist from the transcendental idealist. In both Poe and Emerson, albeit in quite different ways, the American writer's belatedness is submitted to a logic of supplementation wherein writing is a critical performance at once adding itself to an existing tradition and, by a certain doubling of the letter of the text, incorporating but not sublating it. Riddel identifies this American genre as "critical performance," interpretative writing that, in its alterity, produces its priority, a priority that is always futural.

What, then, is this undoing of not only the logic of cause and effect so essential to traditional literary histories but also the precedence of the creative text over the critical? We must begin with Riddel's statement that "American thought seems to originate in the need to think our own originality. It begins by an act at once acknowledging and denying its own belatedness, by writing itself as the end and fulfillment of history and yet the 'beyond' of history, a powerful exception to what it represents. It repeatedly begins again by staging its own origin as an exception, as a reflection on its unique difference. Yet, even this very difference is a projection of what American thought and literature would be if they could but realize themselves" (79). Riddel would distinguish his concept of belatedness from Bloom's dialectical transumption wherein the belatedness of the poet is resolved in a process of incorporation and transformation. For Riddel, American literature is a belated future—it is always already still to come. The introduction of reflection into literary history—an oxymoron—signals what I am tempted to call the end of literary history, but perhaps we can say that it signals the beginning of a history that is, indeed, literary. Or rather, it signals a reading and writing that does the difficult work of thinking what is history. In a self-reflexive manner, the literary text acknowledges its belatedness but in thematizing belatedness can deny it. This ideal of self-reflexivity evokes the hermeneutic circle in which the grounds of existence are taken over in the act of interpretation so that the given, the always already, is assumed by the interpreter who then makes himself responsible for what was first the conditions into which he is thrown. The closure of the circle comes in the critical undoing of the givenness of the precursor or the condition of belatedness, and this critical dismantling of the given becomes the creative act. "American literature," Riddel argues, "inevitably stages itself as a clearing of the ground before the beginning of a new literature, but at the same time projects itself as a future free from the old ground. It must be critical before it can be creative. . . . That is why it seems never to conform to the old genres but to violate every law of genre; to be a hybrid, that is, something without a proper parent" (79). "American" literature remains the stepchild of its European antecedents. Idealists, such as Bloom, would define American literature by its exceptionalism, its dialectical self-engendering. For Riddel, however, self-reflexive coherence, along with self-engendering, is an illusion, a function of the aporia that marks the work, the po-em, as criticism, which always has a performative force. As a critical performance, the work has a double modality; it repeats what it comes after and displaces what it comes before. This question of an American genre is a question of quotation and originality. In its alterity, the critical performance produces what it quotes—otherwise. The reflexive grounds of writing displace the hierarchical and logical orders of history and fashion the work as other to the same reflexive effect that makes it possible. In other words, reflexivity remains a critical component of the work, but totalization and closure are dismissed not simply as an idealization of literature but as a fundamental misconception of writing. And American writing, determined by its difference from European thought, repeats, after a fashion, a family romance of descent and dissent from the parents, only to produce a kind of hybrid offspring that tropes/quotes the laws and genres of literary tradition.

We leave it for Riddel to explore the hybrid texts of Poe's hoaxes and *Eureka*, of Emerson's quotations and essays, Hawthorne's imitative ruins in *The Marble Faun*, Adams' entropic theory of history in the *Education*, as well as works by William James, Peirce, Stein, and Williams. Here we would like to return to Poe, as Riddel's metonymic figure for a certain notion of literature. Riddel finds in Poe two contradictory traditions as mapped out by Eliot and Williams. Nevertheless, both plot a certain chiasmatic crossing that has Poe return from France, in Eliot's version, or turn away from France, in Williams', to invent American modernism. This belated translation of Poe from France to America, from critic to origin, describes the very pathway of American writing as the beyond and the after, a text of original quotation that becomes, by virtue of its transformative effects, at once a copy and a writing against the grain.

15

This is why Riddel may be said to find himself always already inscribed in Poe, encrypted, we might say, in the riddles and cryptograms Poe leaves for us to decipher, to unriddle. But if, Poe tells us, the cryptograph, when recognized as a cryptograph (and Riddel examines the great efforts Poe took to disguise his own works), can always be deciphered, it cannot be done by following any rule. It is only "in regard to the general structure of language," Poe writes in anticipation of Saussure, that a cryptograph is decipherable.[8] The proper name, however, is another thing altogether because it does not belong to language as system, but its erasure within a system makes writing possible, above all when it is so improper as to be a riddle, a word and not a name. The riddle of the proper name is one of essential difference, "a marriage riddle," as Williams puts it in *Paterson*, but also a song of death:

> Indifferent, the indifference of a certain death
> or incident upon certain death
> propounds a riddle (in the Joyceian mode —
> or otherwise[9]

The inscription of the proper name sends us back to a thematics of writing that has come to us from France and carries a name, "Derrida," and a word, *deconstruction*, which are not necessarily synonymous. And if Riddel is correct in arguing that American literature has always been modern, then we can say we have always been French. As Williams said, "We are moderns—madmen at Paris." For if we can say Poe founded French modernism, and the French misreading of Poe returned a certain modernism to America, then we might say Riddel's work has brought a certain deconstruction to America and sent it back to France. After all, Derrida has said "America *is* deconstruction."[10] The chiasmatic crossing of deconstruction and America in what Derrida calls an "allegorico-metonymic figure" may well be the riddle of the po-em, the intersection of the divided inheritance of the two key figures in this book. Riddel is no more nor less the child of deconstruction than Baudelaire is the child of Poe. It is a matter of difference, "a marriage riddle," a marriage that has Riddel and America returning deconstruction to France. We can only conclude, as Williams does in his section on the Puritans in *In the American Grain*, "Unriddle these things."

8. Edgar Allan Poe, "A Few Words on Secret Writings," in *Essays and Reviews*, ed. G. R. Thompson (New York, 1984), 1283, 1291.

9. William Carlos Williams, *Paterson* (New York, 1963), 105 .

10. Jacques Derrida, *Memoires for Paul de Man* (New York, 1986), 18.

1

PURLOINED LETTERS

SOME NOTES ON THE "FUTURE" OF "AMERICAN" LITERATURE

Representative American verse will be that which will appear new to the French
. . . prose the same.
　　　　　—William Carlos Williams, *The Great American Novel*

Let me indulge the American habit of quotation.
　　　　　—Ezra Pound, as quoted by Williams, in the Prologue to *Kora in Hell*

I

There is a "scene" recalled in one of the autobiographical "Envois" of
Jacques Derrida's *The Post Card* that might remind us of the displacement
"literature" effects within contemporary discourse, and the performative
role that Poe in particular, but also American literature in general, and even
the place and name "America," are made to play in that discourse.[1] It is a scene
and story of place and displacement, an allegory, as it were, of history, discourse, criticism, and of a certain problematics of accounting—of reading
and writing the dead. The card, dated June 20, 1978, is an address, in one
or more of its senses, of an "I" to a "you" and recounts the "return" to
Zurich of the sender who has been met at the airport by someone named
"Hillis," an otherwise anonymous friend who transports the writer to a
nearby cemetery where the two pass some time walking about in conversation, happening upon Joyce's tomb and speaking, to quote the card, "I

---

1. Jacques Derrida, *The Post Card: From Socrates to Freud and Beyond,* trans. Alan
Bass (Chicago, 1987), 148–52. Jacques Lacan's famous Seminar on "The Purloined Letter"
first appeared in *Ecrits* (Paris, 1966); a partial translation appeared in *Yale French Studies,*
XLVIII (1973), 39–72. "The Purveyor of Truth,"Derrida's reading of the Seminar and "The
Purloined Letter," is one of the sections of *The Post Card.*

believe, about Poe and Yale, all that" (148). They also happen upon the tomb of one Egon Zoller, inventor of the "telescripter," but fail to discover the resting place of Szondi, the European Romantic scholar.

Two critics at large, we suspect, and doing what critics do, conversing with the dead and trying to direct messages to the living. Or is it that simple? Who reads whom? and who sends and who directs or redirects the message? and what is direction? what is destination? and where is the beginning and end of the circuit? Certainly not the cemetery, nor the crypt; and not the grotesque "phallus of modernity," as the sender calls Zoller's funerary monument, a proper sign for someone who has invented so current a writing/reading machine as the "telescripter." And then we recognize that all the signs are and have been, in one way or another, not only signs of signs but signs of transmissive systems, and of the interfaces of systems. But within this circuit, the sender of the card, or at least the translator, is only a part of the circuit, in which the two walkers also are movers and on the move. The writer of "Envois," for example, cannot or does not determine whether Zoller's monument signifies the inventor or his invention, or is only another of several deformed signposts within this grotesque scene of crossings, signs which are at once indicators of the place, its ritual inscription of the desire for continuity and communication with the dead, the past, memory. What crosses here is not simply a certain "catastropics" of modernity, signified by the ideals and necessary distortions of telecommunications, but a kind of provocation or instigation of writing. There are certain common, if radically different, elements in the cryptic system, where signs come from all discourses and cross one another chiasmatically, producing what the writer of the card calls "deformatics." For the cemetery is only one of several scenes of communication or crossing in the text, and like airports or telephones or postal systems, a place where messages pass through, from past to present, present to past, person to person, text to text. The cemetery is a scene of writing, a crossing point of texts in which signs from apparently different genres are in-mixed with randomness, noise. It is a scene of entropic crossing or, one might say, of criticism, since criticism is not made up of its own discrete signs but of those it takes from other texts, and so on. Do we receive a certain message here, that the self-exiles Poe and Joyce, those inventors of modernism, might like the critics just be, have been, strangely decentered middle men, chips in an information loop that never quite closes? Much like the place Zurich and its funerary monuments, very much like Baltimore or even New Haven on the most ordinary evening? And what is the difference between creation and invention, and invention and intervention, in the posture, position, or postal code of modernity?

Throughout the "Envois," Poe is evoked as a metonymic figure for a certain notion of "literature," and one of the names, but not the only one, for "America," and even in a more specific sense, the United States. The latter two are not exactly the same, though each denotes a kind of otherness of what might be called European or, more generally, Western thought. America seems to be, on the one hand, an excess or beyond of Europe, and the culture that Heidegger had indicated could be blamed for the technological catastrophe that had befallen German thought. Recall that curious postcard, and the note to it, which details the gratuitous phone call from the States from one Martini Heidegger, as the muddled name seemed to suggest, a call refused by Derrida on the grounds it was a joke—a message, in one way or the other, that made the "States" either an echo or an uncanny place where distortion would play itself out. On the other hand, "America" has provided the texts of Poe, which have resisted all psychoanalytic appropriation, especially Jacques Lacan's efforts to employ Poe's story as a literary model for the analytic methodology. Throughout *The Post Card,* this question of the relation of "literature" to philosophy, or the example/model to the general method or science, is at stake, and Lacan's borrowing of Poe is only the latest case of a French thought that has returned to itself through America. In any case, as if to resist Freud's conclusion to section five of *Civilization and Its Discontents,* that he did not "wish to give the impression of wanting . . . to employ American methods," Derrida enters what he seems to consider the already deformed dialogue between psychoanalysis (or philosophy) and literature, from the margin of an "America" and a kind of "literature" that is neither philosophy nor literature.[2] It is Poe, his texts, his crypt, that at once resist and motivate the analytical performance, reading and writing, because they will not themselves be read, mastered, by the methodology they seem to exemplify. For as Derrida says, what kind of science or reflexive clarity is obtained when the literary example provides a clearer scene of analysis, of reading itself, than the science that has to deform it or misread it into a perfect case of method, a method that is complete and total in mastering what it reads, its own example.

2. Sigmund Freud, *Civilization and Its Discontents,* trans. and ed. James Strachey (New York, 1961), 63.

The inscription of Poe into *The Post Card,* as a kind of thematic intervention into the very ideal of thematics, a theme that is at various times variously repeated as "a letter can always . . . never arrive at its destination," has indeed had a "complex fate" (to use Henry James's term for the American, and especially the American writer). The theme can only exemplify an athematics, an anathemia anathema to the technocrats of analysis or methodology. For the theme has to do with the fracturing, deflection, and feedback of a theme, the undoing of its itinerary or destiny. It becomes a gesture in the effort of writing, or rewriting, what Derrida will call in another context, borrowing from yet another chapter of psychoanalysis, a "theory of errata," of Abraham's *anasemia,* the paleonymic tracking of concepts through different degrees, if not kinds, of discourse.[3] For while the debate between Derrida and Lacan stands in the larger text as a never-ending, because never properly begun, dialogue between literature and philosophy, and, more narrowly, as a debate over the "question of method" (one might say, European methods), the reception of the message in "America," in its earliest form as "the Purveyor of Truth," seemed to isolate it as a parochial if sophisticated argument between two kinds of (poststructural) literary criticism, hermeneutics and deconstruction, with the proper reading of a Poe story as the proof of the methodological efficiency and hegemony. The "American" dissemination of the letter had already suspended the negative necessity of Derrida's axiomatics, and had produced a quite different dialogue over the body of "literature" and, one might say, over the writing of "America."

I do not, however, want to concern myself at this point, if at all, with either the Lacan-Derrida intervention or the question of reading a single and singular writer, Poe. I would prefer not to speak of interpretation or method, as such, but rather of the place or position "America" has been made to play in the narrative of literary history and literary theory, a place and part, strangely enough, that it has just as often as not written for and of itself. One might call it, quoting Eliot, the "play and place of criticism," but this would be to quote perversely, or in the Emersonian sense of quoting originally, performatively; for I would have to argue that "American"

---

3. Nicolas Abraham's definition of *anasemia* is contained in "The Shell and the Kernal," *Diacritics,* IX (1979), 16–31. See also Derrida's introduction to the article, "Me-Psychoanalysis: An Introduction to 'The Shell and the Kernal' by Nicolas Abraham," in the same issue of *Diacritics,* 4–15.

literature, as distinct from literature written in America or the United States, is as Emerson said a "critical" or self-critical literature, and addressed to a certain degree to the problematics of clearing the ground for something "new" which has not as yet appeared, and perhaps cannot ever appear as such, that is, *the new*. Perhaps this is to say that the "American" literature I am talking about is no more than a vaguely apprehended "other," but a futural other, to which the actual literary texts we have and study are kinds of prefaces or notes toward; prologues written both after and before the fact, before the letter. They are necessarily written, then, in the old received letter, in the old words and forms, and are in a sense quotations of them. But they are no less, by a kind of ironic reinscription, quotations of the future, of their own potential otherness. The "America" letter, which so much American writing is condemned to describe by anticipation, is a letter never yet written, a metaleptic letter.

I will begin, then, with still another face of Edgar Poe from the one precipitated into current "French thought." In the penultimate but clearly summary chapter of his *In the American Grain,* entitled simply "Edgar Allan Poe," Williams metonymically reinscribes into the American canon a writer who in his view has not only been systematically excluded or repressed, but exiled in the body of his own texts to Europe, particularly France, where he has been recuperated or made to exemplify the return of the repressed.[4] Poe shares the end of Williams' book with a very different figure, Abraham Lincoln, though both are significantly in Williams' view emancipators, that is, historical performers who have by a kind of resistance yet capitulation to the very thing that victimized them—democracy, "America"—inaugurated a "perverse flowering" or new beginning for American letters. If Lincoln's death marks the end of a period, and the end of Williams' book (the very last word is *period,* followed by the mark period), Poe has already, before Lincoln, written the paradox of endings into the teleology of literary and national histories. Poe's work inscribes the nonidentity of democratic man, and redoubles it. Excluded from the canon even before it had been enacted and legislated, and forced to play the exile from all successive canonical reformations and periodizations, Poe had always returned, not to signify the perversity of the enterprise, the effort toward a national identity, but to reveal that such an impulse lay in every attempt to define the "new" in relation to an alien "tradition" or European past that precluded

4. William Carlos Williams, *In the American Grain* (1925; rpr. New York, 1956).

originality. Poe is Williams' name for the perversity that refutes Eliot, and for a strange and perverse reason. Eliot's attack on the provincialism of American letters, and his own expatriate posture, only denied American nationalism in terms of the greater nationalism of the West, of Europe and tradition. For Eliot, America was the wilted flower of European institutions, and Poe would eventually for him become the name of its adolescent madness who anticipated, before Valéry, the modernist dilemma, "self-consciousness": "the extreme awareness of and concern for language . . . [Eliot writes of the crisis faced by both Poe and Valéry] is something which must ultimately break down, owing to an increasing strain against which the human mind and nerves will rebel."[5]

Williams' attack on Eliot, despite its indirectness, comes in the form of a quotation, or perverse quotation. *In the American Grain* appears to be, and has been read as, one of those curious American documents—itself an imitation or close quotation of D. H. Lawrence's *Studies in Classic American Literature* (1923)—that call for a national literature that would be itself unique, new, primordial yet complete and closed, like an epic or a narrative history. Of course, a unique national literature is a postulate in the form of an oxymoron, something that seems to be obscured by the way we write literary history in terms of national languages and then periodic categories, mixing the two comparatively, as if we were not composing hybrids, and as if we could avoid the theoretical question of the mixture and the hybrid: that the concept of the hybrid is modern, the concept of the graft, and that it is not quite a concept at all. The hybrid belongs to the age of relativity and entropy, for the hybrid cannot be representative, nor symbolic; the hybrid bears no evidence of its origin. It has no genealogy, and evidences no father. It is cultivated, and constructed, and will never know itself in its child. It bears within itself no memory, no traits of the precursor. It could not suffer the "anxiety of influence," but only a certain anxiety of the future, of its destined anonymity and non-identity or displacement. Its future is not its child, but the new that signs its death.

But what about Williams, and Poe? Poe, says Williams, is "American" in that what he does, however it seems to repeat the "gestures" of a classical literature, is a "gesture" or "movement, first and last to clear the GROUND" for a new literature.[6] The French, therefore, could never have

5. T. S. Eliot, *To Criticize the Critic* (New York, 1965), 42.
6. Williams, *In the American Grain,* 216, Williams' emphasis.

understood Poe's "originality," Williams argues, because whatever they think of in terms of originality must be, like Eliot's, presumed to derive from a nascent and nostalgic Western tradition, which celebrates originality either by lamentations of its belatedness or efforts toward slavish imitation, that is, discipline. Decadence is thus one of the modes of this French notion of belated originality, as is a return to, or nostalgia for, the primitive. In an earlier section of the book, Williams recalls a conversation with the French writer Valéry Larbaud in Paris, during one of the American's visits with some of his expatriate artist friends (105–20). Larbaud, like other of the avant-garde writers of the Continent, was an admirer of Americans, but tended to identify them most by their industry and moral conservatism, and found Puritans like Cotton Mather exemplary. But the Puritans, Williams had responded, and Mather foremost among them, were the furthest thing from the "American." It was the Puritans who were responsible for importing the customs, institutions, and languages of the Old World into the new and reducing those forms to slavish and empty or ascetic repetition, imposing their own repressive temperament upon the pagan potentiality of an "America" most clearly embodied by the Indian. Thus we Americans, Williams continued, "recognize no ground our own" (109), meaning by *ground* something like a national identity rooted in a place, a *genius loci*. America has no origins or roots except what have been inherited or appropriated from Europe, and so it has been the American's responsibility, in order to be American, to clear the false ground, or separate him- or herself from what one might call the European grammar. This act of clearing, of detaching the self, and thus of "destroying" (Williams' word, repeated throughout his prose and poetry) the inherited or imposed structures of the Old World, has depended on a certain kind of performance, a certain kind of thinking against the grain that will be the American signature.

Poe is for Williams the name of that act, moreso even than Whitman, though in their difference the two dramatize the common dilemma of the American: the task of inventing, one might say, the democratic poem, the atom of a "simple separate person" in the form of an epic embodiment of national identity. It would require this new language and form, a reflexive atomization of the old languages, the paleonymic names, the received tradition. But even so, it would still have to be written in those words. Before there could be the "American" poem, there would have to be an antithetical writing, a methodical undoing of received methods. This is the way Williams describes Poe's achievement, against the way he has been appropriated in Europe, by first Baudelaire and Mallarmé, and later Valéry and Williams' avant-garde contemporaries (remember that this rejection of the French Poe preceded by some time Marie Bonaparte's psycho-biography and Lacan's Seminar, not to say some of the more recent retrospections upon American originality by Deleuze and others):

> Lowell, Bryant, etc., concerned poetry with literature. Poe concerned it with the soul; hence their differing conceptions of the use of language. With Poe, words were not hung by usage with associations, the pleasing wraiths of former masteries, this is the sentimental trap-door to beginnings. With Poe words were figures; an old language truly, but one from which he carried over only the most elemental qualities to his new purpose; which was to find a way to tell his soul. Sometimes he used words so playfully his sentences seem to fly away from sense, the destructive! with the conserving abandon, foreshadowed, of a Gertrude Stein. The particles of language must be clear as sand. (221)

In short, an "American" literature would demand a theory and a critical method before it could be written: an originating theory, but in a certain sense atheoretical, since "literature," that is, the literature of the West, is an institutionalized method and model, a tradition, slavishly followed by popular American writers. Paradoxically, however, those who would write or invent a "new world writing" were compelled not simply to clear away the old, but to theorize the future poem, to write a preface before the letter. For example, writing in 1872, Whitman is still calling for the poet of the modern, the poet of the future, long after the beginning of his unfinished poem, which itself is a kind of assertion of the poem's becoming. By this time *Leaves of Grass* was largely being expanded by revisions, rewriting, and reinscriptions—that is, by self-quotation. And just as Whitman had repeated Emerson's "call" for a new poetry, Williams must repeat Whitman's and Poe's, and in a kind of writing that fits no generic definition except that it marks its distortion of all generic laws, often by a kind of mimickry or parody. That is, he writes in hybrid. In his epigraph to *In the American Grain,* Williams repeats what he claims for Poe, and what he does for Poe in the chapter that reclaims him from the French: "In these studies I have sought to re-name the things seen, now lost in chaos of borrowed titles, many of them inappropriate, under which the true character lies hid. In letters, in journals, reports of happenings I have recognized new contours suggested by old words so that new names were constituted. ... [I]t has been my wish to draw from every source one thing, the strange phosphorus of the life, nameless under an old misappellation"(v).

Thus like Poe, the American writer will proceed by a double strategy of imitation and distortion, of generic rigor and abandon, and his or her work will appear at the same time conative and performative, representational and parodic. If Poe was Emerson's "jingle man," he was Williams' most authentic and serious writer, pursuing the "ground" within the geological strata of language: "He has a habit, borrowed perhaps from algebra, of balancing his sentences in the middle, or of reversing them in the later clauses, a sense of play, as with objects, or numerals which he *has* in the original, dissociated, that is, from other literary habit" (221–22). Poe is a kind of adolescent, but as Williams noted, the place of all new thought was adolescence, and "America" was one of the names of that "place." America was the adolescence of history, or its preconscience as it were. Poe writes against the entombment of the letter in the book. He literally steals away the letter, by parody, citation, doubling, quotation, even blatant plagiarism, so that we see the "performance" of "eccentric genius." He produces, Williams concludes, the "HISTORY of the locality he springs from" (223), rather than representing that history, and that "HISTORY" *is* his language, not what his language stands for, refers to, or apparently names. Language, his new language, is his "soul." Dissociating words or names from ideas, he precipitates them into a new field of associations, a field defined by "play" and not speculation. His soul is not an "essence" but a text, his corpus; he produces the "interiority" of the crypt, which is "America" for Williams. The history of Poe's language is the history of the future or, one might say, quotations of the "future." We see this today, Williams seems to imply, when we experience Poe's words' return from the continent with, as Emerson said of those who seemed to quote him, "a certain alienated majesty." But may we not also say that his miscarried letters, in the habitat of still different discourses, induced the atheoretical theory he could not write?

II

I do not suggest, with Harold Bloom, that the defining characteristic of American literature is a visionary or prophetic voice, a definition that Bloom, by the way, employs to exclude Poe and Williams, among others, from the canon. Neither do I think it definable by certain forms of nativism, that it is a "homemade world," in Hugh Kenner's sense of an architectural bricolage, to be judged good or bad according to whether the writers followed the models sent back from Europe by our expatriates who had, as Pound countenanced in Canto VII, wiped the dust off the funerary monuments of the West.[7] That judgment, too, forced exclusions, so that one might include Williams but not his Poe. Nor am I going to argue that the one American obsession is proleptic, or spatially the desire for a "world elsewhere"; it is "projective," maybe, in the way formulated by Charles Olson, but not proleptic, not an attempt to answer an anticipated question about its lack or failure. There is, as Bloom argued, always the haunting problem of belatedness, and hence of originality. If I had a word, or a name, for the problem, it would probably be the word, not the name, *American* itself, which as Henry James's Prince Amerigo pointed out, was a misappellation, or literally a misplaced metonymy, not a name given to what Columbus thought he had discovered, India—for that, too, would have been a misnomer—but a name taken from one of his, that is, the Prince's, ancestors, who followed long after Columbus to become the "god-father" or "name-father."

Indeed, the word *America* or *American* is the cryptic figure upon which the American writer seemed transfixed—but not paralyzed. It is, one might say, his or her *logos,* but it is also a prompt for performing, a word not simply reversed in itself but simply an odd coupling of before and after, an old name that contains the destiny of destroying itself, becoming anonymous. Hegel situates the name as problem nicely in his Introduction to *The Philosophy of History:*

America is therefore the land of the future, where, in the ages that lie before us, the burden of the World's History shall reveal itself—perhaps in a contest between North and South America. It is a land of desire for all those who are weary of the historical lumber-room of old Europe. Napoleon is reported to have said: "*Cette vieille Europe m'ennuie.*" It is for America to abandon the ground on which hitherto the History of the World has developed itself. What *has* taken place in the New World up to the present time is only an echo of the Old World—the expression of a for-

---

7. See, for example, Harold Bloom, *Agon: Towards a Theory of Revisionism* (Oxford, 1982), and Bloom, *A Map of Misreading* (Oxford, 1975), and Bloom, *Wallace Stevens: The Poems of Our Climate* (Ithaca, 1977). See also Hugh Kenner, *A Homemade World: The American Modernist Writers* (New York, 1975).

eign Life; and as a Land of the Future, it has no interest for us here, for, as regards *History* our concern must be with what has been and is.[8]

"America" here and now, Hegel indicates, is nothing more than a sublation of the ruins of the past, and even dialectical inevitability can only project its destiny as self-overcoming, an abandonment of *the* "ground" in its desire for some new ground. Is it to be "America's" fate and history to be beyond History, that is, to fulfill the ultimate goal of Spirit, Freedom, by working out the idea of Democracy? If so, Hegel quickly abandons concern with that future to focus on what is present, and in so doing abandons that "future" America for the present one, which embodies a contradiction within itself. Present America is the "echo" of the Old World and foreign Life, at once a new kind of State and the place where the State may be abolished in the abolition of classes. To depart from Hegel and take up de Tocqueville, we would note that the incompatibility of individual freedom and equality inscribes another contradiction: the appearance of the "simple self" brings with it the threat of total anonymity, in which every writer is his own poem, beginning and end, atomistically reflecting every other. The future of the idea of democracy follows in its way the law of entropy, *non-difference*, rather than the dialectic. We know Melville's meditation on this, and later Henry Adams'.

One might say, then, that the fate of American letters is inscribed in the words *America* and *future*, the fate of having to meditate on what Melville called in *Pierre* "Young America in Literature," and it involved, as in that novel, the question of the father and of origins, genealogy and narrative. The American novel, as Pierre concluded, might be nothing more than a repetition of the generic form of the novel, a "federated" work, he said, federated in the "fancy."[9] This novel would not so much advance beyond or displace the Old World genre as efface its echoes; out of the "lumber-room of old Europe" it would confect, by a kind of federal imagination, the future "novel"; and it would do this by a kind of quotation or appropriation of the old that at the same time would reveal and remark the artifice of the theft, as, for example, the section on "Chronometricals and Horologicals" mimes the invention of transcendentalism out of the illusory systematics of German thought.

Although it is unlikely that Emerson had read Hegel's speculation on

8. G. W. F. Hegel, *The Philosophy of History*, trans. John Sibree (New York, 1956), 86–87.

9. Herman Melville, *Pierre; or, The Ambiguities*, ed. Harrison Hayford, Hershel Parker, and G. Thomas Tanselle (Evanston, 1971).

America by the time he wrote *Nature* (1836), he seems almost to be quoting it in the opening sentences: "Our age is retrospective. It builds the sepulchres of the fathers. It writes biographies, histories, and criticism" (*CW*, I, 7). In fact, he is echoing an American contemporary, Daniel Webster, among others, in issuing the first of his several pronunciamentos against our reliance upon Europe. But by the end of the essay, having urged us to "enjoy an original relation to the universe" rather than groping "among the dry bones of the past" (7), he proposes, in the section interestingly entitled "Prospects," the kind of strategy involved in producing that relation: "The American who has been confined, in his own country, to the sight of buildings designed after foreign models, is surprised on entering York Minster or St. Peter's at Rome, by the feeling that these structures are imitations also,—faint copies of an invisible archetype" (40). He then proceeds to exemplify the possibility of recuperating the arche from them by quoting George Herbert's poem on Man. The quotation has the strange effect of transporting Herbert's Renaissance configuration, making Man or the self a sign of some future perfection, beyond his ideal da Vincian configuration of symmetry and proportion. Man becomes a figure not of perfection, but of his own potential for self-overcoming. For Emerson, if "man is a god in ruins" (42), a kind of synecdoche of perfection, the part has the potentiality to displace, to supplement, to go beyond the whole. For man has an imagination, the capacity to make fables and thus figurations or allegories of a law beyond the law of reason: "Every spirit builds itself a house, and beyond its house a world, and beyond its world a heaven" (44), he exhorts, but this heaven of perfection will be more and other than the old heaven. It will be an excess of perfection.

To put it in terms of another, later essay, Man quotes, and by quoting supplements the individual self. In a sense, s/he quotes the future. But s/he cannot think closure, because in quoting or reading, s/he is only a prospective, sign of the circle and not its symbol, pointing *beyond* self; Emerson's Oversoul, like Nietzsche's *Übermensch* after it, is not some transcendental possibility, but already that which signifies in its limit, its sign, the circle, that it is an excess of itself, a circle outside a circle, and thus a quotation. "There is no outside, no inclosing wall, no circumference to us," Emerson writes in the essay "Circles" (*CW*, II, 181). This can, of course, be read in the familiar terms of transcendentalism as a somewhat unsystematic philosophy, as a conative assertion, an affirmation of the metaphysical circle or dialectical overcoming. But the question of the individual self, the freedom yet imperfection of the "god in ruins," remains. For if we simply build in imitation, and add nothing to the whole, we are governed by what we quote, by the origin we are beyond and which is behind but also ahead and beyond. Thus poetic or originary language, Emerson notes, functions in a quite different manner from repeating the old words, as does the poet or genius, he who "realizes and adds" (*CW*, III, 7). The poet, and language itself—Orphic song, says Emerson—performs not only speculatively but prospectively. In a "large sense," as he writes in "Quotation and Originality," "there is no pure originality. All minds quote. Old and new make up the warp and woof of every moment" (*W*, VIII, 178). If there is no originality, there is also no pure priority, except God. All else is quotation; only God does not quote, but He who has enacted or created the world and man cannot repeat that act, with self-quotation or becoming original. Thus man, who is condemned to quotation, does realize the possibility of inventive originality, self-quotation. The self is a quotation, doubled within itself. Every new philosophy finds itself returning to "some prophetic maxim of the oldest learning," and there is "something mortifying in this perpetual circle" (179). In literature, in fact, even "the originals are not original." The "first book tyrannizes over the second" (180). But this tyranny of precursors may turn out to have a curious motivational effect, or to re-motivate, as it were —not, however, in a manner that can be mapped by some kind of genealogical law or fable like the "family romance," nor even a map of misreading.

If every quotation tropes, it does not necessarily vanquish or displace, or even sublate. In fact, while "Quotation confesses inferiority," it acts like a "parasite" (188), incorporating the better or higher in a different, unpredictable, lower site, a kind of parable of origins. It renders, translates, transposes. And no law of genre can rule quotation; it is fabulous, fabulating, carrying things away into their other. What Emerson named in another essay as "creative reading" (*CW*, I, 58) here becomes "creative quotation," an act of the Genius who embodies and reinscribes, "realizes" but also "adds." The Genius as parasite is both letter (language) and letter carrier (*facteur*). Among Emerson's several names for Genius are the Poet, Will and Inventor. These are the ones who repay their debt to the Past by projecting it beyond, by composing it in a present cipher that anticipates, or foreshadows, the "future." And that future, too, will be some parasite of the present sign, another factor. Genius purveys; it is both letter and letter carrier.

But if Genius is not only the quoter but the quoted, the quotation, it is a force or factor that cannot authorize or determine the destiny or effects of its own act. Emerson's Genius is not consciousness or intention. And his individual self is not simply an atomistic psyche. The poet is in one sense a representative Man and a "simple separate person," and the cause of his "anxiety" is not exclusively the weight of the Past and precursors (the influence of the Genius that is quoted, that is in the quotation). His "anxiety" is not a problem of identity, the responsibility to act for the present or represent the past, but to overcome him or her (it)self. As with the Whitmanesque division of the poetic self between the "I" and the "en-masse," the representative man acts not only *for* the latter but *beyond*. Otherwise the "I" is abolished in its representative function. To read this problematic out of Emerson and Whitman, and even Poe, who is engaged in trying to isolate some pure interiority within the suffocating nonidentity of the democratic mass (see "The Man of the Crowd," and Benjamin's reading of it against Baudelaire's *flaneur*[10]), one would have to return, probably, to Hegel's ruminations on sign and self and consider them in terms of certain poststructural readings. For now I can only assert that the American writer seems to have invented him- or herself out of some need to fulfill philosophy's and theology's prophecy, that some redemptive hero must come to give the nation identity and direction so that he or she could in turn derive identity from it. And the problem, the obstacle, quickly became, as a kind of "shock of recognition," the problem of every modernism, of how to "turn the tradition" (Pound). And thus how to write a history, produce history, rather than represent, describe, or narrate one, since indeed "America" was an old name for a new world that had no history. As with Williams' Poe, America's history would be its language. How, then, can the American writer avoid being an echo, as Hegel said, since Man is always already a quotation? And Emerson's answer, at the end of the essay "Circles," is a way of breaking out of the circle, the hermeneutical circle, to exceed, to go beyond, the circle by an uncanny repetition, by drawing yet "a new circle." One must, he says, circle the circle, quote it, circumscribe and thus transcribe its law—outlaw its law:

10. Walter Benjamin, *Reflections: Essays, Aphorisms, Autobiographical Writings*, ed. Peter Demetz, trans. Edmund Jephcott (New York, 1986), 155–56.

The way of life is wonderful; it is by abandonment. The great moments of history are the facilities of performance through the strength of ideas, as the works of genius and religion. "A man," said Oliver Cromwell, "never rises so high as when he knows not whither he is going." Dreams and drunkenness, the use of opium and alcohol are the semblance and counterfeit of this oracular genius, and hence their dangerous attraction for men. For the like reason they ask the aid of wild passions, as in gaming and war, to ape in some manner these flames and generosities of the heart. (*CW*, II, 190)

Quoting Cromwell, Emerson transposes and projects Protestant "enthusiasm" into a new site. Lurking within his appropriation is a new sense of "passion" or fire, a new sense of energy, which would shake the nineteenth century and radically revise the notion of "history" and of the "self." But art only circles, echoes, parodies this "enthusiasm"—it is a semblance of performance. Yet simulacrum (like quotation) is not the repetition of the same. It is originary, differentiating.

In calling for a national literature and language that must, in Bloom's term, "transume" rather than repeat the Past, Emerson in effect dismantles the very illusion of nationalism and its hermetic borders and celebrates the extraordinary contradictions of any notion of "originality." Yet if literature, like dreams and drunkenness, only "apes" the ecstatic Orphic or Dionysian performance, the originary act of Genius is always already a quotation, and quotation is originality. We can see in Emerson's formulation the eccentric argument for the eccentric Genius, that he performs originally by a deft repetition or miming that produces abandonment. Literature, or better, Poetry, or better, the imaginative performance mimes our desire to be original and thus produces the idea of originality. Originality is an invention, a poetic idea before the letter, already inscribed in the letter. The paragraph just quoted, the conclusion to "Circles," begins thus: "The one thing we seek with insatiable desire is to forget ourselves, to be surprised out of our propriety, to lose our sempiternal memory and to do something without knowing how or why; in short to draw a new circle" (*CW*, II, 190). This kind of willed abandonment, like Nietzschean forgetting, must also risk the other sense of abandonment, leaving the performer like Poe's figures, or many of the characters of American writing, orphaned. Emerson thus writes an allegory of American writing as strategic translation, as the abandonment of the old grammar in the ecstasy of performance. But this orphaning of the "American" self is only a prelude to another myth of origins or origin, the allegory of auto-insemination.

31

Autobiography, in a sense, would be *the* "American" genre, for it is already a hybrid, a parody of the genealogical paradigm and thus an intervention into the poetics of the "family romance" that had long shadowed the "American" writer, defining him as orphan and outcast but yet defined by the father-language of old Europe. The "American" writer could only account for him- or herself as origin, as native, by breaking the order of self-reflexive thought that defined the Western family of nations. If Emerson's poet not only "realizes" but "adds," he doubles the old laws of genre and exposes the genealogical fable to supplementation. The "American" writer, then, would not so much need to verify his nation's and her own identity as to create that identity; and that meant putting in question all the old formulations of identity and nation. By quotation he will reinvent "America" as a future grammar, the grammar of the future anterior—it will have been.

III

Two American writers of very different "enthusiasm" were forced to confront, at more or less the same time, the early decades of the century, the crisis of turn that Emerson, without knowing it exactly, had been forced to theorize. I refer to Henry Adams and Gertrude Stein, both of whom, as much as Henry James, were forced to meditate upon the exiled American's "complex fate" and thus on the overdeterminations of the name "American" itself. For economy, I will concentrate on *The Education of Henry Adams*, limiting myself to one particular reading scene and the issues of that scene which erupt in the later part of the text.[11] I refer to the moment of Adams', or his persona's, account of his arrival in Rome, sometime after his graduation from Harvard and after having made what he defines as one of the two choices remaining for every young American nurtured in the Eastern states: the American must either head west and "grow up with the country" or turn back toward Europe, even though a third choice might be the most prudent. He could remain in the East for which his education had fitted him—fitted him, that is, for comfort and compromise but not for the twentieth century, since American education in the mid-nineteenth century had left one, he now recognized, "in essentials like religion, ethics, philosophy, in history, literature, art; in the concepts of all science, except per-

11. Henry Adams, *The Education of Henry Adams* (New York, 1931).

haps mathematics . . . nearer the year 1 than the year 1900" (53). The East remained an *echo* of Europe, or so it seemed.

Adams has arrived at Rome after a long itinerary that has carried him from Harvard to England, Germany, and Italy—bypassing France—and through repeated failures to find on the Continent that liberal education that will allow him to read the future out of the Past. English politics and German philosophy numb and dumbfound him, and France, which he circumvented because of its "wicked spirit," a combination of energy and decadence or aestheticism, was too dangerous a lure. The thought of Kant and Hegel, with which he had grappled in Germany, remained a foreign and unreadable language despite the attractiveness of its systematic unfolding, its genealogical fable. But no sooner had he reached Rome than he found himself gazing over a scene that has already been organized and explained by his formative education. The Rome he confronts is a Rome already filtered through the historian's received ideas of historical unfolding, for example, the narrative history of Gibbon, and thus a Rome whose pagan force (that is what he has been seeking) lies repressed beneath understanding, that is, subdued to the teleological laws of a historicism that explains its inevitable displacement by the great Western institutions. Language and law have in every instance failed him because in every instance they have been too successful. A self-defined child of the eighteenth century, Adams finds himself at the end of a spiritual quest that has taken him to a crux and crossroads of history's false origin, in a Rome already annexed to the metaphysical story of the West. But despite Gibbon's narrative of rise and fall, Rome remains an unreadable text for Adams: or perhaps because of Gibbon's text, because of its power to make sense of contradictory signs. Rome cannot be seen except within Gibbon's metaphysical paradigm, which turns out to be the paradigm of tragedy, a classical law of genre. Yet Adams senses that Gibbon's frame, his national *Bildungsroman,* does not finally account for everything inscribed upon Rome, which appears to offer a subtext within the mastering text of the historian. Reflecting from a present standpoint, the turn of the century, Adams now can write what the young Adams only sensed, that a new paradigm would be needed. As he puts it later in the text, acknowledging the scientific, political, and social revolutions that convulsed the century, he has seen beneath Gibbon something that defied narrative and genealogical explanation: "Physics gone stark mad in metaphysics" (382), as he was to describe such ruptures as those produced by thermodynamics and the discovery of radium. The young Adams had sensed what the older would have to live through. What the new physics had done to metaphysics, we might translate, is what the modern historian, philosopher, literateur, will have to do to the old disciplines.

In apparently remounting the stream of time, Adams finds himself in Rome discovering that he has done nothing more than make a philological journey, an etymological retreat. But that has served to clear some ground. He has been transported by a series of texts and paradigms back to a point that is not so much a ground as a chiasmus. And he can only conclude that Gibbon's writing of Rome was based on a habit of reading—the paradigm of "sequence" or genealogical succession—that provides a certain satisfaction as long as the methods or assumptions remain unquestioned. But reflection, or, more precisely, autobiographical reflexivity, can no longer work within the paradigm. Like dialectic, in apparently confirming and closing the paradigm, the circle, self-reflection turned upon itself, and not simply as Marx had seized upon Hegel to effect a reversal. (Indeed, the chapter in which Adams insists that Harvard must come to terms with Marx is one of the most amusing and prophetic in the text.) Adams probably could not have reflected, as Jean Hyppolite was to do later, that Hegel's philosophy, or at least the *Phenomenology,* was perhaps a *Bildungsroman;*[12] but he had, in his autobiography, signified the end of that genre, and perhaps also the end of autobiography, a hybrid and not a genre at all. America was an open-ended autobiography, a history without closure. Adams' conclusion, then, that America and the American can no longer find either identity or destiny in the Past, leaves him with a question about the very concepts of identity and destiny themselves, and thus with the question of America's future. Perhaps "America" is only the overdetermined name of the "future" that has to be thought in a new way. In any event, Adams discovers, as he says, that his thought can only go as far as Hegel's, and not beyond, and his first trip to Europe concludes at the limits of humanist understanding, of dialectical thinking.

The second part of his life and of his story, and there is some question of whether the two are distinguishable, entails a kind of return over the

---

12. Jean Hyppolite, "The Structure of Philosophic Language According to the 'Preface' to Hegel's *Phenomenology of the Mind,*" in *The Structuralist Controversy: The Languages of Criticism and the Sciences of Man,* ed. Richard Macksey and Eugenio Donato (Baltimore, 1972), 157–69.

same ground but this time with a certain difference. An older man, Adams makes another tour of the Continent and finds it energetically engaged in self-questioning. In effect, during his first circle, the trivium, the liberal arts, had failed him; and during the second, the quadrivium, the old sciences, were found similarly lacking, but in a strikingly different way. For at least the sciences were engaging and, in a provocative way, surviving the traumas of self-critique imposed upon them. Ironically enough, Europe is more modern than "America"; it is in Europe that revolutionary and revisionary thought is playing itself out in radical games of displacement, dissociation, and discontinuity, and industrial and humanistic revaluation. Europe has done with genealogy. Adams finds the new model to be physics, mathematics, statistics, and its preoccupation with transformational models, the consequences of which seem to throw out the old grammar, even both trivium and quadrivium, and supplant it with a volatile model of transformational thought. Like Nietzsche, Adams recognizes that "God" and "grammar" are one, and that the new science, the science of the sun (thermodynamics), requires a new mathematic: "Radium denied its God" (381). Yet chaos is an intolerable, unthinkable condition. And the sciences that had displaced the liberal arts nevertheless could not abide a thought without discipline. In a chapter titled "The Grammar of Science," Adams takes up the problematic of the new dynamics in terms of the old word for system, and while he understands that one cannot put Humpty Dumpty together again, the problem of writing the law of chaos, of catastrophe, would involve a kind of self-revisionary performance. The sciences had long since abandoned the model of the arts, and efforts like those of the French mathematician Poincaré to maintain the old relation of the two was the last desperate effort to maintain the humanist paradigm. As Maxwell's Demon registered, the possibility of a controlling metaphor of transformation seemed gratuitous. It stood for a desire of science, its hope for the future—perhaps even as the dream of future field theorists.

Adams, of course, has no answers; and his texts, like those of his heirs a century later, have been read on the model of a skepticism and nihilism that seems to find his theory of entropic history an ethical betrayal of the nostalgic theory of redemptive history: for example, those readings that assess his nostalgia for the Virgin and confusion over the Dynamo as a clear insistence of the paralysis of modernism. But for Adams, the modern self really does not reflect and choose; it acts and reacts. In admitting to a certain primacy of nature as force, as woman, as sexuality, Adams unveils a new figuration of the genetic, at once desirable and unsettling. And he senses that if, like old historians, he and Gibbon had had the resources of the new theory of transformations—a theory the grammar of which cannot quite be written or completed—he might have been able to read Rome as the originary force of paganism, and in reading mine it, mime it. But more important, he discovered that those who were writing the new theory were themselves a part of the force they were describing, and that he, a childless son of an old American genealogy, could only write an end to that figure or paradigm. "America," the democratic self, and so on, must appear as the name of the future, that is, of a catastrophe theory of history. It is too late for Adams, the reactionary. But the new "self" must be reactive, not reactionary; its emblem would be the Dynamo, the reactor, but both less and more a woman than the Virgin.

In 1911, hardly a year beyond the date Virginia Woolf gave as the break of modernism, Henri Bergson delivered a series of lectures at Oxford, later collected under the title *The Creative Mind*.[13] He announced that the one surviving and vital idea of the nineteenth century still living itself out toward its destiny of "freedom" was the idea of democracy; and in keeping with his usual resistance to Hegel and the dialectic, Bergson chose to define the notion of identity and creativity on another model, on another notion of "beyond." In one of the essays, on the pragmatism of William James as the exemplum of American thought, he acknowledges in this philosophy, so different from his own, one common impulse or thrust: "Philosophy has a natural tendency to have truth look backward: for James, it looks ahead. . . . [W]hile for other doctrines a new truth is a discovery, for pragmatism it is an invention" (255–56).

One can imagine Gertrude Stein listening to those lectures, especially the one touching on her old mentor, James, as she certainly did listen to Bergson lecturing in Paris; and we might well wonder what she derived from this distinction between "discovery" and "invention," between the notion of finding something that seemed to be there waiting to be found and enacting the kind of performative thought that not only cleared the "ground" or site of the new but in some strange way "invented" the future.

Stein's writings are at once simple and impossible to begin writing about, to start analyzing, that is, from some outside. To mention her writing is al-

13. Henri Bergson, *The Creative Mind*, trans. Mabelle L. Andison (New York, 1946).

ready to use it, in the distinction of speech-act language; to quote her, even a word, is already to quote a quotation, to quote her quoting herself. There seems no generic identity, no reflective position that may offer a vantage point or point of entry to her texts, for one is never outside what has no inside. Her writing is not ruled by genre, and indeed might be said to cross-ventilate genre. It is "American," and describes itself as "America," or as that other name of American multiplicity, the "United States." "What is the United States of America," she asks without benefit of question mark, in her "essays" *Four in America,* in which she *portrays* Henry James as a "general" (he would have to be a European general) and George Washington as a novelist: "It is not a country surrounded by a wall or not as well by an ocean. In short the United States of America is not surrounded." Her texts, like her States, provide no circle for the hermeneut to enter. Except by quoting, miming, which is not so much repeating as separating out (recall Williams on Poe). The American mode, she writes of Henry James in *Lectures in America,* is a mode of dissociative repetition, which she mimes: "but the disembodied way of disconnecting something from anything and anything from something was the American one" (53). "America" names a kind of genre-cide, a dismantling of frames and borders: *Four in America* is not a series of essays; *Lectures in America,* not exactly lectures; *The Making of Americans,* not a narrative, and thus not quite a novel; *How to Write* is not the pragmatic instructional pamphlet it claims to be, not quite a grammar, and thus it is a potential (that is, new) grammar; her plays are not scripts for performing, but performances upon the idea of a script; and "a rose is a rose is . . ." not quite a poem, even when arranged in a circle.[14]

To say that Stein's writing is an undoing or overwriting of genre and yet a kind of productive, germinal hybrid is to stress more than anything else its performative force, but also to underscore a special notion of performance. The poem poses a question of beginnings, in the sense of which word might be itself unquoted, which "rose" a first rose, or whether the beginning is not already a repetition. Its grammatical coherence does not suspend grammar, or freeze it, any more than its emblematic circle represents a repetition of the same. It is not, therefore, a spatial icon of temporality, the circle, but a supplementary mime of the circle, of a subject become its own

14. Gertrude Stein, *Four in America* (New Haven, 1947), 169; Stein, *Lectures in America* (Boston, 1985); Stein, *How to Write* (Barton, Vt., 1973); Stein, *The Making of Americans* (New York, 1966).

predication *ad infinitum*. It makes one think the grammar of grammar, the law of law. One might even say that it belongs to the Bergsonian deconstruction of spatiality, which depends on a revisionary grammar of time. Certainly, when one reflects that Stein's poem writes into its displacements the name of her maid and the pseudonym of that master deconstructor of modernism, Marcel Duchamp or "Rrose Selevy," one recognizes that it is a one-sentence abstract that undoes the universal narrative signified by the circle and the sentence. Throughout non-essays like "Composition as Explanation," with its assertion of writing as a production of a "continuous present," Stein repeatedly asserts that a narrative does not describe a history but repeats it, not in the manner of representation but in the manner she calls "happening." Thus she tends to resist Ezra Pound's later return to the primacy of presentation over representation, in order to avoid the old sense of immediacy inscribed in the old concept of the present as becoming. As in the mock-handbook, *How to Write,* instruction is also example, or a repetition of the exemplary that puts it under erasure. For instance, in sections like "Saving the Sentence" and "Arthur A. Grammar," she will rewrite the notion of a sentence as a complete thought by inscribing first the word *sentence* in the position of the subject of the sentence, thus describing the whole by the part that governs it; and then, proceeding by a set of repetitions that are governed by the strange logic of this grammatical law, force the sentence, at once the subject and predicate, to parse and multiply itself. The lesson of how to write advances by the capacity of the word to assume multiple yet related senses and functions, to sentence itself, as it were. Syntax displaces semantics, and relation defines position rather than vice versa. In the section "Arthur A. Grammar," she will appropriate the proper name for function of an author whose role in the unfolding text is to expand the very notion of grammar, by a kind of repetitive supplementation, without effacing the word-concept entirely. The law of grammar, like the law of genre, is never overruled, and is amended by grafting onto it that excess it cannot account for. A sentence once begun, or falsely begun by quotation that masks itself, will in a way author itself, though now the old notion of authority is suspended. The subject no longer rules writing but is displaced throughout the linguistic field.

One can find this outlaw writing in such tomes as *The Making of Americans,* which, far from detailing the genealogy of a family, undoes or deconstructs the very idea of genealogical succession and reveals how it be-

38

longs solely to the uninterrogated realism of narrative. In *Lectures in America,* she claims that *Making* is one of three modern novels that dispense with narrative, the other two being Proust's *Remembrance* and Joyce's *Ulysses.* They are exemplary, then, of the modern; and yet in their difference cannot simply be examples. They mark the multiplicity of the modern, the unity of a heterogeneity, one might say. As such, they no longer represent the singularity of a nation and language. Europe has no priority over America or the American experiment but has been quoting America all along.

Stein begins her *Lectures in America* by forging what at first appears to be a sharp distinction between English and American literature: the former characterized by its representations of what she calls its "daily island life," and the latter by a topo-geographical form almost without boundaries, a space that cannot be narrated. This is less a description of two kinds of space, one rigorously circumscribed, the other elastic and expansive, than it is a revision of the notion of "space," and hence of representation. The lectures move from this curious equivocality or discontinuity, which indicates that America is not the simple "other" of England, to engage and put in question all the major grammars and genres that have served the writing not only of literature but of literary history, with its notion of successive periods and orderly transformations. Under Stein's analysis, the notions of successive periods and orderly transformations, both grammatical and historical, collapse or rather reappear in her uncanny descriptions, her performative miming of repetition, a repetition with a difference. This is not a linear progression of changes. The present is continuous, a duration, yet this *durée* is not simply composed of a simultaneity of differences. It is made up of "multiplicities," which are neither successive nor simultaneous, and while they have relation they do not necessarily have a singular direction. At least narrative *telos,* which simply follows some ideal of successive spatial events, is not adequate to capture or represent this "heterology." Moreover, the law of succession allows for no real intervention, no belated genesis or beginning, but only infinite subdivision.

Stein's notion of a "continuous present," of "beginning again and again," owes much obviously to Bergson's concept of duration, a notion not without its problematics. For Bergson's *durée* is not, as popularly employed, the idea of a unity or singularity, not a psychology but an ontology of consciousness—thus not an argument for either individual identity or individual creativity. In his quarrel with Einstein, Bergson would argue that the theory of relativity only apparently overcame the limits of the old physics, which defined matter in terms of extension and thus spatial difference and succession. Einstein, Bergson insisted, had only added a fourth dimension to the other three, so that the fourth dimension of time was hardly more than another notion of space. Scientific duration, therefore, defined reality by quantity or as the spatial relation of numerical multiplicities: an object is that which can be divided infinitely without altering its nature, and thus changes by degree and not by kind. But human time, not quite "subjective" time, must be thought on another order, as a question of qualitative change. And this would imply the possibility of change of nature, necessary to the ideal of identity and creation. Bergson's project, then, was to account for this time and transformation, in terms of a duration that was not so much constituted as mixed, an interaction of the qualities of past and present, memory and matter—a notion of related "multiplicities" capable of change, transformation, evolution, etc. While these were old concepts, inscribed in the old metaphysics, Bergson would describe their interaction according to a new grammar.

According to Gilles Deleuze, in his brief and condensed analysis of the dominant concepts of Bergsonism, Bergson like Einstein did not simply go back to the metaphysical tradition in order to worry out a new concept of time.[15] Each in his own way appropriated the formulations of the German mathematician Georg Riemann, whose theory of "multiciplities" or of the transformation between different, discontinuous, but adjacent planal (spatial) surfaces is an instrumental radical reformulation that makes possible the "turn" of modern physics and may provide a general analogy for what we today call the turn toward language. I am incapable of describing, let alone elaborating, the Riemannian rupture that overcomes rupture; but I might suggest that one finds its consequences and issue not only in relativity and indeterminacy theory, but in the geodesic structures of Buckminster Fuller, in cybernetics, and even in the poetics of the open field of Charles Olson —for example, in his poem, "The Kingfishers," he not only inscribes by reference the "factors" of "feedback" of information theory but he quietly alludes to the mathematician Riemann, who makes possible Norbert Weiner's "machine."

15. Gilles Deleuze, *Bergsonism*, trans. Hugh Tomlinson and Barbara Habbarjam (New York, 1988).

Bergson's notion of a *durée*, of the active coexistence of past as trace and of present supplementation, of a memory that is simultaneously a contraction of the past into image and an expansion of the image in a kind of continuous repetition, must always produce a reading of him that asks but can never answer the question: is duration "one or several"? Is the "self" one or many, simple or complex, a homogeneous essence or a heterogeneous potentiality? The Bergsonian monism of time is an expanding monism and thus not a monism at all. It is a monistic multiplicity, an oxymoron, focusing on the play of the image and thus on the genetic force of an active image, a new kind of writing. Nor is Gertrude Stein's appropriation of it a simple miming of its law. Instead, she is compelled to name and repeatedly name "America" as duration, as writing, or as Williams said of her sentences, a grammar of "conserving abandon." We call it today the "modern," the "postmodern" already inscribed in the "modern." But whatever we call it, by whatever misnomer or metonymy, we will have quoted, not the past but the present, not the present but the future. Quotation has no before or after, but it inscribes the project of the future, what Charles Olson was to call "projective" writing, writing writing itself. Philosophers, mathematicians, and poets knew it already, Poe and Derrida, Emerson and Einstein, that the abandoned letter bore wings, and when stolen steals away —*la lettre volée,* as the French translate "The Purloined Letter." "We" Americans, Charles Olson has noted, "are the last, first people"; and it is because we cannot have been the first quoters that we can be said to be originary.

2

EMERSON AND THE "AMERICAN" SIGNATURE

Pray don't read American. Thought is of no country.

—Emerson, *Journals*, XII, 40

I

Appropriately enough, the (belated) "father" of American thought was also the first to reject it, thereby in the same gesture defining it: as a double inscription. But his argument against a "foolish consistency" in the name of self-reliance and his reification of contradiction, which would permit his own poetic son (Whitman) to evolve the "simple, separate person," were destined for its own "complex fate" or what today's critic might call a "fate of reading." Emerson's parenthood, of course, can be historically contested. Literary histories, like histories of ideas, inevitably pass through so many "crossings" (Oedipal and catachrestic) that the genetic moments and myths they reify must finally appear as only arbitrary beginnings. A criticism of origins reveals only the false origins of criticism.

The scandal of "American" thought is that it has always appeared as "poetic"—primordial but anti-intellectual, idealistic and pragmatic by turns, above all, nonsystematic. Either of the party of Hope or the party of . . . The scandal is no less a notoriously limited canon, the issue, one might argue, of "Emerson's" alleged authority or, more precisely, of the way Emerson has seemed to determine his own reading and even the reading of those who disparage his enthusiasm. The philosopher who evolves into a skeptic at first determines his own negation, compelling the "power of blackness" or the nihilisms that allow the canon to derive from yea-sayers or nay-sayers (say, Whitman or Melville) a historical dualism that admits few exceptions. Thus the notion of an *American Renaissance*, either book or concept, will precipitate into the notion of *A World Elsewhere*, either book or concept, a "world" destined to repeat and resolve in one pattern or another all the crossed figures of mythical history. Thus the notion of the *Virgin Land* and a frontier, as Henry Nash Smith observed, is more mythical or poetic than historical, a garden that will inevitably admit the machine of its own undoing, but only as prelude to a complete mystery.[1] Thus the fundamental dualisms that allow us to think *The Continuity of American Poetry* as a divided but unequivocal history, of the privileged Adamic voice against the reaction of received tradition; or that version of modernism that sees our avant-gardists divided between those who took nurture in the forms and ruins of Europe and those who in all innocence produced as if out of nature *A Homemade World* and called it "new." Thus a canon that excludes Poe, or includes him as a mode of deviant behavior, or regards the circuit of his influence, via a French capacity for inspired misreadings, as a symptom and prefiguring of what our criticism would become. Each inscribes "American" literature in a Romantic (or genetic) history that Paul de Man calls the "prospective temporality" of literary history.[2] They make "American literature" the repetition of a teleological order working out its own unique end from its own unique beginning, itself an organic circle.

I have had recourse here to a condensed metaphorics only in order to suggest that every effort to define the exceptional or original nature of "American literature" has in its turn had recourse only to the most ordinary notions of literary history. In this regard, even the democratic and inclusive canons of the old historical scholars can only be repeated in the exclusive canonics of the formalist New Criticism, even when it proposed to correct the old historicism and return us to the "text"—an indication, perhaps, that the two opposing modes of critical thought are more homogeneous than antithetical. It is as if "American" literature originated in a self-reflexive moment of naming itself, in a manner that might efface and correct the flawed genealogy that marks its finding and founding, that simple misreading and misnaming of both the native (the Indian) and the native ground

1. Henry Nash Smith, *Virgin Land: The American West as Symbol and Myth* (New York, 1959). See esp. the final chapter, "The Myth of the Garden and Turner's Frontier Hypothesis" (291–305), the metaphors of which I will return to a few pages hence. See also Richard Poirier, *A World Elsewhere: The Place of Style in American Literature* (Madison, Wis. 1966), and Roy Harvey Pearce, *The Continuity of American Poetry* (Princeton, N.J., 1961).

2. Paul de Man, *Allegories of Reading* (New Haven, 1979), 80–81.

(as "virgin" and "ground"). What Faulkner would later expose as the condition (always already) of miscegenation that characterizes every American myth of grounding and precludes a corrected genealogy, a condition that John Barth can parody as the very origin of the idea of a great American novel, might be said to be the enigmatic sign that "American" thought originates in its own *irony,* and that what American literature represents, in the very figure of "Man Thinking" or the "central man," is critical thought itself —a thought that mythologizes itself in the very gesture of disguising and effacing its "poetic" nature and its mimetic link to all the old myths of origin it has rejected.

But Americanist criticism has tended to resist the notion that its literary history, not to say its literature, germinated in the anomalies and confusions of irony. Even Bloom, who offers the most elaborate sense of the misprision that inhabits every tradition, has had to purge irony along with the nostalgia for origins in order to arrive at an American lineage of prophecy and power, a canonic reading of the American "self" that survives all those deaths of God and self that signify the exhausted European thought of the nineteenth century. Curiously enough, then, Bloom recapitulates the very historicism, not to say formalism, he begins by repudiating —and in the peculiarly American style of reversal. For the sake of economy, one might exemplify the discourse of this restaging of the American tradition in a moment that could never have taken place: let me call it Emerson's misreading of de Tocqueville. I do not mean to attempt the historicist's illusion here, to trace the effect of de Tocqueville's prophecy upon subsequent readings of the democratic tradition (as a radical attack upon tradition). But upon that singular notion of the "simple, separate person" turns in antithetical unison the conservative criticism of Van Wyck Brooks and Lewis Mumford (once thought liberal) and the unmitigated liberalism of Vernon Parrington.

When F. O. Matthiessen, in his ground-breaking *American Renaissance,* challenges the priority of history to literature by arguing that we must study not the "background" but the "foreground" of American thought, he presumes to effect a reversal from thought to aesthetics, from ideas to expression, and to follow the Emersonian argument that the great American invention is a new language to express the invention of a unique American consciousness.[3] Yet this radical theory, that there is a uniquely

3. F. O. Matthiessen, *American Renaissance* (New York, 1941), ix .

American "consciousness," not to say idiom, has its linguistic origins in Romantic epistemology (an appropriation of Coleridge's appropriations). The consequence of this apparent reversal of historicism, in which a belated American "renaissance" derives from romanticism's closure of the Enlightenment, is to provide another historicized myth of origins, a literary or poetic myth in which a poet at the end of history recuperates the primordial moment when the "word" is "one with the thing" and literature once again closes the distance between art and "nature." This, Matthiessen argues, will reveal that "the transcendental theory of art is a theory of knowledge and religion as well," and hence originates in the same metaphysics as the old historicism.[4] A decade and a half later, Charles Feidelson would complete Matthiessen's thesis by arguing that the genetic moment of American literature was its recovery of the privilege of "symbolic" language, a discovery verified by a literary modernism (especially T. S. Eliot's poetics) that had finally written the closure of literary history. And, Feidelson would insist, American literature, in its Emersonian origins, had always been modern, in the sense that it had discovered the primordial economy of language, a self-reflexivity that poetic language alone had at once represented and exemplified and that philosophical language or criticism could only idealize by lamenting the historical trials of the word.[5]

This privileging of literature as a force for working out a historical movement and thus recuperating lost meanings, and yet as an originary force for disseminating meanings, is a common paradox found in Emerson but surely not original with him. On the other hand, the tendency of our literary criticism to see itself as situated at the exhausted end of a very specific, condensed history has led not only to the privileging of literature but to a schiz-

4. *Ibid.*, 31. Matthiessen entitles this subsection on Emerson's language "The Word One with the Thing." It is an uncritical commentary on Emerson's "specific observations on language," which Matthiessen considers a coherent, unproblematic theory of "expression," even though Emerson turns Coleridge's "explicit statement about semantics" into "hyperbole" (30). Thus Matthiessen affirms the renewed American language as "organic," new even though it is derived from the Romantic theory of the "symbol."

5. Charles Feidelson, *Symbolism and American Literature* (Chicago, 1953). See esp. the concluding chapter, where Feidelson argues that Eliot's "autotelic" theory of lyric completes and ratifies the American development of the Romantic symbol. Therefore, he concludes, American literature had always been modern, that is, a fully developed self-reflexive theory of art. Though texts like Melville's *Pierre* may fall short of the maturity of Continental examples, like Gide's *Counterfeiters,* and though it may elaborate the negative side of Emersonianism, both its formal and thematic self-reflexivity, he concludes, are in the American and modern grain.

45

ophrenic reading of that "literature"—making it at once representative of the literary "tradition" (and that means the tradition of Western literature) and a radical exception, completion, and overthrowing of that tradition. Eliot's paradoxical title of "tradition" and the "individual talent," a paradox he will efface rather than elaborate, by the way, provides a metaphor for the modes by which our literary history has tended to be written, as an exception that not only proves but sanctifies the rule: the law of self-reflexion and self-reflection; the individual as a true renaissance of history.

Since it leads directly to a reading of American literature in what one might call the Emersonian "eye," I want to offer at this point a representative instance of the problematic inhabiting any attempt to stage that literature, at once inside and outside history. "The history of America," says the professorial figure in Richard Chase's *The Democratic Vista*, "has been a history of continuing revolt."[6] In the comfort of his summer retreat, with neighbors from middle America instead of recalcitrant undergraduates to serve as "sure questioners" (Stevens), Ralph Headstrong delivers a liberal critique of the waning of the American spirit, as evidenced, of course, in its brief literary history. The decline is most indelibly marked in the increasing elitism or distance between modernist art and its public, and magnified at the social level in the schismatic life-style of the American bourgeois (increasing suburbanization). The implication that our literature originally touched a kind of pastoral note, the word rooted in nature, as some critics intimate, is rejected, and yet maintained. The American imagination, says Headstrong, could produce only a literature of "brilliant fragments, of melodrama, humor, pastoral idyll, and romance" (4). Leaving aside, at least for the moment, the fact that Chase himself may have defined by repetition the most characteristic quality of American thought, by consigning that thought to "literature" and "literary history," one is left with the most familiar argument of the modern crisis as a split between self and society, a schism already doubled in the crisis of a divided self, caught between an everlasting "yea" and "nay," between optimism and pessimism. But, indeed, the most characteristic reflex of Chase's dialogue pivots upon what he concludes to be another opposition or dualism, wherein the historical schematic of a Parrington, setting liberalism in privileged opposition to conservatism in the twin "currents" of American "thought," is supplanted by a modern or dialectical historicism (for which, incidentally, Lionel

6. Richard Chase, *The Democratic Vista* (New York, 1958).

Trilling's "liberal" imagination is evoked as authority)—as if to suggest, and not altogether wrongly, that "American" thought is only another retelling of the nineteenth century's "end" of history.

Chase's dialogue would remain today as little more than a forgotten chapter of American humanism were it not for its curious effort to make the bourgeois communism of the transcendentalists into a radical Nietzschean prophecy. In Ralph Headstrong's words: "I have tried to give new striking power to the tradition of radical criticism in this country—the tradition of Emerson, Whitman, Henry Adams, Veblen, the early Van Wyck Brooks, and others. In order to keep up a steady dissent from the conformism and middlebrowism of the time, I have shown how little these are justified by the best traditions of American culture and American literature" (175). Even the references to Nietzsche, which provide the text's model of "radical" criticism, evoke only the nihilisms of critical thought, Emerson's "central man" and "Over-Soul" evolved into Trilling's modern *literatus*. The negations of critical thought, then, wait to be repaired once more by literature.

A belated and now endangered American literature, then, awaits in Chase's view its "new Tocqueville," a foreign critic who will "not return to a Europe convinced conservatism." This critic is "Rinaldo Schultz," "optimist, engineer, and newly naturalized American," who promises to "stay here and help to reconstruct a radical democracy—America" (178). It is hard to say what happened to Rinaldo, engineer rather than bricoleur, except that he may be the head of some American studies department (or even 1960s president of the MLA), of any program long since known for its suspicion of the nihilistic thought of Europe. He has become what Headstrong calls one of the "new dialecticians," and since dialectics, whether in its Hegelian or Marxian mode, leads inevitably to recuperative hope and despair, or to the genetic myths of a conservative imagination, his history is already written. Chase's dialogue, then, becomes in itself the reflexive form of American thought, caught up in the irresistible illusion that it had realized, not only for the first time in history but for the first time, like those sailors at the end of *The Great Gatsby*, the possibility of an unmediated "vista" opening upon ever-new breasts of endless green worlds—the open-endedness of history and thought returning upon itself in a way that reveals only the present to be a tragic decline—and that such lost or violated "frontiers" are at least renewable in imagination. Thus American "thought" would be mythopoeic.

Chase makes it clear that American literature was always inscribed in, even originated in, a margin. It was always already a fragment—at once a derived and reinstituted figure. As Smith showed in *Virgin Land,* even Turner's historicism thesis of the frontier revealed the interpreter's (and mythographer's) hand, since the frontier makes sense to history only as a reclaimed myth of origins. But, to make a clean breast of it, frontiers that are only metaphoric are like Chase's suburbs, those regretted modern frontiers, doubled within themselves. In the American mythopoeic, the frontier as nature is *genius loci,* that place which is only another name for language. The American scene or grain, then, even the American frontier, could never be pastoral or utopian, neither beginning nor end, closure or opening. And the frontier is only another name, at last, for a new literature, of an overcoming that is not a sublation but only another ironic twist or trope. The frontier, suburb, or horizon in and of American thought can only signify a dialectical gap or the undoing of dialectics.

Or to put it another way, if there is American thought, it is poetic in the most "radical" sense. And it takes the double name of Man and nature. All of the centralizations of Emerson and Whitman as the patronyms of American literature come to this: to the figure Man, or to figure itself; and they re-mark the problem, posed as early and as late as Emerson, of how to read that figure of the "central man" after all the mystifications of theology have been subverted or a myth of origins, of an origin already inscribed in language and disruptive of the Logos, has been rephrased and poeticized in the idioms of the philosophical subject. Which is to say, however cryptically, it is at once trans-parent (original) and trans-lative (belated), a language not easily figured out.

II

For Emerson's readers, with the possible exception of Bloom, humanism has never been put in doubt, and even for Bloom the figure of will and power, the genius, has continued to verify the strength of anthropocentrism. Thus Emerson's refusal of system or systematic thought becomes a transumption of it, a triumphal will to power. For most of his critics, however, Emerson's power remains a dangerous solipsism; he is a man of solitude rather than society. Yet transcendentalism, whatever else one says of it, anticipates and even fabulates a social or communal utopia, though Emerson doubted if it were at the end of history, let alone at Brook Farm. Community would have to admit nonconformity; otherwise it was a conspiracy against self-reliance. At the center of things, he would argue, is "Man Thinking," or the "Thinker and Actor": "An institution is the lengthened shadow of one man" (a phrase that would haunt Eliot into reaction); "Every true man is a cause, a country, and an age"; "Where he is, there is nature" (CW, II, 35).

The rhetoric is familiar. Man is not an issue, an effect, but a cause. But to be made the "centre of things," or subject, man has become a rhetorical figure, a metonymy, a cause freed of its effects, an entity unto itself. Yet at this very moment, one of his most programmatic affirmations, Emerson turns to a "fable" of this man at the center—and tells us the story of a sot who, found dead in the street, is brought to the duke's house and dressed out as a prince. This cultivated image, which "symbolizes so well the state of man," must today, he continues, displace the "colossal symbol" of the King as the "hieroglyph" that measures at once the state and man's estate —the sign, that is, of the meeting point of "aboriginal self" and historical form, of intuition and its representations (CW, II, 36). Thus the "aboriginal self" is that which is not simply repressed but is (in two senses) redressed as the ever-presence of human "Power." It is a figure of language, of figure itself—not the "phraseology of some old moldered nation in another country" but the figure of a new language, the "lengthened shadow" of a man, a "giant" or colossus. He is at once of nature and an excess of nature.

Man never appears in Emerson outside of this double inscription, the figure at once of center and circumference, emperor only when inscribed in his clothes, yet signifying beyond himself—like the "eye" of the essay "Circles," which is a first circle forming the "horizon" of a second: a "primary figure" from which infinite ripples of circles or horizons may be projected, but an origin originally figural and eccentric. The "centre" or the first (we will have occasion later to think of C. S. Peirce's notion of firstness) is in man so long as he is in nature, in nature so long as it is in language. It is therefore cipher and sign:

Every ultimate fact is only the first of a new series. Every general law only a particular fact of some more general law presently to disclose itself. There is no outside, no inclosing wall, no circumference to us. The man finishes his story— how good! how final! how it puts a new face on all things! He fills the sky. Lo! on the

other side rises also a man and draws a circle around the circle we had just pro-
nounced the outline of the sphere. Then already is our first speaker not a man, but
only a first speaker. His only redress is forthwith to draw a circle outside of his an-
tagonist. (*CW*, II, 181)

Even the notion of "outside" is a self-effacing figure, a "re-dress" inscribed
in a previous cipher and in turn inscribing it. Emerson's circle is open and
antagonistic, an agon or trope. The only point of origin of the circle is therefore inscribed in a circumference that has no existence or is not a thing-in-
itself. And Emerson has a name for it: "literature." Literature is the horizon, a "point outside of our hodiernal circle through which a new one may
be described," a "platform whence we may command a view of our
present life, a purchase by which we may move it" (185). Literature, therefore, is "wild nature," but it is already divided within itself; it is a present not
present to itself, a force. And like Nietzsche's force, it consists of equivocal and irreducible differences. Thus, what Emerson calls the "eternal procession" of cause and effect outruns the grammar that would close it or return it to the center.

Literature, as we will see, is not only a text, but intertextual. But there remains the question of whether it can be described by the tropological economy. In "Quotation and Originality," a relatively late essay that has until
recently been more or less ignored—perhaps because it tends to undermine
its author's more famous negations—Emerson argues that since there is
no way to think pure originality except by thinking a first speaker, every
beginning is already a quotation: "All minds quote. Old and new make the
warp and woof of every moment. There is no thread that is not a twist of
these two strands" (*W*, VIII, 178). In literature, the "originals are not original. There is imitation, model and suggestion, to the very archangels, if
we knew their history" (180). As with Nietzsche later, the original is the
result of an active forgetting of the metaphoricity of firstness. It is this for-
getfulness that has produced the myth of the fall, of men as "off their centre," exiles in nature, copyists; so that "quotation confesses inferiority"
(188). Yet Emerson would save originality, and the genetic fiction of self,
if only in a mode that must bridge and efface the vertiginous abyss that
opens up a quotation beneath every quotation. As he says in his journals, "Me-
diator mediation. There is nothing else; there is no Immediate known to
us. Cloud on cloud, degree on degree, remove one coat, one lamina, and
another coat or lamina just like it is the result,—to be also removed. When

the new symbol is explained the new truth turns out to be only a symbol of ulterior truth" (*J*, XI, 424).

However, it is not the emptiness of origins that disturbs him; not nostalgia, but the fear of entropy or the successive inferiority of quotation. Thus his notion of the genius (and as we will see, the poet) as center, as that figure or trope which in turning from itself perpetuates quotation or difference, in a scene that Emerson calls the present, the "new": "The profound apprehension of the Present is Genius, which makes the Past forgotten" (*W*, VIII, 201). Genius is, therefore, the Will, or "original force," and it belongs not to an individual consciousness or to the self in the colloquial or psychological sense, but to the "aboriginal self." Genius is without question inscribed in rhetoric, the voice of the "oracle" or "words of some god," but these are only metaphors for a poetic language that "high poets" may borrow (or quote). Quotation (and translation) is the activity not of an individual but of language itself, that "prodigal power" of which Man and/or Poet are the names. Voice, then, is never extricable from quotation, or figurality. Originality never precedes quotation; it is appropriation (propriative), what Emerson calls "noble" borrowing—an activity that involves not only the breaking of a precursor, as Bloom indicates, but reinscription, through which the original or earlier is marked in all its figurative firstness to the inferior quotation that marks its limit. Emerson here would seem to pose a question to what Bloom calls the movement of transumption. Poetry is therefore originarily a figural weave, and (as becomes explicit in "The Poet") a mis-transcription of its origin, the pure poem that nevertheless cannot properly precede it. Genius is not the particular author, subject, voice, but the transitive or tropic firstness that Emerson calls "nature." Genius and *genius loci,* language and nature, are woven together as the irreducible text of things—voice is the issue of the play of figurality. Any evocation of God or pure origin will find Him already woven into what calls Him.

Not only do all men quote, all men are quotations: "Every book is a quotation; and every house is a quotation out of all forests and mines and stone-quarries; and every man is a quotation from all his ancestors" (*W*, VIII, 176). This is the epigraph of "Quotation and Originality," itself a quotation, Emerson's self-quotation. In writing, his signature is its own ancestor, and nature the quotation of a text.

III

Emerson's quotations of idealist thought are neither a repetition nor a reversal of metaphysics, nor can his own development of transcendentalism be described as a history of ideas, evolving from unmediated optimism to mature skepticism. Emerson was never innocent, and never simply idealistic. And for this reason Bloom has been able to insist that Emerson cannot, or need not, be deconstructed: "Deconstructing Emerson is of course impossible, since no discourse ever has been so overtly aware of its own status as rhetoricity," Bloom writes in his book on Stevens.[7] Bloom, however, does not intend this as evidence of the originally deconstructed rhetoricity of poetry (de Man's notion). On the contrary, Bloom resolutely submits Emerson to a dialectical tradition in which the deconstructive moment of discourse is only a negative moment, anticipating its own self-overcoming. I must leave aside here, at least for a time, the question of Bloom's dialectics, or why he chooses the notion of metalepsis and transumption (rhetorical and even quasi-theological concepts) rather than the philosophical term *sublation,* in order to show that the negative moment has at best little force in Emerson, even in his emphasis on the Fall into mediation or "illusion," and in order to argue that Emerson's metalepses, his turning of subordinate things into metonymies, open the circle or dialectic of his thought in a radical sense even Bloom will not follow. The "Lords of Life" that he acknowledges in "Experience" (an essay once to be entitled "Life") are the limits of an inevitable temporality of Spirit, and therefore are related to "history," but in a manner that refuses the agon (and tragedy) of Hegelian history. One might even call "illusion" the texture of life itself, or at least its inter-texture, the play of interpretation: "God is reality & his method is illusion" (*J*, X, 355); "God's ways are parabolic projections that do not return into themselves" (*J*, IX, 172); "All experience has become mere language now" (*J*, XI, 374). A cento of Emerson not only does not return upon itself, but does not transume or transcend that which it quotes.

"The only sin is limitation," Emerson wrote in "Circles" (*CW*, II, 182), and limitation is the inevitability of illusion, of "method." Moreover, as he would repeatedly insist, there are no negatives in nature, a prospect which would open up for Ernest Fenollosa and Ezra Pound a "new" theory of poetic language. The circle, therefore, while the archetypal Emer-

7. Harold Bloom, *Wallace Stevens: The Poems of Our Climate* (Ithaca, 1977), 12.

sonian figure, is parabolic and not self-reflexive, and we understand it only in parables. The meaning of any circle is the interpretation, or quotation, that must be drawn around it. Conversation, perhaps dialogue, is a "game of circles"; circles are grammatical and therefore inscribe the illusion (method) of "cause and effect," or the play of analogy that does not return upon itself. Thus when Emerson avers in one of his very late essays, the apparently triumphal "Illusions" of *The Conduct of Life,* that there is "no chance and no anarchy in the universe. All is system and gradation" (*W,* VI, 325), we might pause for a moment over the rhetorical chain that has led to this overcoming. Since "method" as God's "illusion" has become origin and end, the circle is only an illusion; method and trope distribute.

Chance and anarchy are not illusory negatives or absences. They would only be intermittent or transitional disturbances. Illusion is not a negative but the figure of a discontinuity that is overcome by that most transitive of forces, grammar. Grammar inscribes illusion only to triumph over it by providing an order of relationships. Grammar is nature; or nature, grammar. Rather than chance or anarchy, the universe is a "power" that exceeds the limits of every descriptive grammar. God's method is a grammar that bears its own excess, that distributes. There is no negation, no dialectical return, in the parabola of "nature."

In an essay called "Nature," which follows the more classical early one of the same title, Emerson, while seeming to confine himself to a physical or manifest nature in contrast to the more idealist notion, offers a characteristic subversion of his interpreters. While "nature" is continuous and "always consistent," he writes, she still "feigns to contradict her own love": "Exaggeration is in the course of things. Nature sends no creature, no man into the world without adding a small excess of his proper quality. Given the planet, it is still necessary to add the impulse" (*CW,* III, 107). And the "impulse" is a "little violence of direction," an "excess of direction." If all things betray the same calculated profusion, if the teleological law inscribes its own surplus, the circle can never return upon itself, but is originally distorted, parabolic, and prospective: "Our music, our poetry, our language itself are not satisfactions, but suggestions" (110). This disseminative effect is neither continuous nor discontinuous. An excess of direction similarly characterizes Emerson's own aphoristic texts and undermines the very genetic myths they perpetuate: in Emerson's case, the famous metaphysical theories of analogy, correspondence, and compensation, of a closed, self-reflexive, organic nature or even an open history. Thus if "Nature is a language & every new fact that we learn is a new word," and if all we see "taken together is not . . . merely a language but the language put together into a most significant & universal book" (*J*, IV, 95), this conventional reference to a Book of Nature at the same time marks the "excess" of its system. It is a reference to a reference book: "My garden is my dictionary" (*J*, V, 326), and an incomplete, open system.

IV

Nature as a "dictionary" would be nature as an arbitrary assemblage of metonymies. It would be a book without a center. Despite all the idealistic and theocentric protestations, there is no one center in Emerson. Everything is a center, a sign. And if man appears as the center of centers, the reader of the dictionary, he, too, is one of its entries, a sign or representation. Representative Man (men)—there is no center outside representation, no representation except in the play of this figure. Man/nature/language are never divisible in the Emersonian rhetoric. And of all the representative men, the Poet, and not any one of his particular names, is most central: "He stands among partial men for the complete man" (*CW*, III, 4), the "man without impediment," the genius. But even that without impediment, this "sovereign" who "stands on centre," this "sayer" and "namer," is also "interpreter," is divided within itself: "The man is only half-himself, the other half is his expression" (5, 4). He is a "doctor" (6).

Moreover, the genius of representation does not merely stand in place of; "genius realizes and adds" (7); just as language is not simply an expression or an image of nature but an addition or "second nature, grown out of the first, as a leaf out of a tree" (13). The organic metaphor inevitably inscribes not a simple analogy but that "excess" of metamorphosis that turns the circle of nature from itself and its tropic return into a parabola. Nature like language is a presence only because it is never really present to itself. Similarly, poems, as Emerson argues in various places, are inevitably a mis-writing of some ideal poem that can have its being only in that transcription which adds itself to ideal presence: "And herein is the legitimation of criticism, in the mind's faith that the poems are a corrupt version of some text in nature with which they ought to be made to tally" (15). Poems are irreducibly intertextual, not only in the sense of marking their inadequacy to some uninscribed or unuttered ideal, but in the sense that they inevitably inscribe a double language: "All languages are inter-translateable" (*J*, VII, 302), he will remind himself, just as in "Quotation and Originality," all literature is quotation. And therefore every poem is a translation that inscribes a critical as well as a genetic moment: "Literature is now critical," he writes in his journal: "Well, analysis may be poetic" (303). Thus he quotes Goethe to the effect that literature is a "fragment of fragments," and even of that which has been written down only the "least part remains" (*J*, V, 143). By the same token, the doubleness of language, that "exuviae of a foregone World" (*J*, VII, 207), as he says, allows the always already derived sign ("Literature is the only art that is ashamed of itself"—*J*, IX, 45) to exceed itself in a second nature. Genius and rhetoric are Emerson's names for this force; and literature, which in one moment is deprivileged, returns as that center on the horizon that, not being present to itself, surpasses itself.

In "The Poet" this is expressed as the "fluxional" or "vehicular & transitive" nature of the "symbol," a language at the same time image and voice, creative and analytical. As we have seen, Emerson is never so powerful a dialectician as Bloom thinks. Or to put it another way, his power resides in a play of rhetoric, between voice and figure, in the kind of irony Paul de Man has found in Nietzsche, but without nihilistic despair. Moreover, as I will argue, this notion of literature as "fragment" appears as early as the idealistic *Nature* and reverberates throughout the Emerson canon, perhaps to be contained, or at least effaced, in the powerful rhetoric of an ephebe like Bloom.

Nature is a text that escapes the categorizations of either philosophical or literary discourse, that breaks the clear generic demarcations criticism makes between the two in order to master its own discourse on them. We might even say that it puts the genre "essay" in question or disturbs the law of genre. As we know from the journals, while Emerson worked over the formal organization of the text in a way that would not be appropriate to later pieces intended for oral presentation, he thought of this early work not simply as one "book," but possibly as two, "Nature" and "Spirit." Notwithstanding the commonsensical fact that neither section achieves the independent coherence or substantiality of a self-contained discourse, the two parts, breaking between sections five and six, "Discipline" and "Idealism," repeat and cover over that transcendental moment we have come to call "natural supernaturalism" and reify as organic form. Thus the essay continues to be read as an instance of Emerson's youthful Platonism and an eccentricity of the Romantic tradition, even in Bloom's sense of Emerson as self-demystified prophet of the "American sublime."

One does not want altogether to abuse (even in Nietzsche's sense) this reading, the idealist reading—only unsettle it. This, however, may necessitate taking the bloom off it. At least one wants to begin by insisting that it is not altogether wrong to call Emerson a Platonist or Hegelian, but it is not altogether right either. Certainly, the insistent formal symmetry that the essay imitates—particularly by attempting to divide each section into a logical triad and marking the progressive advance from lower to higher forms in a hierarchical schema—would seem to suggest that the text is, if nothing else, a natural-supernaturalist's prose-poem, and not quite even a philosophical fable. It writes an American footnote to the closure of metaphysics, from Plato to Hegel. It transcribes philosophy back into poetry. It is therefore a quotation, a purloined letter that does not simply reverse or close metaphysics, but reintroduces into thought the poetic addition philosophy had systematically tried to contain.

For quotation, as we have seen Emerson argue, has a cryptic or indigestible effect. Quotation, and what we today call intertextuality; quotation, and what Emerson called "nature"—is only another name for Man. Emerson, of course, is very defensive about this belatedness or retrospectiveness of American thought, and *Nature* addresses the question in its opening sentences. There is something at once naïve and eccentric in a beginning that calls once more for the recovery of an "original relation to the universe," a "poetry or philosophy of insight and not tradition," in view of the fact that all previous theologies had mis-written that history, and American thought had fallen into sepulchral retrospection in its very birth. To presume a first philosophy, to offer a "true theory" that "will explain all phenomena" and reflect the "not-me" in the transparency of the "me," is to be original only in innocence, or by forgetting. Yet Emerson's own beginning within the concepts of ontotheology, the only language he has, already marks the problematic of immediacy or transparency by recognizing that he must conduct his new discourse in an old language, or must reveal the new as an intertranslation of the old.

The "not me," as he must observe, is already both "nature and art," or in the Kantian sense, "nature" and "intuition," and both have only one

name, NATURE. "*Nature*, in the common sense," is the physical plural-
ity that is an essence because it is "unchanged by man" (*CW*, I, 8); in contrast to that nature which bears the imprint of man's will (or intuition), his
"art," even the physical is inscribed as concept and trope. Nor is "art,"
which is will or intuition informing "nature," devoid of "nature." The "not
me," which is "nature and art," is a weave of doubles. NATURE, then, is originarily "relation" or language, a text, in some sense—a metaphor, then,
enfolding both "form" and "power," essence and will, the relation of reference and the relation that trans-poses and dis-places things as if things
were already inscribed in a grammar. Despite Emerson's repeated evocation of Unity (God or Spirit beyond its becoming), the "original relation" is
originally different from itself and irreducibly a "relation," in two senses. Nature (and here one does not know which of the terms Emerson would use,
since he marks it differently for its different, for him, meanings) is at least both
"property" and "poetic," hence figural.

Emerson's opening remarks on the failures of metaphysics and his own
appeal for a "true theory" that will "be its own evidence" already indicate
that he thinks of a true theory as preceding dialectics and as being the equivalent of a primordial poetry, self-reflexive in the unimpeded sense that dialectics only promises to recover or arrive at some future unity. Therefore,
when the essay points out all the "phenomena" that remain to be explained
by a new theory, it names as the inexplicable "language, sleep, madness,
dreams, beasts, sex"—all of which, with the possible exception of "beasts,"
would include both "nature and art" and which have resisted adequate explanation or a meta-language. Since NATURE, then, is already "both nature
and art," or the redoubled inscription of words and things, the failure of
science or metaphysics is revealed as the provisional failure of language,
its fall from an ideal of self-reflexivity that Emerson evokes as an ideal of
vision or perception, the "transparent eyeball." It remains to see whether
Emerson can sustain this illusion of the ideal moment, either of remote Past
or envisioned Future, the moment when "Universal Being" circulates through
the finite self. For this moment will inevitably be figural, the moment when
God appears inscribed in the "ruins" of man, or in poetic figuration. The
essay's rhetorical movement from a lower to a higher "nature," therefore,
evokes the progressive closure or intermediation of nature upon itself, of
a restoration of words to things. But the ideal or transcendental moment
of closure, the recuperation of unity from nature's dualities, is deferred by

the very moment of language (also, nature) that prophesies it. Emerson argues that idealism or the idealist theory cannot disbelieve in the permanence of natural law, or the permanence of nature as the irreducible play of "me" and "not me," of nature and art, of nature and man "indissolubly joined." Even the figure of transparency ("transparent eyeball") is only an ideal figure of figure, of a self-reflection or perfect alignment between the "axis of things" and the "axis of vision"—a metaphysical dream of perception as transcendence that corrects the "ruin or the blank that we see when we look at nature," the "ruin or the blank" that is "in our own eye" (CW, I, 43). That moment of perfect perception can be rendered only in "fable": "We make fables to hide the baldness of the fact and conform it, as we say, to the higher law of the mind. But when the fact is seen under light of an idea, the gaudy fable fades and shrivels. We behold the real higher law. To the wise, therefore, a fact is true poetry, and the most beautiful of fables" (44). Fable at last must tease us out of thought, or efface itself, to return as poetic fact—itself already re-marked as "fable."

We will return to this ecstatic moment of forgetting later. For now it is sufficient to note its occurrence at the end of the essay, after the evocation of the Orphic poet whose song is to "repair" this disjunction of the axes apparent even in fable. The essay has progressed, then, not simply from the dualism of nature to the self-transparency or unity of NATURE. In becoming a fable of identity, a poetic story whose truth resides in its power to supply illusions of unmediation, it has become a self-commentary on its own fabulation and on the necessity of metaphor or indirection. Nature, then, advances from a question of language toward an idealization of language (really voice), or toward the self-reflexive ideal of "poetic" language. The transcendental moment (first marked in section six) is precisely the moment in which the poet and philosopher, imaginative and cognitive spirit, perceives a reciprocity in figural thought. But it remains, this "poetry," no less critical or analytical than prophetic, and hence doubled.

Perhaps because of Emerson's notoriously casual way with philosophy there has been little challenge to his equation of poet and philosopher in *Nature,* his argument that each seeks the same end, though for each it bears a different name: the poet "proposes Beauty as his main end; the other Truth" (CW, I, 33). Plato especially, but also Aristotle, are his authorities: "The true philosopher and the true poet are one, and a beauty, which is truth, and a truth, which is beauty, is the aim of both. Is not the charm of one of Plato's or Aristotle's definitions strictly like that of the Antigone of Sopho-cles?" This poetic telescoping quite disregards the distinction each philoso-pher made between philosophy and poetry, the superiority of the former to the latter or Truth to Beauty that the metaphysical tradition would sus-tain up to Hegel and that even Heidegger only begins to disrupt. It is not simply that Emerson is ignorant of this deprivileging of poetry within meta-physics. He notes elsewhere Plato's argument against writing as a crutch of memory, and even in *Nature* refers to the philosopher's argument for the superiority of poetry to history. But here Emerson not only ignores the hierarchical distinctions of Plato; his reprivileging of the poet also reverses an argument of degree made earlier in this same context. "Beauty" (sec-tion three) is the second stage or degree of nature's spiral, its temporal phase, a stage of nature sublated into through art's innate dialectic: physi-cal beauty, as the perception of natural forms, being raised to a higher level by the recognition of a "spiritual element," and to a still higher degree by the intellectual and intuitive. The "creation of beauty is Art" (*CW*, I, 16), so that art, which is already in and of nature, is a force that turns or creates its own surpassing. But, he continues, "beauty in nature is not ultimate"; and if "Art [is] a nature passed through the alembic of man" (17), "art" is itself transcended in the next stage, "Language," that famous section when Emerson sets forth his dialectic of the "sign," his condensed version of the poetic origins of language. (Of this, more later.)

It is not surprising, then, that Emerson's strategy at the end of *Nature* is not simply a reversal of the Platonic deprivileging of the poet, but a rein-scription of the poetic within pure thought. This double inscription marks the irreducible figurality in the discourse of idealism, and resists any ulti-mate sublation or effacement of nature within Spirit. It also marks the tem-poral play of figure and discourse that limits transcendentalism to the realm of "aesthetical" thought. Rather than a search for what Emerson, quoting Plato, calls the "end" of thought, Truth conceived as the "ground unconditioned and absolute" or Logos, Nature returns to a "ground" of language that is unconditional only in its play. One thinks, for example, of Kant's remarks in the *Critique of Judgment* on the nature of certain languages that inscribe both concept and its figuration (as an "indirect presentation," or hypotyposis), like the German word for "ground" (*Grund*).[8] For Emerson, the American idiom *nature* offers an even more resonating example of a concept at once

8. Immanuel Kant, *Critique of Judgment*, trans. J. H. Bernard (New York, 1951), 196–99.

literal, conceptual, and figural, in which, as Kant writes, "judgment exercises a double function," and in this case, offers a poetic economy. If Kant, however, tends to suppress the problematics of hypotyposis, the criticism of deconstruction has not. We will return to it in a moment, though now it is necessary to remark that the problematics cited by deconstruction have their precursor in Nietzsche and, I would add here, in the broken circle of Emerson's theory of "natural" signs. Therefore, one must heed Bloom's caution about the thrust of Emerson's demystifications, that his overcoming of philosophy demanded that he demystify (or even deprivilege) literature, but only as a means of restoring the aboriginal and originating power of trope.

Bloom's most salient advance in the radical reading of Emerson as a primal scene of interpretation (or Instruction) has therefore to repeat that ultimate idealist fable of the word as the medium of recuperation, the dialectics of voice. Thus Bloom's argument that while Emerson comes close to deconstruction, deconstruction is only a negative phase that the "Poet" employs to redress vision: "On this Emersonian implicit theory of the imagination, literary energy is drawn from language and not from nature, and the influence-relationship takes place between words and words, and not between subjects. I am a little unhappy to find Emerson, even in one of his aspects, joining Nietzsche as a precursor of Jacques Derrida and Paul de Man, twin titans of deconstruction." And so he wills the Emersonian transumption or dialectical overcoming of all negations: "Dialectical thinking in Emerson does not attempt to bring us back to the world of things and of other selves, but only to a world of language, and so its purpose is never to negate what is directly before us."[9] But, as Bloom then must conclude, Emerson's dialectics is less than rigorous and must be supposed by Europeans (philosophers?) to be "plain crazy." For Emerson restores meanings by evoking the haze of prophecy, by throwing his voice, as it were; so that Bloom can declare an American triumph of re-centering, or troping, over the entropy of Europe:

I think Nietzsche particularly understood that Emerson had come to prophesy not a de-centering, as Nietzsche had, and as Derrida and de Man are brilliantly accomplishing, but a peculiarly American re-centering, and with it an American mode of interpretation, one that we have begun—but only begun—to develop, from Whitman and Peirce down to Stevens and Kenneth Burke; a mode that is intra-textual, but

9. Harold Bloom, *A Map of Misreading* (Oxford, 1975), 174, 176.

that stubbornly remains logocentric, and that still follows Emerson in valorizing eloquence, the inspired voice, over the scene of writing. Emerson, who said he unsettled all questions, first put literature into question, and now survives to question our questioners.[10]

V

Bloom attributes Emerson's refusal of the abyss to an American spirit of pragmatism, with which one wants to agree, if allowed the qualification that makes pragmatism intervene in metaphysics in a way that a negative dialectics cannot—that is, in a way that disrupts what Bloom calls transumption or reveals transumption to be only a figural illusion. *Nature* concludes with a kind of "afterword" called "Prospects," which takes up once again the American experience of living within imitated (retrospective) forms derived from "foreign models." Only, Emerson adds, if one were to return to the European originals—"York Minster or St. Peter's at Rome"—he would discover that they "are imitations, also—faint copies of an invisible archetype" (*CW*, I, 40). That archetype is "Man," the ideal form in which "head and heart" are at one. We might interpolate: Man as figure, as hypotyposis, symbol of ground or nature, and ground of symbol. Emerson proceeds to appropriate a sizeable part of George Herbert's metaphysical poem celebrating this "symmetry of figure" (Man) that incorporates the universe; that is, he inscribes Man in his essay by quotation.

Now, as scholars of seventeenth-century poetry have observed, this quotation is a radical dismembering of context and a reinscription that makes Herbert's poem undercut its own theological ground. It is, of course, Man as the figuration of the center, and hence master of proportion, that Emerson's quotation extricates. Man is therefore the synecdoche, or symbol of God, become in "song" the metonym of a poetic universe. Man is inscribed in the poem as the poetic origin itself, as the genitive center, which urges its own elaboration or reading. The "voice" is inscribed in figuration. Thus the poetic voice originates "imperfect theories" and undoes received or "digested systems" (*CW*, I, 41) by an ex-centric appropriation of old signs. The proportion or ratio between this symmetrical center and the "imperfect" it projects, as "fable," escapes any final understanding as a self-contained, self-reflexive, closed em-

10. *Ibid.*, 176.

blem of Truth. The new is a quotation; symmetry, fabulous and figurative.

But more crucial to our purpose here is the fact that this genetic moment in Emerson is an aesthetic moment: "genius realizes and adds," to quote again his line from "The Poet," and poetry is the exteriorization or bodying forth of genius (spirit) that is always already a trope. The poet, then, is not simply a medium through which beauty realizes itself as truth; he is not a transparency or even a proper parent but, as we will see, is a figure in addition. Genius-spirit is never disembodied, and never fully body: "We are symbols and inhabit symbols," he had said in "The Poet"; "each word was at first a stroke of genius" (*CW*, III, 12, 13). The poet/genius that strikes the word also inhabits it; he seems therefore to reside where there is tropic begetting, where one figure is translated into another, its "second nature." The sense here of a teleological movement toward ever "higher" forms, and the consequent production of a hierarchy of languages, fulfilling the urge of a primordial poetic language, is cautiously qualified by Emerson. The genius who creates is only an "activity" that "repairs the decays of things" (13), and therefore is only a force within "nature." Genius is language, and language cannot finally surpass its temporal, aesthetical relation: "Like the metamorphosis of things into higher organic forms is their change into melodies," a "freer speech" that Emerson calls "organic" or "liberated," yet a mode of "indirection." The "daimon or soul" that stands over everything (the Over-Soul?) is "reflected by a melody." It is never outside reflection or the realm of the symbolic. And so all poems are the "corrupt version of some text in nature" (15), melodies that do not "tally" with the "text" of which they are "second" nature. The melodies cannot efface themselves to reveal the uncorrupted text. Instead, all poems call for the supplement of criticism in order to produce a formal symmetry or "tally."

Anyone seeking the philosophical precursor of Emerson, then, would not look to Plato but to the more contemporary transcendentalism of Kant— and indeed it might be claimed that *Nature* is but a condensed (mis-)quotation of Kant, or more precisely, of that moment in Kant when man (and genius) become the fulcrum of dialectic. It is in the second part of the *Critique of Judgment* where man is confirmed as the "final purpose of creation, since without him the chain of mutually subordinated purposes would not be complete as regards its ground" (246). But the teleological centering of man (as purpose or "subject" of nature) is achieved dialectically only through the careful construction of an aesthetical hierarchy that introduces the third

Critique. And it is this centralizing of man, as the figure that allows Kant to think the unity of sensible and supersensible, that still today tyrannizes critical thinking. Art, then, is at once the genius of nature and that through which man in his exceptional nature (genius) imparts via intuition the aesthetical yet self-transcending, or moves from aesthetical to teleological judgment. It is not the rigor of Kant's dialectic, however, but the problematics of his notion of aesthetical concept that seems to vex the analytics of the age of critique he inaugurates.

The third Critique is most famous for its analysis of the beautiful and the sublime, though it has become a primer for modern contextualist criticism more because of its powerful recentering of the "subject" (Man) and its privileging of poetry (and poetic language) as the highest of the arts. The central and transforming place of man/genius/art in the Kantian aesthetic, then, must finally come upon a transcendental moment that is inscribed in and inextricable from an aesthetical or figural moment—that doubled moment that opens his text to the kind of reading Derrida performs in "Parergon."[11] In Derrida's reading, philosophy itself, and particularly its categorical imperatives, is discovered to be interweaved with questions of genre, of demarcations or boundaries, frames and edges, or in short, aesthetical moments that confuse and cross out every possible closure or categorical demarcation. For our purposes here—far more modest than the Derridean analysis of the aesthetical or generic—I need to confine myself to the notion of figure, not simply the human figure or optical average that emerges as the primary Kantian example of the aesthetic ideal, but his notion of a poetic figurality or poetic language which, as Derrida shows, is always presented as the figure of the human body (115–16). The analytics of the sublime, as Derrida argues, develops according to a "violent incommensurability" between formal presentation and the concept of ineffability, of the colossal, everywhere marked as a problematics of representation and aesthetic containment (of framing, bordering, edges, generic space). The problematic becomes critical in the famous paragraph 59 (referred to earlier) on the figure of hypotyposis, which elaborates the necessary incommensurability of imagination and understanding, or intuition and concept, in representational forms. Hypotyposis (*exhibition,* illustrative figure, either schematic or symbolical, an "indirect presentation") is, therefore, at once the crux and question of Kant's aesthetics, the linguistic moment par ex-

11. Jacques Derrida, "Parergon," in *La Vérité en peinture* (Paris, 1978), 21–168.

cellence in which his earlier argument for the "free play" of poetry can be elaborated into the higher moment of moral judgment.[12] This moment of the symbol, when "free play" becomes "analogy," makes possible the transition or dialectical surpassing of "sense," the aesthetic and linguistic limit.

By paragraph 59, then, Kant has arrived at the pivotal moment of the "symbol," the "sign" or figure that is at once a grounding concept and its "indirect presentation," that which at once presents and calls for "reflection." Hypotyposis marks the boundary or obscured margin of any tropical dialectics; that is, it interferes with that self-reflexion (and self-reflection) it perpetuates. Emerson's circular figure of language in *Nature* would seem to obviate any such problematic, since the economy of the sign appears to make possible a transcendental progress of reflection. Yet, "Language," which is the "third use which Nature subserves to man," reveals that "Nature is the vehicle of thought, and in a simple, double, and threefold degree" (*CW*, I, 17). Emerson's famous circle, which argues for the origin of words in "natural facts," not only marks words as "signs" of facts but as the "transformation" and hence metaphoric "frame" of fact. So "words borrowed from sensible things" are also reflections not only diverted upon other objects but "appropriated to spiritual nature," irreducibly double and figural —and if Emerson's best examples of these words of natural origin include the word "*transgression,* the crossing of a line" (18), the example of trope itself, his definition of the word as analogue of fact at the same time marks

12. In his discussion of the necessity of symbolical hypotyposis, Kant offers us an observation that we may relate to Emerson's final break with his Unitarian ministry: "If we are to give the name 'cognition' to a mere mode of representation (which is quite permissible if the latter is not a principle of the theoretical determination of what an object is in itself, but of the practical determination of what the idea of it should be for us and for its purposive use), then all our knowledge of God is merely symbolical; and he who regards it as schematical, along with the properties of understanding, will, etc., which only establish their objective reality in beings of this world, falls into anthropomorphism, just as he who gives up every intuitive element falls into deism, by which nothing at all is cognized, not even in a practical point of view" (*Critique of Judgment*, 198). De Man seizes upon the problematic of hypotyposis in Kant as an undecidable rhetorical moment. In "The Epistemology of Metaphor," *Critical Inquiry*, V (Autumn, 1978), 13–30, esp. 26–29, he argues that when Kant insists that symbolical hypotyposis has no necessary relation between the icon and what it symbolizes (in contrast to schematical hypotyposis or abstraction, for example, a triangle, in which form and concept have a direct relation), he introduces the problematic of rhetoricity into the figure, no matter how confidently he ignores the question or resolves it by the introduction of intuition into the gap opened up by indirect presentation.

the word as metonymic transcription, chiasmus, and catachresis. Emerson's circle, therefore, can never advance beyond its exempla and the "radical correspondences" that interrupt the line of any circle that would return upon its beginning. Every sign, including natural fact, is folded upon itself originally, so that any lines (or reflection) that project from it also recross it: as Emerson said of "God's ways," they cannot "return into themselves" (*J*, IX, 172). Fact is the "end or last issue of Spirit," thus, a starting point and a circumference that is a center (or ex-center, horizon), from which only another circle or figure can be projected, a frontier at which we are left to "contemplate the fearful extent and multitude of objects" in the form of grammar (*CW*, I, 23). There is only a "radical correspondence between visible things and human thoughts"; and "savages" who spoke the "first language," "picturesque" and efficient, conversed in "figures" (19): "Hence, good writing and brilliant discourse are perpetual allegories" (20).

It is not Kant, then, but Nietzsche whom Emerson should recall. In Emerson, the Will to Power does not issue from any bottoming out. The negative, even in his most sceptical moments, is never a force, and the perpetual play of allegories never a vertigo but an "open book" (23). Power, then, does not inhabit dialectic, but surpasses or overruns any systematic containment. Power has no place or center, except in the crossings or transgression of borderline. What most critics define in Emerson as the subject ("mind"), the power or force that overcomes (transumes, or even sublates, if one employs the language of philosophical dialectic), is rather a force distributed throughout "nature," and man is the transitive of nature. Power, then, belongs to the sign, or the play between signs, a circle/line that transgresses itself or is in excess of itself. Emerson's transcendentalism will not close upon the Unity it pre-figures, but radiates or disseminates from word to word.

Emerson's next step in *Nature,* then, is not a transcendence of "Language," but a meditation on the power of interpretation compelled by language. And language can be nothing other than genius or Man. "Discipline" in Emerson should not be read as expression of law and limit, nor even as a hermeneutics of uncovering, but as a marking or decisive inscribing of law and limit ("action" as the "perfection and publication of thought"), and the correction of a language that has become "rotten," in which words are not connected to visible things. Thus language is the "action" or grammar of "nature," and Emerson, like Nietzsche later, would see this inscription of action (grammar) as the sign of God or Spirit. Yet God is seen only in terms of man, the "fragment" or sign that He inhabits: "Words and actions are not the attributes of brute nature. They introduce us to the human form" (28). But one cannot leap to the humanist (secular) affirmation here, to the conclusion that Emerson's poet repairs the rift in things to their "morning lustre" (21). The "human form," which seems everywhere in Emerson to authorize the "central Unity" of a humanist thought, becomes a verb of nature —that which at the same time mends and analyzes. To find the "first languages" again, an American idiom, would be to find a critical language, but not quite in Kant's sense.

If Emerson seems to appropriate the Kantian "circle," his metaphor does not function, either in *Nature* or in the essay "Circles," to effect a transition from the subjective and aesthetical to teleological purpose, which is another way of saying that his moral thought remains aesthetical and parabolical. Each turning of the "circle" in Emerson reinscribes it within another and marks its limit, its significance; so that even transcendental progress or the movement from lower to higher remains within a lustrous indefinite "horizon," that is, a figure that is a double inscription. That which moves from "center to the verge" does not simply displace the center with another, but doubles the center so that it is always at the "verge." The center was never anything but a verge, that is, a margin or crossing, a catachresis. The center is originally misnamed, a center in name only. The present is never present to itself. The Emersonian voice is irreducibly figural, and dialogical: "Conversation is a game of circles" (*CW*, II, 184), a circum-scriptive agon. Or as he put it elsewhere: "All conversation, as all literature, appears to me the pleasure of rhetoric, or, I may say, of metonymy" (*J*, IX, 231). We must now understand *metonymy* in Nietzsche's sense, as abstractions torn away from their contexts and made to stand autonomously as entities or phenomena when they are affections or figurations that owe an existence only to our feelings. Emerson's rhetorical elevation of the center or cause, his discovery once again of a primordial grammar that inscribes the subject and hypostatizes mind, turns out to be a reversal of the ideal of poetic language from effect or representation into cause, which can only reveal for us that poetry does not originate in things but in rhetoric, that "fact" and "spirit" are grounded in, not linked by, "symbol." The ideal of nature's form, center and circle, is only poetry hiding its "face."

We might best understand Emerson's eccentric resistance to "idealism," therefore, in the terms of a thinker who, despite his protestations against the influence of transcendentalism amid which he literally grew up, might be called an ephebe of Concord. I mean, of course, C. S. Peirce.[13] If Emerson could insist that "I write metaphysics, but my method is purely expectant" and thus argue that "every man is a new method" (J, XI, 267, 374), Peirce more precisely shows how any new advance in thought has to divest itself of metaphysics (self-reflection, dialectics) by a method he would call "pragmaticism" (as against the colloquialization of "pragmatism"): "The truth is that pragmaticism is closely allied to the Hegelian absolute idealism, from which, however, it is sundered by its vigorous denial that the third category . . . suffices to make the world, or is even so much as self-sufficient." It is within the Hegelian triad that Peirce situates his theory of the sign as a disruption that advances thought, because it does not confine the movement to systematic closure. Peirce's sign, therefore, is as vigorous an attack upon the notion of the symbol, from Kant's aesthetics to Hegel's, as is Nietzsche's almost contemporary deconstruction of the thing-in-itself. Or as Peirce would argue, all ideas depend on previous ones, the metaphoricity of which we may have forgotten: "and so on back to the ideal first, which is quite singular, and quite out of consciousness. The ideal first is the particular thing-in-itself. It does not exist as such. That is, there is no thing which is in-itself in the sense of not being relative to the mind, though things which are relative to the mind doubtless are, apart from that relation."[14]

There is not space here even to attempt a résumé of Peirce's recondite theory of the triadic sign, other than to outline its emphasis on relation and reinscription and its undoing of the Hegelian triad, or sublation, as well as of Kant's intuition. Thus Peirce's argument that Kant's categories take the

13. See *The Philosophy of Peirce: Selected Writings,* ed. Justus Buchler (New York, 1940), 339: "I may mention, for the benefit of those who are curious in studying mental biographies, that I was born and reared in the neighbourhood of Concord—I mean in Cambridge—at the time when Emerson, Hedge, and their friends were disseminating the ideas that they had caught from Schelling, and Schelling from Plotinus, from Boehm, or from God knows what minds stricken with the monstrous mysticism of the East. But the atmosphere of Cambridge held many an antiseptic against Concord transcendentalism; and I am not conscious of having contracted any of that virus. Nevertheless, it is probable that some cultured bacilli, some benignant form of the disease was implanted in my soul, unawares, and that now, after long incubation, it comes to the surface, modified by mathematical conceptions and by training in physical investigations."

14. *The Philosophy of Peirce,* ed. Buchler, 266–67, 247.

form of "propositions" and Aristotle's form themselves as "parts of speech" make way for modern semiotics, and arguments like Emile Benveniste's for the ground of philosophy in language[15]—hence the notion of Being as "a conception about a sign; a thought, or word" and not universal because it is not applicable to every sign or word. Peirce's hypothesis holds that, without exception, "every thought-sign is translated or integrated in a subsequent one," and therefore that every sign is inscribed in a threefold interpretative relationship, without origin and end, a circle or triad which is nevertheless a chain that does not return upon itself. Emerson's circle of "fact," "sign," and "symbol" cannot, finally, transcend this semiotic limit.

Peirce undoes the logical chain by which a thought would fulfill itself in its own end or death (a concern Emerson recognized in his own version of circumscription) by situating thought not in the subject or intuition but in the discontinuity of linked representations, or in the play of interpretation. The particular interrelations of Peirce's triadic sign—the sign or representamen "which stands to somebody for something in some respect," that is, in relation to a second sign/object, demands yet another or third sign, an interpretant, which also has a relation to the second, thus permitting no purely dyadic structure[16]—compose a broken circle that not only denies the priority or absolute determination of firstness but resists both the thought of transcendence and the despair of entropy.

Peirce, then, inaugurates a peculiarly "American" attack on the "subject," or on the Emersonian "self," though as I have argued, Emerson has already prepared for that attack by inscribing genius in rhetoric. Our "thought," Peirce insists, is not the issue of a subject, but the subject the issue of a sign: "When we think, then, we ourselves, as we are at that moment, appear as a sign. Now a sign has, as such, three references: 1st, it is a sign to some thought which interprets it; 2d, it is a sign for some fact to which in that thought it is equivalent; 3d, it is a sign, in some respect or quality, which brings it into connection with its object" (233). Thus, as he says in "Logic as Semiotic: The Theory of Signs," the triad connects representation to ground (at once object and idea) and both to the interpreta-

---

15. See Emile Benveniste, "Categories of Thought and Language," in *Problems in General Linguistics,* trans. Mary Meek (Coral Gables, Fla., 1971), 55–64. Also, see Derrida's deconstruction of this argument in "The Supplement of the Copula," in *Textual Strategies,* ed. Josue Harari (Ithaca, 1979), 82–120.

16. *The Philosophy of Peirce,* ed. Buchler, 99–100.

tion, or incorporates as semiotic the notions of pure grammar, logic, and pure rhetoric (99). The interpretative interrelations of signs, which situate man in a nexus of "judgments"—Peirce thus refutes Locke's "association of ideas" by showing that they are "association of judgments"—demystify the solipsism that haunted Emerson's genius, and in a way that might allow us to indicate why Emerson was seemingly undisturbed by the abyss of language that we have seen open up in his own theory of the sign. Thus Peirce: "the very origin of the conception of reality shows that this conception essentially involves the notion of a COMMUNITY, without definite limits, and capable of a definite increase of knowledge" (247). What does it mean, then, Peirce asks, to say "Man" if man is not already a word: "Consistency belongs to every sign, so far as it is a sign; and therefore every sign, since it signifies primarily that it is a sign, signifies its own consistency. The man-sign acquires information, and comes to mean more than he did before. But so do words. . . . Man makes the word, and the word means nothing which the man has not made it mean, and that only to some man. . . . In fact, therefore, men and words reciprocally educate each other; each increase of a man's information involves and is involved by, a corresponding increase of a word's information"; therefore, "the fact that every thought is a sign, taken in conjunction with the fact that life is a train of thought, proves that man is a sign; so, that every thought is an external sign, proves that man is an external sign" (249).

Peirce concludes this essay, "Some Consequences of Four Incapacities," with a verse on "man" who is a "negation" insofar as he insists on his "separate existence" or denies his communal "essence." On the contrary, man is inscribed in a relationship (hence community) of signs. Emerson had concluded *Nature* not simply with a quotation from Herbert's "little poem on Man," but with what the appearance of that quotation/transcription had inspired, an increase of meaning in the "cycle of the universal man," in its American relations. The quotation of Herbert activates an "Orphic" utterance (what a "certain poet sang to me"—little matter that Emerson, as some say, is referring to Alcott in particular), a prophecy that extends or draws yet another circle of the "traditions of man and nature" (*CW*, I, 41). What Emerson calls "Prospects" (a pro-spective, or throwing forward) does not transcend man to ineffable spirit, but returns to the "form" of man, a "god in ruins," to man in his "infancy" or limit, "disunited within himself," a center on the verge always in need of some completion; in need of "marriage," a "relation" with the universe. We might now recall one of those axiomatic passages from the journals, on his favorite figure, "Croisement": "Nature loves crosses . . . : and marriage is a crossing" (*J*, X, 45). The context here makes indelible the notion of marriage/love as a trope of trope, and "the value of a trope is the hint it affords of trope or (in) transmigration to the mind of the reader itself" (44). Quotation is reading; reading is translation; translation is a re-crossing. The "song" of prophecy is intertextually inscribed in a circle that does not return upon itself or break out of itself, the "traditions of man and nature." The play of trope is most irreversible when the reversals and crossings are most vigorous.

The "song" that the Orphic poet sings to Emerson, which Emerson translates into the "prospects" that make certain another crossing or troping, resists the very transcendental moment it forecasts. That is, the "song" resists its own effacement by calling forth its interpretant, like a voice always already a representation or figure. The figure of the poet, therefore, is a figure of a "blind man," who tells us (like some critics) "fables of voice" that tempt us out of thought, that lure us with fables of identity. But Orpheus is doubly pre-figured in his own "song"—as the failed interpreter whose very turning marks the problematics of all recuperation and teleology, and the ideal of perception they entail. Orpheus' loss suspends the end of the genetic myth. For Orpheus is the victim of his song, the prophet of his own dismembering. Orpheus, who is most crucially identified with voice, or mythopoetics, is inextricable from the sign, the crossing or a marriage that is never realizable except in the aberrational play of tropes. Poetry reenacts this figural moment of translation as an action of interpretation that Peirce calls "semiosis," and Emerson, more poetically, "method": "Every man is a new method, & distributes all things anew" (*J*, XI, 374).

When in "The Poet" Emerson tells us that "poetry was all written before time was" (*CW*, III, 5), he introduces us to a myth of origins in what he calls "primal warblings," a common myth of figure emerging from voice, of poetry as the origin of language—an argument for poetic origins that we have already witnessed in the "Language" section of *Nature*. But as in *Nature*, in "The Poet" man's reception and echoing of these "warblings" is a translation not from silence to voice and from voice to words, but an indication that the one could never exist outside of or before the other, and that such questions as outside and inside are only the issue of some mistranslation of "thought" out of primal "words." Words are originarily tropes; nature is a quotation, a sign and a crossing. Man is a metonymy that literature (poetry) resituates as origin, but only in the sign. He is language, and "Language is fossil poetry." Transcendentalism's myth of origins originates in a translation it cannot cover over. And man is at once origin and issue of this (his own) signature, the power of rhetoric; that is, of poetry. Man is a god in ruins, but not a fragment of the god of perfection. The ruins or fragment, the metonymy reigns, is King. And "first philosophy" originates in the (his) sign.

3

THE HERMENEUTICAL SELF

NOTES TOWARD AN "AMERICAN" PRACTICE

"Man is a method."
—R. W. Emerson

"Man is a sign."
—C. S. Peirce

"Man is a force."
—Henry Adams

For E. D.—still, a force

Having no history, the American writer has regularly found her- or him-self in a kind of double bind: needing first to invent that which could then be represented. This is particularly true of the nineteenth-century writer who was repeatedly engaged in genealogical fabrications, producing fables which at the same time constructed family histories and made the theme of a family history or "romance" problematic. In *Pierre,* Melville under-scores the irony of the enterprise when he has his titular hero confront the dilemma of providing his editors and publishers a biography though the young writer has in effect had no life to recount, certainly none worthy to represent in his own writings. Yet his first publications are to be his "col-lected works," produced, as his editors enthusiastically note, in the "Li-brary Form." His writing will imitate the idea of a life, which is to say, the unity of a book, or "literature." Stein, with a kind of disarming naïveté, states the problem as something less than the "anxiety of influence," but as nothing less than the question of writing. "It has always seemed to me a rare privilege, this, of being an American, a real American," she writes at the beginning of her massive genealogical fable, *The Making of Americans* (1966), "one whose tradition has taken scarcely sixty years to create. We

72

need only realize our parents, remember our grandparents and know our-selves and our history is complete." And she continues: "The old people in a new world, the new people made out of the old, that is the story that I mean to tell"(3).

She does not want to report or record a history, but to engender one, and this means virtually to perform it into some semblance of a family lin-eage, something like a narrative. It is uncertain whether the notion of nar-rative derives from the reality of human history, or whether the fiction of that history is derived from our habit of thought, our tendency to under-stand things as a continuity, as narrative—as "her-story." Unquestionably, as Stein will prove with the monotonous repetitiveness of her account, the history is constructed out of some belief in grammar, but at the same time the story proceeds by putting extreme stress upon grammar. If "composition" is "explanation," as Stein argued, the explanation is at once representa-tion and interpretation. The writer does not repeat "what was in the script," to recall Wallace Stevens' line in "Of Modern Poetry," but in writing en-acts the very "stage" on which the performance takes place. A genealogy is not natural, it is constructed—the "making" of Americans.

For Stein and Stevens, poetry is a performance that exposes the prob-lematics of modernism. Since what it engenders is its own stage, a writing that writes itself, it at once proceeds along the lines of an old grammar and revises or disturbs the grammatical law. In "Poetry and Grammar," Stein offers one of her curious non-definitions of the interventions of writing, approaching the subject of her title in the only possible way, in a prose that must first define the other of poetry, prose itself.[1] Prose, she says, is an art of balancing sentences and paragraphs, or statement and senses, meaning and its emotional or sensory elaboration. Because "sentences are not emotional and paragraphs are" (223), or because paragraphs tend to open the peri-odic closure of the sentence, the writing of prose seeks some kind of equilibrium between a logic of description and the rhythmical extension of fact—be-tween the cognitive and the performative. (We might note here that in an-other context she described the eighteenth century as an age of sentences, the nineteenth as one of phrases or fragments, and the twentieth as one of para-graphs, thereby defining history as a change of modes but also as a kind of radical revisionary break [158–59].)

1. Gertrude Stein, "Poetry and Grammar," in *Lectures in America* (Boston, 1985), 209–46.

In *The Making of Americans,* she claims, "I tried to break down this essential combination of sentences and paragraphs by making enormously
long sentences that would be as long as the longest paragraph and so to see
if there was really and truly the essential difference between paragraphs
and sentences, if one went far enough with this thing with making the sentences long enough to be as long as my paragraph and so producing in them
the balance of a paragraph not a balance of a sentence, because the balance of a paragraph is not the same balance as the balance of a sentence" (223).
Far from being a description of prose, this is a sentence performing its own
revision and violating the grammatical law. The new equilibrium she posits
will not occur as a logical balance but as a rhetorical excess and re-petition. Sentences, she insists, depend upon nouns, that is, on names, and to
open sentences to the emotion of the paragraph is to give the noun a history, to make it verbal and adverbial. In this Stein anticipates the Ezra
Pound/Ernest Fenollosa recuperation of the Chinese written character, in
which they find the verbal reinscribed within the nominal in such a way as
to reintroduce time or dynamic into the sclerotic logic of Western phonetic
languages.

Stein then proceeds to a description of poetry, or the shorter, condensed
rhythms that contrast with the expansive and emotional performance of
paragraphs. And she offers a definition precisely the opposite of Pound's. "Poetry has to do with vocabulary just as prose has not," she says. It is a "vocabulary based on the noun as prose is essentially and determinately and
vigorously not based on the noun": "Poetry is concerned with using with
abusing, with losing with wanting, with denying with avoiding with ador-
ing with replacing the noun. . . . Poetry is doing nothing but using losing
refusing and pleasing and betraying and caressing nouns." To caress the
noun is also to trope it, to infuse it with a sense-effacing sensation, to disturb
its referentiality, to lighten its semantic load and distribute it through the
time of enunciation, even to render it *anasemic.* But at this point, she cites
or recites her own famous poem as example, and I quote her in prose:

> When I said
> A rose is a rose is a rose is a rose
And then later made that into a ring I made poetry and what did I do I caressed
completely caressed and addressed a noun. (231)

If poetry is the ardor of caress, it also appropriates or takes possession of an other, a name. It detaches the name from what it names, and precipitates it into a phase or time of its own. Giving the noun its own property, it suspends the proper name. The rearrangement of the noun into its own circle of relations, or into an improvised grammar—here a circle—repeats the old grammar and violates its law. For the sentence has no end. The circle does not return upon itself, but expands infinitely, a repetition with a difference, producing a genealogy of names without origin or end. Blanchot said of the "poem" that it is "the locus of a perverse contradiction," the double emblem in which are entwined trope and something more or less than trope (en-tropy or ana-tropy), what Derrida calls "a flower of rhetoric without properties, with no proper meaning, a repeated self-quotation."[2]

Stein credits her mentor William James with the method of incremental writing that she was working out in *The Making of Americans,* insisting that her purpose was, like the scientist's, to account for the greatest possible amount of information, to totalize it by exploring relations and affinities. But this meant defining not what was inherent in the information; it required producing a new vocabulary, a new mathematic of relations—at once a new genealogy and a new genre. This writing would be a pragmatic, not an ontological, description, and thus a "method" that would more satisfactorily account for the logical gaps in relations than could the old grammar. When James describes pragmatism, he calls it a "method" rather than a philosophy, that is, a way, but not the only way, of taking account of the moment of *transition* between two vocabularies, or two senses of things: the moment in which an old language gives way to the necessity of a new. That moment, he observes, must appear at first incomprehensible if not simply "mad," as if the old words were being torn from their moorings and set afloat. Pragmatism would be the atheoretical theory of *transitions* (a word he heavily emphasizes), and hence an action that must appear to reintroduce the powerful effects of the irrational into the old logic that had thought itself beyond the primitivism of language's birth. Pragmatism, therefore, speaks not of "truth" in the singular but of "truths in the plural," says James, and these latter are not "real truth"—that is, not *the* absolute correspondence.[3] On the contrary, pragmatism is an ac-

2. See "Border Lines," note to Jacques Derrida, "Living On," in *Deconstruction and Criticism* (New York, 1979), 157–58*n.*

3. William James, "What Pragmatism Means" (lecture two of *Pragmatism*), in *Pragmatism and Other Essays,* (Cambridge, Mass., 1975), 104.

tion that produces the only truths we can know, or need to know, those which belong exclusively to our thoughts, or better, our vocabulary. New truths, then, are produced by a change of vocabulary—or a vocabulary in change—and the action is in effect translation. It is within the moment of this translation that pragmatism encounters what Stevens calls the "irrational moment," the poetic rather than scientific understanding that inhabits all language.

For James, however, the transitional moment would only be an interval and not a discontinuity, and if subjective still no threat to the new-sense. "New truth is always a go-between, a smoother-over of transitions. It marries old opinion to new fact so as ever to show a minimum of jolt, a maximum of continuity" (35). But even granting that it can cover over the logical "jolt," if "new truth" does not fully displace the old—the "influence" of the latter, James says, is "absolutely controlling"—it does nevertheless suspend for the moment the determining force of the past. For truths lie not in the "content" of facts but in "what we say about them," and what we say about them are words in the endless process of self-translation. The pragmatic actor may select and rearrange, but he is not a single subject whose thoughts govern and determine the changes of meaning. Pragmatism is an experimental method, and like Stein's experimental writing, the language in a certain sense writes itself. Or at least language is the only possible model of mind. The problem remains, however, of the plural and contradictory models of language.

It is the moment of *transition,* then, which James finds the greatest threat to pragmatism's methodological claims, the moment in which it appears most poetic and even "mad," that is, dependent on metaphor: "truth is satisfied by the plain additive formula"; that is, its new vocabulary supplements the old as it transforms it, though it adds nothing to the nature or content of what it presumably addresses. James then describes an uncanny scene of translation from old to new:

But often the day's contents oblige a rearrangement. If I should now utter piercing shrieks and act like a maniac on this platform, it would make many of you revise your ideas as to the probable worth of my philosophy. "Radium" came the other day as part of the day's content, and seemed for the moment to contradict our ideas of the whole order of nature, that order having come to be identified with what is called the conservation of energy. The mere sight of radium paying heat away indefinitely out of its own pocket seemed to violate that conservation. What to think? If the radiations from it were nothing but an escape of unsuspected "potential" energy, preexistent inside of the atoms, the principle of conservation would be saved. The discovery of "helium" as the radiation's outcome, opened this way of belief. So Ramsay's view is generally held to be true, because, although it extends our old ideas of energy, it causes a minimum of alteration in their nature. . . .

A new opinion counts as "true" just in proportion as it gratifies the individual's desire to assimilate the novel in his experience to his beliefs in stock. . . . When old truth grows, then, by new truth's addition, it is for subjective reasons. (36)

What is startling in this passage, beyond the ease with which James interprets the new truth as giving pleasure and not authority, is his choice of example: the discovery of radium, which at first disturbed the old paradigm and then was assimilated to it, "grafted" onto the old, as James says, in a continuously unfolding metaphor that tries to accommodate this new idea of the sun to the old organic notion of the sun as source and center, and more important, to smooth over the "jolt" of the new arrangement of understanding. This is not exactly the ease or pleasure that all interpreters of the new dynamics would derive from it, as we will see. For "radium" is only one of a number of new scientific discoveries that convulsed the nineteenth century—discoveries at once necessitating a new vocabulary and disturbing the old. But perhaps more important, the discoveries motivated a rethinking of the crises they signified, the rethinking of theories of change —a thinking perhaps of the unthinkable, of chance, catastrophe, catachresis.

Here is Emerson, more than a half century before James, recognizing the question, even as he smoothed it over in the old language of continuity:

There are no fixtures in nature. The universe is fluid and volatile. Permanence is but a word of degrees. . . . The Greek sculpture is all melted away, as if it had been statues of ice; here and there a solitary figure or fragment remaining, as we see flecks and scraps of snow left in cold dells and mountain clefts in June and July. . . . The Greek letters last a little longer, but are already passing under the same sentence and tumbling into the inevitable pit which the creation of new thought opens for all that is old. The new continents are built out of the ruins of an old planet; the new races fed out of the decomposition of the foregoing. New arts destroy the old. See the investment of capital in aqueducts, made useless by hydraulics; fortifications, by gunpowder; roads and canals, by railways; sails, by steam; steam by electricity. (CW, II, 179)

But it is not easy for his readers today to maintain Emerson's composure in the face of these "jolts" or displacements, or to sustain the metaphor of organic continuity in the face of the recognition that the new concepts of energy might truly be what Henry Adams called "radium," a "metaphysical bomb." What "radium" had introduced into the laws of conservation, the new science had bequeathed wholesale to the historian who sought, in Adams' metaphor, to sustain the law of historical "sequence," of narrative and genealogy. We begin to read in American thought the "jolt" of having to think its own newness, of having to rethink the solar myth from where it stood in the twilight of Western thought, like a belated reflection and repetition. From Poe's *Eureka* to Williams' call for a "new language" and its "new measure," American thought would have to take account of what Pound called this "thermometric cyclone." If "radium" forced the scientist to think the problematical difference between matter and energy, rather than sustain his old faith in their continuous transformation, the new science forced the observer of nature and history to rethink the relation between the two, and eventually to rethink the difference between the self considered as an essence, substance, or origin, and the self as a force or an action—the difference between the "central man" and the an-archical performer.

It has always seemed a paradox to think of American "thought" or of the uniqueness of "our literature," and not simply because we encounter the old contradiction between the claims of universality and the claims of nationalism. We do not have the same reservations in speaking of the universality of Western thought, or of the differences between, say, German and French thought. The Hegelian model, which makes such thinking not only possible but inevitable, is not, however, altogether appropriate to the American exception. For certainly one of the identifying characteristics of American *thought,* even if we now recognize the term to be a euphemism, is its thinking of itself as an exception, and even an excess—that is, in James's terms, as a kind of "additive" to this history of the West. We do not lack for cultural historians and critics who make this or that claim for the uniqueness of the American experience, and the strangeness of the American signature. Whether it is democracy's unique transformation of social structures and its institutionalization of individualism, or some unique and gothic twist our culture performed upon its religious inheritance, or even some massive cultural repression we suffered by recognizing our difference, as Leslie Fiedler has suggested, which at the same time animates and enervates our writers;[4] or whether

4. Leslie Fiedler, *Love and Death in the American Novel* (New York, 1960).

it might be the result of our particular geography, our "space," as Charles Olson put it, that summoned us toward an ever-receding future rather than a determining past and lent us a certain unique sense of our own historicity, making us orphans of the West yet the instruments of its destiny, the one shared characteristic is that American thought seems to originate in the need to think our own originality. It begins by an act at once acknowledging and denying its own belatedness, by writing itself as the end and fulfillment of history and yet the "beyond" of history, a powerful exception to what it represents. It repeatedly begins again by staging its own origin as an exception, as a reflection on its unique difference. Yet even this very difference is a projection of what American thought and literature would be if they could but realize themselves. American literature inevitably stages itself as a clearing of the ground before the beginning of a new literature, but at the same time projects itself as a future free from the old ground. It must be critical before it can be creative—at once self-reflective and an intervention in or doubling of the ideal of self-reflexiveness. That is why it seems never to conform to the old genres but to violate every law of genre; to be a hybrid, that is, something without a proper parent. Like Poe's orphans and Melville's, American literature has repeatedly allegorized the exception of its thought as a strange self-engendering.

"American literature" has always put in jeopardy the very "humanist" discourse it had seemed to fashion as its own unique contribution and character. American criticism, on the other hand, has been just as industrious in covering over the "jolt," even when the story it tells is a dialectic between Emerson's "optative mood," as Matthiessen called it, and the skeptical questioning of the "central man" one finds in Melville's isolato, Poe's orphans, or Hawthorne's sinners. The dialectical reading of Emerson fashioned by Stephen Whicher locates this thematic in one exemplary life or, in particular, in the poetic "self." The "American" thematic has always been grounded in some version of Emerson's "central man," whether he is the religious antinomian or frontiersman.

The point I want to make, before abandoning the generalizations for a closer textual analysis, is that this individualism or Adamism turns upon a monumental installation of the figure of man at the center of things—Emerson's "Representative Man" as a kind of regulating mechanism, governor of the dialectic of history and mirror at once of nature and of God; in a word, the regulator of all self-reflexion, an originating and organizing force. Even some of the more potent efforts to redefine the American tradition as a radical departure from the metaphysical tradition, Richard Rorty's and Harold Bloom's respective efforts to identify a unique American tradition in terms of a discursive practice that is pragmatic and rhetorical rather than epistemological and logical, merely revise but do not radically question the consensus of our humanist lineage.

According to Rorty, American pragmatism belongs to one of the two major paths open to nineteenth-century philosophy—one turning to the question of language in order to complete the Kantian project; the other taking the direction laid out by Hegel and later Nietzsche that leads to recent Continental philosophy and is characterized by what Rorty calls "conversation," a discursive practice that questions the old philosophical questions and rejects the scientific and systematic obsession for truth.[5] Conversation turns us away from epistemology, or the search to make our representations adequate to some extra-linguistic reality, and toward hermeneutics, which is no longer concerned with the recuperation of truth or with the adequation of representation and represented. It is concerned rather with prolonging the inquiry or with the limited usefulness of the practice—hence it is a method of inquiry that provisionally subordinates the purpose of method to the pleasure of the practice. And Rorty associates it with its recent manifestation in the regional discipline of literary criticism. Like Bloom after him—though Bloom's notion of pragmatism is not so rigorously defined—Rorty employs a psychological model of this discourse, so that "conversation" is an activity that leads us not toward some end but toward the satisfac-tion of some momentary understanding. Bloom amplifies this as a scene of psychic warfare, both internal to the individual and among cultural forces, best exemplified in the dialectics of literature, an "agon" or struggle that can be understood on the model of trope or performative language. And Bloom argues vigorously that what is at stake here, as in all literature, is the "self" or psyche, the stage of human history. This conversational self, as Rorty tends to define it, may be performing at the end of history, and may be the last resistance to that end; but Rorty's story, and his discursive and hermeneutical heroes, are pressed by less anxiety than Bloom's. Nevertheless, what remains of humanism survives in this privileging of the literary conversation as psychic event.

There is not space, however, to rehearse further this latest critical fable,

5. See Richard Rorty, *Philosophy and the Mirror of Nature* (Princeton, N.J., 1979), and Rorty, *Consequences of Pragmatism* (Minneapolis, 1982).

and besides, I wish to tell a slightly different tale: to argue from certain individual texts where a "self," even an "American self," seems to have its advent, that it appears only as the simulacrum of an occulted theological origin, or as theology itself. It appears as a provisional substitute of the old myth of the center, bearing all the marks of its grammatical origin. And thus it prepares for its own undoing. I want therefore to recall my three epigraphs: Emerson's assertion that "man is method"; Peirce's that "man is a sign"; and Adams' that "man is a force." It would be tempting here to suggest that they compose the trajectory of a history, from a kind of secular humanism to its eventual degradation and self-annihilation, which parallels and represents a general nineteenth-century history of ideas. And in a sense that is the way our canonical literature has been read. (One might note that so-called American thought has almost always been read through its literature rather than through its philosophers or philosophy, presuming there are any, and that it is almost uniquely defined, as Emerson claimed, as "poetic" and practical at the same time.) Though Emerson is unquestionably the metonymic figure, if not the actual father, of the myths of American individualism, of the American Adam, and Henry Adams is as surely the nihilistic voice of its vulnerable innocence and colossal failure, the textual space that relates the one to the other no more describes a pattern of rise and fall or a dialectic of our thought than it does an end of innocence. Indeed, as I will argue, it constitutes a massive critique of that kind of understanding, and calls for a new interpretation of interpretation.

Emerson poses to us from the beginning a question of "reading," of an interactive or "creative reading" that will free us from the received ideas entombed in "books" and libraries. But how does one read this admonition? as a statement or directive? or as a rhetorical ploy, a performance? Emerson's texts repeatedly pose this problem of how to read him: as philosopher or poet? If the first, he is surely derivative and unsystematic; if the second, rhetorical and hortatory (Bloom interprets him as prophet and visionary). Or perhaps we are witness to a double discourse, the one folding back into the other, troping the other, producing effects that cannot be traced in the economy of Bloom's revisionary ratios. Still, Emerson makes statements that conform in a certain way to moral philosophy, even when they exhort one to a vision "beyond" philosophy or when they celebrate contradiction. That is, he writes philosophy in metaphors and aphorisms that enact in reverse what Vico (or even Peirce in a different sense) saw as the emergence of thought out of a primitive poetic language; he wants to reintroduce into philosophy or cognitive discourse the very figural contaminants it sought to pass beyond or overcome. In *Nature,* he can advocate a return to "first philosophy" and to a "transparency" of thought, only to conclude that the nearest form of transparency we have is the poet's voice, so that *Nature* turns into a philosophical fable that discovers the origins of Spirit in the voice of the genius, the poet, the central man, or Man Thinking, an activity inseparable from figuration and from a certain notion of discursive practice.

But in Emerson, the installation of Man at the center doubles the center and precipitates it upon the ex-centric horizon. As a reflection of both Spirit and nature, Man stands in the place of the sign. But the sign has no place—it is both a positing and a provisional substitution, a position and a translation. "A man is a centre for nature, running out threads of relation through everything, fluid and solid, material and elemental" (*CW,* IV, 6). But this representative center is not quite the subject; it is the verb of grammatical relations, a transitional center that acts, a predicate: "Men have a pictorial or representative quality" (6), but they are not the figures of the ineffable or transcendent. Man is the interpretation of the invisible, a kind of translation: "The possibility of interpretation lies in the identity of the observer with the observed," Emerson notes, but this is only an ideal possibility: "Each material thing has its celestial side; has its translation, through humanity"(7). The ideal of translation, of the pure transparency of the sign, is complicated by Emerson's awareness of what the representation necessarily adds to, even as it deflects, the represented; for otherwise the representation would have no identity, just as the poet could not be a creator himself, that is, could not be free to act. The representation can be neither a transparency nor a perfect correspondence of what it represents. It is at once more, a "power," and less than itself. Emerson's rhetoric is poised upon this contradiction. It must yet cannot be self-effacing. It must show a face. Face or figuration is not simply a name for the origin, it is uncannily pre-original.

As a "central stance," "man" is an "analogist" charged with regulating nature's pairing rhymes. But analogies and rhymes also reflect a fundamental difference; they reflect a world not of stable relations but of transitions and transformations, and thus de-flect or produce alterity. If the ideal poet were a man "without impediment," things would be unchang-

ing. If man did not deflect as well as reflect, or add something to every translation, nature would be a still life. Unlike Kant's man, Emerson's is not an
end in himself, nor does he exemplify the purpose or end of nature. He is
instead a kind of instrument by which nature extends itself and transforms
itself. If man is a centre for nature," he is nevertheless "incomplete": "we cease
to look in man for completeness"; the "individual is temporary and prospective" (19–20). If he is an analogist, he produces "radical correspondences"
rather than unmediated visions. Such self-contradictions proliferate in
Emerson's texts like the self-canceling aphorisms that they comprise. Thus
the Orphic utterances of his essays turn out to be endless self-quotations,
comprising or recomposing poetic sequences of tropes.

Man may stand at the "centre of beings," but he is himself neither a center nor a being. He is a "method," a gathering and diffusion of forces, an
organization of "immense instrumentalities" (W, VI, 55). That is why Emerson's *Representative Men* are exceptional: men of action, heroes, geniuses,
poets. Action, however, has a very special sense for Emerson. Thought is
action; and of all kinds of action, the poet's is the most significant because
his is an action that "turns the world to glass, and shows us all things in
their right series and procession" (CW, III, 12). The poet's words are "actions" and "actions are a kind of words" (6). Thus the poet enfolds in himself a kind of trinity: he is "the Knower, the Doer, and the Sayer" (5), at
once the innocent child of the epigraph who shares "Apollo's privilege"
and yet one who sings "Divine ideas below," or in other words, one who
translates or performs that "privilege" into words. If the knower shares
the immediacy of Apollo's "privilege," the Doer is a Hermes, a kind of thief
or translator: "For poetry was all written before time was, and whenever
we are so finely organized that we can penetrate into that region where the
air is music, we hear those primal warblings and attempt to write them
down, but we lose ever and anon a word or a verse and substitute something of our own, and thus miswrite the poem" (5–6). "Talent may frolic and
juggle," he says; "genius realizes and adds" (7). The miswriting supplements the "primal warblings," resulting in both loss and gain. That is, the
poet's actions (or words) form a double writing. His words, like all words,
are at once "fossil poetry" and transforming tropes; and poetry is at the
same time an act of proper naming and a critical or interpretative reading.

The ideal of such a "tally" or adequation between "primal warbling"
and its translation, as between observer and observed, or even poet and

critic, is deferred in the very figure that should regulate their self-mirroring. The poetic performance is neither an impediment nor a transparency. It is supplementary: "beyond the energy of his possessed and conscious intellect he is capable of a new energy (as of an intellect doubled on itself)" (15). Man is more than a property; he is an "excess" of his own nature, and his actions have an "excess of direction," which is one of his "Spiritual Laws." One goes on quoting Emerson quoting himself, in a series of metaphors that institute man at the center as the name, both metonym and misnomer, for something that is more than original. The center is more than itself, doubled within itself, and precipitated into the margin. Man/poet occupy the same place as "literature" in the essay "Circles": "Literature is a point outside our hodiernal circle through which a new one may be described. The use of literature is to afford us a platform whence we may command a view of our present life, a purchase by which we may move it" (CW, II, 185). It is prospective, not reflective, and it "represents," as it were, the future rather than the past. It is a representation that precedes what it represents. It is not a ground but an interpretation that clears the ground. It represents, that is, the prospective act of interpretation. Emerson's "centre" is what Stevens, in "A Primitive Like an Orb," called a "centre on the horizon," a "patron of origins," a figuration of the sun.[6] But where the sun appears, as we know, metaphor has already begun. The "patron of origins," as Stevens' poem concludes, is a "figure" not complete in itself because it must be occulted and revised in every writing or miswriting. Thus Stevens deconstructs the popular notion of Emerson's "central man," and places there at "the centre on the horizon" the figure of language itself, the "giant ever changing, living in change."

Emerson's figure of the poet cannot be separated from his utterance and from the problematics of the sign. Man is not a "simple, separate person," as Whitman would put it, nor is his poet Whitman's "equable man." Yet our tradition of individual self-reliance has been concocted out of such proclamations of his that seem to claim as much. Peirce's need to disavow transcendentalism in order to begin his revisionary philosophy and to found a science of language is simply another dramatic example that Emersonian thought appeared in its rhetorical sweep to be a regression from reason—to be poetic and prophetic rather than philosophical. But Emerson thought it to be critical: "Literature is now critical. Well, analysis may be po-

6. Wallace Stevens, *Collected Poems* (New York, 1954), 440.

etic" (*J*, VIII, 303). For Peirce, however, literature belongs to the pre-logical stage of language, as did transcendentalist discourse, which if not exactly poetic, was certainly not analytical. Thus Peirce, in making one of the nineteenth century's most unique turns toward language, was blind to the fact that Emerson had preceded him. The putative father of pragmatism had to walk in the rhetorical steps of a still earlier father. For Emerson's philosophy of action, of Doing as Saying, constitutes an intervention into the very metaphysics he is presumed to have voiced. Peirce's attack on metaphysics is more direct, and perhaps, as Rorty claims, it turns out to be more metaphysical than Emerson's version of American "conversation." Yet it is Peirce's own intervention, his effort to ground a philosophy in a general theory of the sign, that now requires our attention.

We must necessarily bypass the question of Peirce's attempt to found a new philosophy (a new logic) on a revisionary critique of the old, specifically of that philosophy of mind associated with Descartes and Kant, or of categorical thought in general. Thus semiotics would close metaphysics in preparation for the opening of science. Peirce begins by putting in question all binarism. His complex notion of the sign resorts to the model of the triangle. But his triangulation is not strictly dialectical. All thought, says Peirce, must be conceived on the model of language, or more precisely on a new model of the sign, a sign consisting of the complex interrelation of three pairs. All signs are representations, but also interpretations; and the signs are objects themselves, though not things in themselves. Peirce's neologisms for this tripartite structure are "representamen," "sign/object," and "interpretant," which he in turn aligns with the notions of Firstness, Secondness, and Thirdness, respectively. Yet, First-Second-Third does not fall into the traditional or arithmetical pattern of sequence or priority. The sign, we will see, inscribes a certain notion of time, even though Peirce thought of it as purely logical, and it is this notion of temporality or change that makes his critique so suggestive. Firstness is not earlier, nor is it thetic; secondness is not later, or simply antithetical; and thirdness is not synthetic, nor still later, but necessary for the possibility of the other two. Peirce recognizes that his triangulation may have affinities with dialectical thinking, that it is "closely allied with the Hegelian absolute idealism." Yet, as he says, it is radically different because of its "vigorous denial that the third category . . . suffices to make the world, or is even so much as self-sufficient."[7] "A

7. *The Philosophy of Peirce: Selected Writings*, ed. Justus Buchler (New York, 1940), 266–67.

sign, or representamen," he writes, "is something which stands to some-body for something in some respect or capacity. It addresses somebody, that is, creates in the mind of that person an equivalent sign, or perhaps a more developed sign. That sign which it creates I call the *interpretant* of the first sign. The sign stands for something, its *object*" (99). The sign does and does not refer, for reference is also interpretation. Peirce denies, however, that the *representamen* precedes and provokes the *interpretant*. Every rep-resentation is already an interpretation, and an "object" exists only be-cause it is an "idea," that is, because the object is related to what repre-sents it and to some idea of it, some understanding or interpretation. Each of the three is related to the other in a binary relationship, and the whole, which can never quite be whole or singular, is composed of a kind of triple doubleness. The triangular sign, then, cannot be dialectical or self-reflexive. It always calls for a new sign, or for its own future.

Peirce's more radical claim is that if all thought exists only in signs, there is no thinker or singularity of mind before or outside the sign, no Being or presence of which the sign is a representation, and no constitutive origin for subsequent signs it will produce: "We get [the notion of Being] by re-flecting upon signs, words, thoughts. . . . The conception of being is, there-fore, a conception about a sign—a thought or word" (240). Pragmatism, says Peirce, is a matter of producing new signs, of signs producing signs. In general, it is the production of a new vocabulary by a revision of the old vocabulary. Hence it is a "method," an "experimental method," but one not concerned with the "truth" of metaphysics, or with the adequation of the sign to some thing-in-itself. It is a method of producing and proliferat-ing a knowledge that is always provisional and, in a sense, prospective. Strictly speaking, therefore, pragmatism denies that interpretation resides either in the self or mind, or in what is interpreted, but that it is a part of a dialogue or action that has always already begun: "a person is not ab-solutely individual. His thoughts are what he is 'saying to himself,' that is, saying to that other self that is just coming into life in the flow of time. When we reason, it is that critical self that one is trying to persuade; all thought whatsoever is a sign, and is mostly of the nature of language" (258). For Peirce, man seems always in the process of translating himself.

In an essay entitled "Logic as Semiotic," Peirce relates the three sides or positions (at once positons and tran-positions) of his triangular sign to the three general branches of knowledge: the *representamen*, or first, with *pure grammar,* the *sign/object,* or second, with *logic* proper, and the *interpretant,* or third, with *pure rhetoric.* Of the third he says that he follows Kant's "fashion of preserving old associations of words in finding nomenclature for new conceptions." Thus the old word *rhetoric* is retained and yet transformed into a new notion of rhetoric: "Its task is to ascertain the laws by which in every scientific intelligence one sign gives birth to another, and especially one thought brings forth another" (99). This new rhetoric is here defined as a kind of interpretative ratio that moves or tropes the sign. Peirce's *interpretant* contains within itself (though it is not *itself* singular) some enigmatic law of translation, but a law, as we will see, that must also inscribe chance, or some excess of law, an illogic or alogic Peirce himself abhors. So he must anticipate some overcoming, or self-overcoming, of the life of the sign, if logic is to complete its destiny, or achieve its destination.

In Peirce's theory of the sign, therefore, one can find neither origin nor end, and certainly not a governing subject or self, though he everywhere posits a *telos* or future of truth. But interpretation or inquiry has long since begun, and we have no access to its origin. The thinking self is only an inference, Peirce says, and that self is not individual. It is collective, or better, linguistic, and must be thought of on the order of the sign, a sign that is self-critical, an indeterminate determinant. Thus Peirce insists that although we must hold out the hope for the ultimate "convergence" of all knowledge (in some projected closure of the sign), he must also project that knowledge toward some infinitely deferred future, and one that cannot be determined with each pragmatic act, choice, selection. The closure of the sign would be the end of interpretation—the death of the sign and the beginning of its self-reflexion. Peirce resists the idealism his theory desires. If "thought in action has for its only possible motive the attainment of thought at rest" (28), and if "we can look forward to a point in the infinitely distant future when there will be no indeterminacy or chance but a complete reign of law" (358), there is nevertheless in every action an errancy, a chanciness.

Rorty has claimed that Peirce's contribution to philosophy, and in particular, to pragmatism, has been vastly overrated, primarily because his insistence on a "general theory of the sign" was never clarified. Moreover, his demand for a general theory, and his belief in the ultimate "convergence" of knowledge, put him on the side of metaphysics and its desire for some ultimate representation of truth, some eventual self-mirroring of knowledge. Yet Peirce's notion of the advance of knowledge, his argument that we advance by "habit" or by a certain repetition, is conditioned by what he called the "doctrine of absolute chance," the risk involved as "every thought-sign is translated or interpreted in a subsequent one."[8] Peirce would, were it possible, write a logic that would nevertheless be a "theory of errata." Such a theory would be caught in the "aberrancy" of interpretation, that is, in the rhetoric of action. Thus when Peirce comes to define the act of thought not as individual but as collective and dialogical—even if it is a dialogue between oneself and one's developing critical self, a self that is not being but becoming—he reinscribes the misdirection of rhetoric into the method or methodical step of logic.

The thrust of his thought, and his theory of the sign, is against the very systematicity or logic he advocated and yet blamed metaphysics for not achieving. The tension in his theory between the movement toward self-reflection and the undoing of a constitutive subject leaves him in the position Henry Adams thought to be emblematic of the nineteenth century: the turn toward science or physics in order to escape the aberrancy and chaos of metaphysics, which can only end by reinscribing metaphysics in physics.

In turning now to Henry Adams, I want to explore this recurrent desire for truth manifest in a "will to interpret," which satisfies itself only by subverting desire. For this is the sense in which Adams would read the nineteenth century: as an age of interpretation, in which the demand for system and instruments of understanding turned out not simply to fail but to exacerbate the problem the instruments were intended to resolve. More important, they do not simply exacerbate by generating a nihilism or despair but by producing an excess of interpretations that begin to feed off themselves rather than containing or controlling the nature of things observed. It sounds like Nietzsche's story, but in the hands of Adams it becomes an American, or at least a modern, one. I want to suggest, then, that *The Education of Henry Adams* might be read more as a fable of criticism than as an autobiography, or if as an autobiography, then as a text that, in questioning the authority and unity of the life it reflects, disturbs the very auto-reflexivity presumed by that generic title, undermining both the genre of autobiography and the progressive ideal of education that can be reflected in an individual "life."

Adams' text poses the question in terms of an old and increasingly sus-

8. Rorty, *Consequences*, 160–61; *The Philosophy of Peirce*, ed. Buchler, 234.

pect paradigm of "education," or the ideal that one can mold a self for the future by shaping it in terms of a past it will repeat and fulfill. This ideal, Adams says, derives from a time when man could define himself to be a purpose and a direction, a time like the Middle Ages that could maintain a unitary theory that resolved or contained all the internal contradictions threatening its architecture and its arche. But the nineteenth century, Adams claims, was marked by a general dismantling of the old architecture, and thus of the old systems for containing contradiction. Ironically, the dismantling was the result not of a general nihilism but of the proliferation of different paradigms or multiple grammars, to the point where the possibility of a general grammar became problematic if not impossible. Instituting Man at the center, the nineteenth century had displaced God, only to discover that it had displaced the center or the very idea of the center, the "dream of unity," by fracturing it into multi-centers. Pursuing education as a way to truth, it had discovered education to be a questioning of truth. Multiplying systems of interpretation, fragmenting the intellectual disciplines, it found that the contending disciplines produced rather than resolved complexity, releasing more energy or conflictual power. Interpretation had been unleashed in the century like a *vis nova* or new force, which traveled by the name of Man. Man had become not an absence but a supernumerary, a contagion of interpretations, a metaphor on the loose.

Man can no longer think himself as essence "dressed out" in a proper expression nor as capable of changing himself through expression, but is now only a "manikin," a pre-shaped idea made for customary fittings. He is no more than a generalization à la mode. Thinking himself what Peirce called a "glassy essence," nineteenth-century man is habited in eighteenth-century ideas of his unity and purpose; his education prepares him only to repeat the past. Just so Adams thought of himself, scion of an original American family, as destined to carry on the family's and the country's history. His education up to and including his undergraduate years at Harvard College confirms that, though he now recalls that world as a contradiction, sometimes as elemental as the conflict of the seasons, of winter and summer, or a life of thought and a life of the senses. The purpose of education, he later recognizes, has been to smooth over such contradictions, and it works by the authority of massive exclusions and repressions. That is, it offers knowledge while ignoring or repressing critical thought. Adams' example is the Harvard curriculum, its institutionalization of knowledge as a history of uninterrogated ideas fulfilling the teleological laws of sequence and continuity. It is dogmatically ontotheological, based on the model of man as the reflection of nature. Thus the core curriculum is centered on the liberal arts, and science on human reason—physics on metaphysics. Adams calls himself a child of the eighteenth century, molded by its faith that man is the anthropocentric emblem of its order. Hegel, he recalls, wrote the concluding chapter to the story of that story—for Hegel seized the dangerous thematic of contradiction, of the negative, and reworked it into a system of unity, thus completing what the Middle Ages had always managed to do by working contradiction and exception into its jerry-built gothic. Adams says he managed to go as far as Hegel in thinking contradiction, though he fails to understand the language of metaphysics. What is beyond it, he has trouble imagining. He can only sense a contradiction in contradiction that he calls the present, and which education leaves out of account. Adams' example of what is excluded from the Harvard curriculum is Marx, his metonymic thinker of social revolution and of change itself. But Marx is only a silence inscribed in Hegel, though his signs are evident everywhere—not simply of a dialectical reversal but of an intervention into all self-reflexive thought.

The story Adams has to tell, retrospectively, can be roughly described in the metaphor Thomas Kuhn employed for the discontinuity of scientific revolutions: the nineteenth century is marked not by a simple change of paradigm that can be described in historical or dialectical terms, but by rapidly accelerating changes of the changes, each leap producing a rupture that poses to a historian the question of how to account for discontinuity when he has only the old language of "sequence," or metaphysics. The problem, he discovers, pervades not only the discipline of history, but all other areas of thought, and indeed is reflected in the rapid multiplication of specialization. The university can hardly contain, let alone account for, what Adams calls the "multiverse." Unlike the medieval church, which could accommodate any aberrance, all its systems are convulsed by accelerating contradiction, which it ignores at great risk, in contrast to the modern multiversity, which expands to meet change and thus promotes more of it. If Harvard responded by ignoring contradiction and repeating the old explanations, as Adams notes, the vibrations were everywhere driving him, pushing him toward self-consciousness and paralysis, though at the time he had no name for them. Even the *Education* as a book, one must observe, deliberately and craftily exploits the contradiction by describing an education in contradiction as a continuous narrative experience, itself parallelling a century that proceeds to undermine every faith in sequence.

Unlike William James, Adams has neither faith in the emergence of "new thought" nor belief that one can find a new paradigm that will "smooth over" the displacement or provide a formulaic language of transition. But ironically it is that belief in a general grammar that Adams finds the most distinguishing characteristic of the century, and one held over from the previous one. Everywhere there is the effort to recuperate systematic thought; everywhere there is interpretation intended to account for the anomalies that have rendered the old paradigms and old names useless. But interpretation exacerbates rather than resolves complexities, exposing them in such a way as to demand new formulations, because interpretation must address itself to the question of system itself, and hence examine its own operations. Science unveils a new notion of energy, and its own activity in search of a theory or grammar repeats the new thought of acceleration. Progress toward the new truth opens up a regressive questioning of origins. So that Adams, who would like to use his own life as an allegory of the century, making it the model for the transition from the eighteenth century's stable view of history (*vis inertia*) to the dynamic view of the present century (*vis nova*), can only remark the irony of a "life," that it is a notion belonging to an old language. History is no longer the "lengthened shadow of one man."

But let's turn to the story Adams seemed doomed to tell. As noted in the previous chapter, by the time he had completed his Harvard education, Adams realized that the American had two choices, to launch out without memory for the West, like Huck Finn, or remain in the East and in contact with the cultural memory of Europe. He chooses the latter, befitting his shaky faith in continuity and sequence, and departs Cambridge to continue his education in the past, in a search for origins. Arriving in England, he discovers that Europe is not the past but a divided present, filled with even more contradiction (the confrontation of old forms and modern energy) than America. Adams does not yet recognize that he, too, has become in a sense orphaned, that his life from now on will be the restless itinerary of a tourist, a student without a firm or stable place. Stopping but a short time in England, Adams travels on to Germany for a period of study, thence to Italy before returning to America on the eve of the Civil War. Later, an older Adams will make a similar pilgrimage, though one that is asymptotic to the first. The two journeys allegorize an uncanny repetition that unfolds as a "life" without origin or end, and hence not a "life" at all, or nothing that will ground his auto-reflection. In England for the first time, Adams is confronted by the paradoxes of the Industrial Revolution, which he sees as dynamic and modern yet markedly characterized by "burnt-out ends of history" (Eliot's metaphor). Trope and entropy are manifest in one scene, or as one figure. In Germany his attempt to study civil law is thwarted by his inability to cope with the language, a problem he will later face with science and mathematics. Moving on to Italy, he encounters the layered text of Rome, a crossroads where he hopes to read and understand the evolution and continuity of Western history, its rise and fall. But there he finds himself reading not Rome but a history already recorded in Gibbon's narrative. In fact, he observes a place that will not answer to Gibbon's story, a mixture of past and present signs that is unreadable, or more precisely, the incompatibility of a narrative text and Rome's spatial palimpsest disrupt the historian's dream. Eventually he returns to America hoping to enter the political system, which despite its difference, should be continuous with European origins. Politics, he hopes, might fulfill the purpose of his education by making him an agent of historical law.

In brief, Adams' first journey takes him through the so-called liberal arts (not yet "human sciences"), which he hopes will provide him the education to account for the revolutionary change that everywhere astounds him. But just as he cannot learn enough German to read civil law, he cannot find in the old humanistic arts anything that accounts for the new "energy" he observes. In short, metaphysics fails him, and he virtually announces the "end of philosophy": "Politics, diplomacy, law, art, and history," he writes, "had opened no outlet for future energy or effort, but a man must do something, even in Portland Place, when winter is dark and wintry evenings are exceedingly long. At that moment Darwinism was convulsing society."[9]

Thus Adams finds himself on the verge of a major discontinuity, the rupture between philosophy and science, the displacement of philosophy by science. Yet he needs to understand the break, perhaps to see it not as a rupture but as a transition. Darwinism is not simply a new life science; it still depends upon the old metaphors, the old ontotheological formulations. Evolution, in either its geological or biological phases, still tries to

9. Henry Adams, *The Education of Henry Adams* (New York, 1931), 224.

account for a continuity within discontinuities, or to provide a developmental history. It is both scientific and metaphysical. But theoretically, Darwinism poses rather than resolves contradiction, or turns back upon itself. It is not only a double theory but a self-questioning, a paradox Adams will repeatedly face as he passes from one to the other of the new sciences, from electricity to chemistry, to the early theories of heat and gases and their reformulations in physics, with a brief glance at the development of psychology. In every case, what remains out of account is the law of transformation from an old science to a new, a grammar of change. In a phrase, the bridge between metaphysics and physics is a *tour de force* that has not yet been written.

Darwinism, which was convulsing Europe, disturbed Adams for another reason than its challenge to religion, since, as Adams saw it, it could be made to conform very well with religion. He was more disturbed by its internal contradiction. In the first place, it blocked rather than opened access to the past. He points to the example of the *Pteraspis,* or ganoid fish, a creature that had ceased to develop at some remote prehistoric point, thus providing a shocking perturbation to the general law of evolution. And this generic fish, which is not quite a species, also blocks access to its origin, since it leaves no account of the evolution that must have brought it to the stage it achieved. It defies all the historical and theological metaphors of evolutionary development or regression, even natural selection, even accident. Darwinism confronts the student with a contradiction between empiricism and theory, but most disturbing of all, it grounds theory in a certain law of chance, itself a contradiction. Rather than providing the historian a metaphor of "sequence" or *telos,* this science suspends the origin in an abyss. And this is particularly critical for the American who has sought his identity in the "past" of Europe: "In the scale of evolution, one vertebrate was as good as another. For anything he, or any one else, knew, nine hundred and ninety-nine parts of evolution out of a thousand lay behind or below the *Pteraspis.* To an American in search of a father, it mattered nothing whether the father breathed through lungs, or walked on fins, or on feet" (229). The encounters with science Adams records in the *Education* turn the shock into a trauma. If literature disguised the abyss of history in fictions of origin, the new sciences exposed the fiction, but at the expense of consuming themselves.

The *Education* is constructed upon a sequence of scenes of reading or, more exactly, scenes of interpretation, in which the bewildered student inevitably comes to the understanding that he doesn't understand, that he cannot translate from one language or discipline to another. Any one of these scenes could be made exemplary of the entire story. Interpretation is restless; it undoes stable perspectives. One could recall the comic scene from the chapter called "Dilettantism" where Adams purchases what he thinks is a small Raphael painting on the word of an authority who later disclaims his own judgment—to extend the irony, the painting bears on its back a poem presumably by the painter; and Adams must go from authority to putative authority, and from specialist to specialist, only to discover that each can authenticate only one part (the handwriting, the language, the style), but not the whole, as one specialist at the British Museum can transcribe the handwriting but cannot translate the Italian. In short, specialization fragments and atomizes, with the same kind of accelerating consequences created by those who in seeking a general theory multiply regional ones. And no one can reconstruct the unity of the whole, the identity of the artist in his work, from the fragment.

But in conclusion I want to turn to another scene, not necessarily a scene of reading but an account of Adams' reflections on the implications of the scientist's attempt to produce what we would today call a "general field theory." Adams entitles this chapter of the *Education* "The Grammar of Science," taking his title from a book (1899) by the English mathematician Karl Pearson, who had tried, in the face of the challenges of thermodynamics, to create a statistical language that would join the new physics with the old and account for the transition between the two. Pearson warned his fellow scientists that they must purge theory of all metaphysics or the "chaos beyond the senses" and concern themselves exclusively with what could be measured. He called, therefore, upon science to try to write a series of local grammars; then a general one would have to be composed of a non-referential statistical language. He was especially concerned that they avoid the mistake of Clerk Maxwell, who fell into metaphysics when he hypothesized upon the possibility of a "daemon," which Adams likens to a "prime motor" or determining power, who might regulate all chance and give a total account where physics had encountered no possible evidence. Maxwell, Adams concludes with Pearson, represents the temptation of the scientist to fall back into metaphysics, something he finds even more characteristic of physicists like Mach. For "English thought," Adams writes, making Pearson his example, "had always been chaos and multiciplicity ... but German thought had affected system, unity, and abstract truth" (453). Thus English and German scientists of the nineteenth century repeat, but in a different phase, the conflict of national philosophies in the eighteenth century between the empiricists and the great system makers.

It is in France, however, and specifically in the mathematics of Poincaré, where Adams seeks the reconciliation of physics and metaphysics—Paris would be the go-between. It is as if he had written a fable for today's critics. Paris, he feels, has ever been a scene that smooths over contradiction: "No Frenchman except Rabelais and Montaigne ever taught anarchy other than as a path to order. Chaos would be unity in Paris even if child of the guillotine" (454). Poincaré might reconcile the conflict between scientist and humanist, producing a world in which "history and mathematics" did not cancel each other, and resolving beforehand what the twentieth century was to inherit as "two cultures." Yet Adams cannot translate from the one language to the other, and Poincaré's reconciliation is not unflawed. Even if it were not, Adams could not read it, for he has no mathematics and thus cannot recognize that there are now two incompatible mathematics at work. But Adams senses the unresolvable contradiction, two equivocal theories posed in an apparently common language. But the common language, of course, will turn out to be two at least.

Adams finds the dilemma emblematized in the latest radical discovery, which he calls the "metaphysical bomb" of radium. After Madame Curie, "there remained no hole to hide in. Even metaphysics swept back over science with the green water of the deep-sea ocean and no one could longer hope to bar out the unknowable, for the unknowable was known" (452). "Radium" introduced a new metaphor of the sun, a new metaphor of metaphor, in the same sense that it made impossible any thinking of the unity of matter and energy. The possibility of a general grammar had been put in question, but not the desire for it, and with the acceleration of desire, metaphysics or a force that exceeded sense measurement rushed back into physics. Only now the notion of metaphysics had been as radically transformed as the notion of energy. The sun took on a new sense even as it made no appearance.

Radium was invisible, and it appeared only when bombarded by its other, a "contaminant." Its light was not a part of it. Moreover, radium was an element of nature, and not nature's origin, a sign of nature's dynamic and its instability; radium was not a new name for nature but the name of a new nature. It was a misnomer at best. At once a trope and entropic, one element in a unilinear sequence or chain that degraded into an entirely different element, the latter bearing no trace of its origin, radium promised no return of the sun. Just as thermodynamics had introduced a new sense of history—unilinear, discontinuous, and moving toward the ultimate disorganization in cold death—radium undid the dream of the metaphysical reflection. There was no privileged place in nature, no position for man: "Power leaped from every atom, and enough of it to supply the steller universe showed itself running to waste at every pore of matter. Man could no longer hold off. Forces grasped his wrist and flung him about as though he had hold of a live wire or a runaway automobile" (494). Nature devoured the systems contrived to contain her: "her forces," Adams writes, "were anarchical" and "little short of parricidal in their wicked spirit toward science"; "Radium denied its God" (381). Nietzsche might have said that it had finally got rid of grammar. And what it offered in return was a plenitude of impossibilities: "Impossibilities no longer stood in the way. One's life had fattened on impossibilities" (494). The past was no longer prelude: "If any analogy whatever existed between the human mind, on one side, and the laws of motion, on the other, the mind had already entered a field of attraction so violent that it must immediately pass beyond into a new equilibrium, like the Comet of Newton, or suffer dissipation altogether, like meteoroids in the earth's atmosphere" (496).

Admitting the new law of irreversible degradation applied both to man and history, Adams sought nevertheless to temper it with the old. If man were no longer an agent or cause, he must be a kind of effect. Yet this naturalism, a term most critics apply to Adams' thought, can take no simple form. Naturalism is only an old name applied to a new dynamics of nature, a nature that is neither determining nor determined. A "dynamic law," Adams had observed, "requires that two masses—nature and man—must go on, reacting upon each other . . . and that any appearance of stoppage is illusive. The theory seems to exact excess, rather than deficiency, of action and reaction" (478). But the new law cannot determine what is action and what reaction. In an "ocean of colliding atoms," no organizing center is discernible, and if there are multiple centers, even the name of the center is no more than an old misnomer. There is no "prime motor," Adams notes, and in effect no true idea of man, that "glassy essence," as Peirce wanted to call his "man-sign." Man is a "force," therefore, an equivocation, and not an equilibrium, like Emerson's figure of man as the "contradiction" and "excess" of nature. "A dynamic theory," Adams speculates,

begins by begging the question; it defines Progress as the development and econ-omy of Forces. Further it defines force as anything that does or helps to do work. Man is a force; so is the sun; so is a mathematical point, though without dimen-sions or known existence.

Man commonly begs the question again by taking for granted that he captures the forces. A dynamic theory, assigning attractive force to opposing bodies in pro-portion to laws of mass, takes for granted that the forces of nature capture man. (474)

But the old mechanical law of conservation no longer provides an "im-age," and the new force does not yet have a language, and stands outside all representation. It stands only for the impropriety of the name, a sun that in Stevens' phrase will "bear no name." Man no longer stands in the sun, cast-ing his shadow. He is not a method, and takes no step either in advance of or to follow the sun. He is part and parcel of a sun, at once action and reaction, equivocal, both trope and entropic. Adams must therefore coin or appropriate an "image," a figure for this figure that is at once action and reaction: "For convenience as an image, the theory may liken man to a spider in its web, watch-ing for chance prey. Forces of nature dance like flies before the new, and the spider pounces on them when he can, but it makes many fatal mistakes, though its theory of force is sound" (474).

This man is no Ariadne, spinning her web, commanding in some lim-ited way the play of chance. It is a figure entangled in its own figuration or limit, a Hermes. Here is theory forced to express itself in metaphor—a the-ory of force is a new theory of metaphor, but interwoven with the old. Any-way, Adams' image is surely a quotation, a "literary" image, and thus a quotation of a quotation. Adams names himself a "conservative Christian anarchist," an oxymoron or figure of contradiction. And that might be what he would say of his namesake, the old Adam, the original hermeneu-tic. In the parabolic saga of American humanism, man does not enter the hermeneutical circle to be instituted there, nor is he innocently entrapped there. The "impossible possible philosopher's man," as Stevens calls him, appears like the spider in the web of Adams' image, in the sense that every theory of force, or shall we say theory of interpretation, demands a figure of the interpreter—but one who is certain to make "many fatal mistakes." One of his names is "American," the metonym of an action without beginning or end. The American *agon* makes an American genealogy unthinkable, no matter how enthusiastically the historian pounces on some evidence of a unique or originary "force," some figure like Man, or Emerson. The solution remains in hieroglyph and calls forth yet more interpretation, another "reading."

4

READING AMERICA

In "The Comedian as the Letter C," Wallace Stevens provides us with an allegory (and a romance) of literary modernism, a story of what it means to be an "American" poet.[1] Among other things, it means that the poet has to invent and not discover, to perform and not imitate, and hence to produce the scene rather than repeat what was "in the script," as he writes in another piece, "Of Modern Poetry" (239). To call "The Comedian" performative, of course, is to recall the form Stevens names as its antecedent, *commèdia dell'arte,* an improvisation that turns from itself and undoes the theatrics of representation. Whatever, it tells a certain story about American poetry, of how our literature relates to "tradition," at once breaking with and repeating a past it hardly remembers. And in this sense it deals with a question of "translation," of the need for a new-world language that remains enchained in an old-world history, and yet is the "beyond" of history. The haunting paradox of Emerson's call for a national literature that would throw off the tyrannous forms of Europe, historical and nationalistic, but only in order to retrieve a still earlier, primordial and universal, utterance, haunts Steven's belated "valet," as it troubles the poet who knew that the American translation could never be either nationalistic or universal, modern or primitivistic, nor a simple reduction of the two to one univocal voice: "So may the relation [and relating] of each man be clipped" (46).

"America" as projected in its literature is not so much a history of what occurred as a dream to be arrived at. It is a point of arrival infinitely deferred by the act of searching for it. Named in advance, by old names, it is at once metonym and misnomer, like Columbus' misnaming of its natives. Columbus was involved in a paradox of comparative culture, and his discovery engendered a history of misprision. Modernist ruminations upon

1. Wallace Stevens, *Collected Poems* (New York, 1954), 27–46.

Columbus' "discovery," from Henry James to Williams to Hart Crane, repeatedly underscore the fact that America is always already a text without origin, a translation of a translation. Its source or past is always other, and elsewhere, and thus a text or archive, but not one that can be read as a concealed or lost meaning. Its past is a text that can only be performed, interpreted, and in interpretation thrown forward, an origin summoning it toward its true "Orient." "America" is not discovered, but invented, and by "reading"; that is, by translation.

Emerson knew this. Even though he appealed to a uniquely American landscape, to a nature at once primeval and universal, yet his nature could be understood as origin only within the history of Western idealism. In what sense could that nature produce or transform an original voice or idiom that would not be expressed in a language imported from a past, a history, a world older, yet in another sense younger? Language, Emerson argued, was "fossil poetry," hence the effluvia and residue or eternal force of a presence no longer present; just as poetry could only be defined as the miswriting of some ideal poem that is itself never realized or present except in the mistranslation of history. But this miswriting, in America often a misnaming, has a supplementary effect, and the poet or genius who hears the "primal warblings" and miswrites them not only marks their temporality but "adds" to what he receives. If "America is a poem in our eyes" (CW, III, 22), then it is at once a miswriting and a supplementation, a translation and displacement not of some past present but of some past translation. America the poem and the American poem would always be formed upon some horizon or margin, not as an emblem of the past, but as a "fluxional symbol" or trope that signified a future present that would mark its own effacement or death. The American poem would not recuperate some past but would project the future. It would be horizonal.

The American language, then, would be some kind of catachresis, a digression rather than a derivation, or in Stevens' terms, an "accent of deviation." Poetry is the privileged name of this natural language that is not so much genetic, a primordial presence, as transformative, tropic. It will appear derivative, a repetition of the old names bearing the old values, but at the same time deformative and transactive, and in this sense, Emerson observes, would be critical as well as creative: again, "Literature is now critical. Well, analysis may be poetic" (J, VII, 303). But if the two functions remain entangled, neither the same nor different, then the text has no identity or specular order, no auto-telic nature—is neither literature nor criticism, is both and neither. The phrase "American literature" becomes an oxymoron, since literature in its classical sense, in its affiliation with truth and meaning, would have to erase its critical, transformative, translative, disseminative effect. Yet Emerson's notion of a poetry that is always inscribed in mis-writing, or in translative effects, denominates "literature" as the deflection of any specular or representational law, and suggests that it is what Charles Olson would call a "figure of forward," a trope related to what he also calls "projective verse."[2] The "figure of forward," Olson says, goes back in order to come forward, or repeats the past as a departure or break in order to project itself beyond the present. This formulation of a literature beyond literature, of a literature that would be mimetic not of the past but, as it were, of the future, a literature in which repetition is also dis-figurement, has come to bear the familiar yet misplaced name of "post-modernism." But in a sense, from its earliest problematic formulations, the notion of "American literature" had always been post-modern, indeed the beyond of modernism, a literature burdened with producing a past it never had, except in the figure of revolution, in order to mime that past into a future it lagged behind. In this sense, it is post-modern, itself posted, a *carte postale,* a kind of postal message passing through a dead-letter office.

From his earliest essays, Emerson chastised his American contemporaries for their nostalgic and sepulchral thought. In *Nature,* after lamenting the prevailing retrospection, he turns to the challenge of writing again this "first philosophy," only to discover that his belated re-writing would itself be "retrospective" were it not also a mis-writing: that is, a return to poetic and not philosophic thought, to Beauty and not Truth, the poetic being at once primordial and horizonal, the "figure" of what Emerson calls our "original relation to the universe." Like Heidegger after him, Emerson imagines this "original relation" neither as a simple unity nor as a simple dualism, but as a transformational moment, a figural moment or crossing, like a chiasmus, in which man and God, man and nature, and so on, even the poetic and the philosophical or the creative and the critical, are at the same time united and opposed, face to face as it were. And Emerson can only think of this relation on the model of an original or natural language, not of the single word but of the trope, a dynamic nature always turning from it-

2. Charles Olson, "Projective Verse," in *Selected Writings,* ed. Robert Creeley (New York, 1966), 15–30.

self. Original and originating art or poetry will appear to be imitative, but it will really be a repetition of the *mise en scène* of trope. This scene is Emerson's "nature." Nature is a name for trope—a trope of trope, and hence is "pre-original" as well as belated or post-original.

Later, in "Quotation and Originality," Emerson radicalizes this activity of mimesis into a kind of program that Pound would call "creative translation," in which repetition becomes at once appropriation and misappropriation, a troping movement that does not so much recuperate the past as "project" it. Quotation and origin are indistinguishable, and thus the origin is a non-origin. The primal scene is "Nature," which is to say, it is "poetic" and "textual": "All minds quote. Old and new make the warp and woof of every moment. There is no thread that is not a twist of these two strands." In literature, the "originals are not original. There is imitation, model and suggestion, to the very archangels if we knew their history" (*W*, VIII, 178). Originality, then, is determined, to extend Heidegger, not by our escaping from this (hermeneutical) circle, nor even by how we enter it, but by how we perform it: "Every book is a quotation; and every house is a quotation out of all forests and minds and stonequarries; and every man is a quotation from all his ancestors" (175). This is the epigraph to the essay, but written by Emerson; Emerson quoting himself, originally.

In a provocative essay in his First Series, entitled "Art," Emerson would indeed define art's "privilege" not as a representation but as a hyperbolic repetition. Art, he says, "never quite repeats itself," and thus, "not imitation but creation is the aim" (*CW*, II, 209). A "new art is always formed out of the old" (210), he continues; but like a *mise en abîme* of quotations, it does not have a history or *telos*, does not advance. It has neither origin nor end. Art repeats and detaches, in the manner, he observes, of "rhetoric": "The power to detach and to magnify by detaching is the essence of rhetoric in the hands of the orator or poet" (211). This "aboriginal power" is therefore not an "origin." It is not Being or Presence, but rather must be thought of as a Power that Emerson finds in "nature's eclecticism." And Power or Force can only be understood as "trope." Emerson thinks of "nature" on the model of language. Art is that which quotes, and in quoting incorporates and translates the old form. Thus Emerson breaks the specular illusion, and undoes or opens his primary figure, "The Circle."

The art of the past, then, may at the same time lead us and beguile us, offer us a paradigm of some unity of past and future and block our access to either. It divides the present rather than composing a bridge from past to future. Its obstacle must be breached or inhabited, so that by inhabiting the received form the imagination rebuilds by adding. Emerson's repeated use of architectural metaphors for this process reveals art to be a supplemented or excessive arche, a house within yet beyond a house. At one crucial point in his reflections, Emerson ironically comments on the apparent absence of a present American culture that drives its citizens to Europe in search of a past, leading them ultimately to cultural centers (or crossroads) like Rome to stand in the presence of the old masters that are presumed to be the mirrors of the culture America will become by historical repetition. But when Emerson himself sees those masterpieces, he is reminded of "the old and eternal fact I had met already in so many forms . . . [and that I] had left at home in so many conversations" (214). "Travelling" in search of a past model for the present, he says, is as "ridiculous as a treadmill" (215). He thereupon cites two of those masterpieces—one literary, the other painterly —that at once lure us toward and block out accessibility to the past: the *Iliad* and Raphael's *Transfiguration,* instances, he says, that allow us to see that great art is not a finished product or closed form but is an "aim" (his word) or a "stream of tendency." Emerson defines art as "never fixed, but flowing," a force that throws "down walls of circumstance" and penetrates boundaries. It detaches, yet is not itself detached: "not detached, but extempore performances" (216). Performance mimics but does not imitate; and like rhetoric, it deforms. Great art, he says, produces or performs, "cripples and monsters."

If Emerson here has introduced the notion of the performative, he has done so, obviously, in a way not entirely compatible with the linguistics of present-day speech-act theory. Yet his association of performance with rhetoric underscores the aporia that opens up within two irreducible notions of rhetoric—rhetoric as trope or figures of cognition, and rhetoric as persuasion—or as we will call it here, the play between representation and re-petition. Art therefore transfigures and disfigures, and in Emerson's words, as later in those of Williams, produces "monsters." This scene of translation is originary but not original and masks a double operation, on the one hand signifying an orderly (historical) continuity and evolution from one culture to another, and on the other marking a discontinuity and digression of signs. And translation repeatedly brings to our attention the failure to transport a meaning in all its unicity or univocality through a displacement of signifiers. This failure, however critical, is not simply negative or nihilistic, in a certain orthodox sense of that concept, but indicative of a radical model of language that Emerson finds in "nature's eclecticism." The scene of translation provides us with a reading moment that is, to say the least, highly agitated.

What I am going to characterize now as "American literature," or the notion of American literature, is only tangentially related to the themes and forms of a literature written (or even produced, in the Marxian sense) in America (even though it is). It is more directly related to that question of literature that takes itself as its own theme or, better, that stages its own problematic as a case of auto-insemination and self-engendering. For the sake of economy, however, I must turn now to two particular "literary" moments that will seem at first as arbitrary as I admit them to be, and intend them to be. Even within the American canon they come from different genres, or hybrid genres, and serve to break the laws of genre. But I have selected them for another reason, for a "moment" they share, a "reading moment" that intervenes in and disrupts the Americans' "treadmill" of repetition.

Despite Emerson's warnings against the ridiculous "treadmill" of Americans running off to European cultural centers like Rome in search of a past that might as well be found, however dispersed, in "conversations" at home, our literature was to take this quest for or pilgrimage to a "visitable" or "usable" past as one of its obsessive themes, as representatively American as the frontier myth or the Adamic hero. Whether it took the parodic psychological form of "innocents abroad" (Twain or James), or of metaphysical journeys like Melville's for pre-Western roots in the Levant and Olson's for a pre-metaphysical language of action in pre-historical cultures, and especially the modernist theme of the artist as expatriate amid a "lost generation"—the obsession with an ever-receding past and ever-fleeting future was always posed upon that cliché of historicism, the absent present. Henry James lamented that we had no representative or central city, and Ezra Pound would make that decenteredness into a modernist poetic. Gertrude Stein's remarks about Oakland may be extended to the American writer's dilemma: "there's no there there." America could not be read because it had no reference point, no representative text. It was an anthology of quotations, detached and dispersed, a digression of history.

But it is just this thematic I want to avoid in turning to the two disparate though not unrelated texts mentioned above, where the theme of the putative American consciousness (always a kind of artist figure, an orphan) arrives at a place where past and present seem to coalesce, where it appears the threads of origin are rewoven and the unity of history can be read, thereby providing the model for America's eventual arrival, the convergence of its history upon a center and the fulfillment of its own prophetic role to complete, by repetition, the history of the West. Early in his most gothic and obfuscated "romance," *The Marble Faun,* Nathaniel Hawthorne has his narrator recount a visit by two of the novel's four main characters to the "suburban" Villa Borghese, an enclave distinguished by the architecture of Michelangelo that in some as yet obscure way connects the "lava stones of the Roman pavement" with the "beautiful seclusion" of a natural landscape beyond.[3] Yet the grounds do not quite lead beyond the city to nature, but inscribe in themselves a nature that "arrays itself in the imagination when we read the beautiful old myths, and fancy . . . more picturesque arrangements of venerable trees than we find in the rude and untrained landscapes of the Western world" (71). The signs of "human care" not only mingle with nature's own "ways and methods" in a way to "prevent wildness" and produce an "ideal landscape"; they do so by referring, not to nature, but to historical pre-texts, to myths. The villa is not a scene where art links with culture, but a palimpsest: "What a strange idea," the narrator reflects, "—what a needless labor—to construct artificial ruins in Rome, the native soil of ruin" (73). These are "sportive imitations" that have themselves, being centuries old, gained a kind of veneration, so that they now signify not continuity but discontinuity, the archives of "growth, decay and man's intelligence wrought kindly together." This vernal, pastoral scene is subject to nature's cycles or to time, but unlike the myths of renewal it suggests, it is haunted by that seasonal miasma of Roman fever. This in-between place is neither nature nor culture, both and neither. The villa is not a bridge or link but a "scene" that undoes such oppositions. It is a place of fragments, and fragments of fragments, which defy any reconstruction of the whole from the parts. The villa is a metonymic displacement of Rome.

Two of Hawthorne's characters visit the scene—the youthful Donatello, an Italian whom the others think of as a natural or even supernatural man,

3. Nathaniel Hawthorne, *The Marble Faun: or The Romance of Monte Beni,* Vol. IV of *The Centenary Edition of the Works of Nathaniel Hawthorne* (Columbus, 1968).

the Faun of Praxiteles come to life, a figure "standing betwixt man and animal, sympathetic with each" (13), his long hair, as they speculate, concealing a "pair of leaf-shaped, furry ears"; and the young, talented artist Miriam, of mixed and enigmatic ancestry, who, "fair as she looked, was plucked up out of a mystery and had its roots clinging to her." Miriam is the subject of many contradictory speculations about her past and her heritage, whether she is Jewish or Oriental, South American or even African, perhaps German (22–23). The other two characters are American—Hilda, an expert copyist of old masters who has come so close to developing a unique style that she threatens to be original and thus to disturb her own American genius for representation; and Kenyon, a sculptor of some talent yet a "beginner in art," who has not yet found his true subject or style and thus imitates all that his customers desire.

Sometime previous to the scene at the villa, the four friends, whom we meet at the beginning of the novel, gather in a "sculpture gallery of the Capitol" (5)—a place where the art signifies a "threefold antiquity" and thus pretends to reconcile the dangerous Christian/pagan rift exemplified everywhere by a Christian art that allegorically employs mythic figures. The four friends make a visit to the catacomb of Saint Calixtus, where, in the labyrinthine tomb, they become for a moment separated, Miriam falling behind the others. When, after frantic effort, her friends finally discover her whereabouts, they see her talking with a "specter," the two face-to-face cast against the halflight of the chapel's chiaroscuro gloom. The male "specter," according to their guide, is a "pagan phantom," and Miriam later calls him an "odd messenger" (29). But like Donatello and Miriam herself, he becomes the subject of avid gossip and speculation as soon as the story of the strange meeting spreads about Rome. As with Donatello, the only hermeneutical method for establishing the "specter's" identity is to relate him to a set of legends, tales, or fables, what Miriam calls "monstrous fictions," each model rendering to the speculator a different identity. Miriam even avers that the specter, once an artist, had promised to teach her a long-lost but invaluable secret of old Roman fresco-painting, the knowledge of which would place her at the head of modern art. Here is underscored the repeated hope of modernism: to ground itself in some authentic, which is to say primordial or pre-historical and thus universal, source, so that it will not only escape the belatedness of representational art and make itself at once the transparency of reality and reality itself, but will complete, by a kind of supplementation, the tradition or history of art; the dream that art will unveil truth, as in what the Greeks called *aletheia*, but in a representation (fresco-painting) that would be at the same time original and belated, like "writing." The "original," however, inevitably turns out to be an old inscription, a "specter" intimately related to each spectator who reads it. The specter, too, is a "figure." Miriam's hope, she says, is that by entering into a dialogue or "controversy" with the infidel she can convert him to Christianity, or in some way translate the mysteriously concealed Being (at once natural and uncanny) into a symbolic representation that will not itself be corrupted by what remains of nature. Her art would thus purify and not transgress, by translating specter into sense. But even this aesthetic would retain something of a haunting doubleness, of the image that not only Miriam but the many contradictory readings of the "specter's" appearance cannot efface. Miriam's modernism would have to be a symbolic art, effacing itself as it converted mystery into meaning.

It is this awful foreboding of both promise and failure that ultimately trips the action of the "romance," the "crime" as it is called, in which Donatello, to protect Miriam with whom he has fallen in love, murders the phantom in a scene observed, if indirectly, by the two Americans—and in that act murders his own innocence in their eyes. From the moment of the "crime," Donatello appears to lose his youthfulness and naturalness, to assume the costume of mortality in a transformation that sets off another round of violent interpretations, especially by the spectators to the crime. Of the three, Miriam's reading appears the most authoritative (one might say, ironically, the most "modern"), for presumably she is not simply an observer of the act but a culpable party to it, Donatello being little more than her instrument. But Miriam's interpretation, if modern, is also the most conventional and traditional, the interpretation that in its way has guided the readings of the novel ever since: "Was the crime—in which he and I were wedded—was it a blessing in that strange disguise?" she asks Kenyon in a later conversation, and proceeds to describe the "pleasure" and "delight" (the aesthetic satisfaction) she derives from "brooding on the verge of this great mystery." The mystery, however, is no mystery at all, since it is already explained, as "felix culpa": "'The story of the fall of man!'" she says. "'Is it not repeated in our romance of Monte Beni?'" (434). Miriam's interpretation takes the form of allegory, though by reversal: the particular event is explained by the universal paradigm, the ontotheological event.

The crime, however, is not simply an event, but already to Miriam a "romance," that is, itself already interpretatively displaced, reduplicating the specular play that is already at large everywhere in Rome, evident not only in every art object that inscribes the aesthetic economy of exchange between religious and pagan, historical and pre-historical legend, fable and icon, but also in the archival and archeological lamina of the city. Inserted into this play, the "specter" shatters the specular economy, supplements it, becomes the mark of its excess, setting off those interpretative mechanisms of which all the facts and artifacts of Rome are the product and the motive. Miriam's interpretation, which results in "pleasure" rather than "truth," turns also on the production of the kind of guilt.

Kenyon and Hilda, the Americans, demur from what first appears as the moral absolute of Hilda's interpretation. One of Hawthorne's most daring readers, Kenneth Dauber, has acknowledged that part of the problem the novel has faced with critics is its heavy-handed interpretative mode—apparent in Hawthorne's strategy of gradually moving the narrative voice away from any one of the characters toward a reflective or speculative observation on the characters' own reflections.[4] Thus, Dauber concludes, Hawthorne finds himself, like the transcendentalists he criticizes, in the position of trying to account for the gothic obscurity and complexity of European art and culture from the relative clarity and purity of American naïveté or naturalness. Hilda's innocence (reflected in her copyist art, her self-effacement) and Kenyon's detachment (his pluralism and thus lack of stylistic identity) are certainly compromised by their participation in the "crime" (presuming it was an "event"); so that they come to recognize the complicity of the spectator in the spectacle: or to put it another way, to recognize that they have always been implicated in the hermeneutical circle. (Hilda, we should note, is a very special kind of copyist, who selectively reproduces sections or parts of larger paintings. Reducing the whole to its parts, or to a kind of synecdoche, she thus interprets the painting by producing a symbol. The symbol no longer represents the whole but the author's "intention," which is to say, it signifies the author's transformative act and the copyist's translative performance, not an original but, as it were, a pre-original art.) This translative displacement no less extends to the narrator's act of narration, which is at the same time "detached" and guilt ridden, since he cannot tell a story without interpretative intervention. In each

4. Kenneth Dauber, *Rediscovering Hawthorne* (Princeton, 1977), 193–219.

instance, an interpretation precedes what is the object of interpretation.

Let's return, then, to the scene of the original crime, supposing it original, that has set off such a violent play of interpretations, at once binding the four friends together in guilt and separating them from their old familiarity of natural acceptance, the illusion that they formed some kind of natural community. The real crime, we are to understand, is not so much the murder of the "specter" as it is his first appearance, an intervention that sets off a chain of interpretations in which everyone tries to identify the figure by referring him to a coherent context, to fables or myths the meanings of which are supposedly self-evident, or which have been made evident by the orthodoxy of historical exegesis. The problem is to give the figure a name, a role. But every attempt to identify the "model" by reference only multiplies the mystery. In the first place, his sudden appearance so violates all expectations that it already foreshadows the repetition of the violence by those who feel violated. Whether he appeared to Miriam by will or accident can never be determined, but that he did appear when she separated herself from the "natural" family of friends is not in doubt. The unfamiliar or uncanny has no origin. One can never determine just where interpretation begins.

Donatello, the murderer, we remember, has from an even earlier but undetermined moment been the subject of the same kind of multiple interpretations, his ambiguous naturalness that makes him half-man, half-faun being resolvable only with reference to legends that have already been transfigured into aesthetic forms, that is, have already been interpreted. (One should perhaps note here that the novel's title was once to have been *The Transformation,* and it still appears as such in England.) Donatello, that is, has his origin in the old vegetation rites, with their sublimated rituals of sacrifice, and he has become historical by a process of metamorphosis. Donatello is at once an anomaly and a magical name—the name he shares with a historical artist, and the one he shares with his almost forgotten legendary origins, the name of manna, of the gift, of the don. In the case of Donatello, we have an originally double nature, at once pure and violent; and if he is the link between man and nature, if he is on the "verge of nature," he is also the margin or threshold that undoes the clear distinction culture would like to maintain between the two. "There was an indefinable characteristic about Donatello," we are told, "that set him outside the rules."[5] He is not,

5. Hawthorne, *The Marble Faun,* 14.

then, simply a figure of nature's purity or nature's plenitude; he is both and neither, not simplicity but complexity. He is, purely but not simply, a figure of "figure." And the problem these artist friends of his have in trying to transform him into their own understanding, to translate his "figure" into their own, is the problem of translation itself. They can only understand him on the model of Praxiteles' Faun, a figure not of nature but of interpretation, a figure standing for the mystery of metamorphosis itself.

Donatello, therefore, is already prefigured in the phantom he murders. At the murder scene, near but not at the Forum, on the threshold yet outside the fragment that signifies the institutionalized law, the three artists see, yet do not see, the violence. Miriam cannot determine whether she is "an actor or a sufferer in the scene," and Hilda hears what she does not see, Donatello holding the specter over a precipice and releasing him into the abyss. In Donatello's words, "I did what your [Miriam's] eyes bid me do" (172), and in that moment he suffers his "transformation" from faun-figure to self-conscious human being. Later they are to learn that the body found at the bottom of the precipice is a Capuchin monk, or at least a corpse dressed in the religious frock of the beggar, and no one is certain whether it is that of the "specter." Even the narrator must report on what is never seen, a transformation initiated by "eyes." The question of who or what is murdered, of what figure or corpse lies in the abyss, carries us back to the specter's first appearance, where like a text or corpus he has set off a sequence of wild speculations. But of all these rumors, the narrator observes, the most probable is that this "beggar" was a "thief," an "outlaw," a "lunatic," and an "assassin," hence like Donatello before he murders, outside the law.

We are now ready to give him a (borrowed) name—Hermes, or more exactly, Thoth (Tot), the Greek's Egyptian predecessor, messenger of the sun god Amon-Ra, god of physicians, mathematicians, thieves, murderers, madmen, and language, or to be precise, writing—the god who engenders through an uncanny mediation. We now know what Miriam "sees" at the murder site, what indeed she has murdered through her eyes—she has murdered, by effacement, the mimicking sign of mediation, the sun's agent, as it were, in the sense of the painter's desire to efface all mediation and to make her representation adequate to her perception, or even more original than perception. Yet the effacement of mediation can only re-mark the corpse or corpus as a provisional substitute, and therefore expose the dream of originality. In the beginning was interpretation, more original than the interpreted. Miriam has desired to murder her own self-consciousness, her own "eye" (I), and this involves the disfiguration of figure. Like Thoth, the specter belongs to a scriptive order that undoes the scriptural law that has always ruled historical Rome. The transformation effected upon Miriam and Donatello is called guilt, but we have learned to call it self-consciousness, or, perhaps, criticism. The violence Miriam has observed, has participated in with "pleasure," is transformation, the troping violence of art.

Rome, then, is a scene or spectacle where the specular illusion is at once staged and undone; it is the *mise en scène* of translation, the transitive forum of Western history that cannot itself be mastered by speculation, or interpretation. Because the American has no history, he goes to Rome to find one, to untangle the knot or mystery of the crossroads. What he finds there, however, is not the origin, but only the sign of origin, the substitution, not the sun but his son, one sign in a complex of signs, a textual crypt, "lamina upon lamina," in Emerson's words, of interpretation. Recall that Thoth, among his other duties, was deeply involved in intrigues or plots—plots of usurpation, plots of narratization, that is, in machinal designs that at once undo and reassemble genealogical orders of inheritance, marking them as fictions of beginning and repetition. A modern American in Paris may recognize that he is a member of a "lost generation"; in Rome he is forced to reflect that the notion of generational continuity itself is always already lost, and the more he looks for his past the more he uncovers signs of severance and reinscription. Rome is not a center but a margin, a marginal text, and its history a plot of discontinuous interpretations refolded upon one another.

One could document this preoccupation of the American writer with genealogical crisis through dozens of texts, from Melville's *Pierre* to Williams' *Paterson,* the latter harboring as a pun within its very title the transactions of language ("a reply to Greek and Latin with the bare hands") necessary for a belated national literature to come into its own. One of Williams' little-known novels, *A Voyage to Pagany,* dramatizes this crisis of the American discontinuity in a scene that repeats, with an uncanny difference, Hawthorne's Roman holiday of interpretation.[6] The novel is based on the metaphor of the journey toward a source or origin of the "word" (Rome as the "place where the word began"), a journey that takes the physician/writer through other cultural centers that have displaced Rome: Paris, where the writer con-

6. William Carlos Williams, *A Voyage to Pagany* (New York, 1928).

fronts the radical experiments of modernism that he recognizes to be mimetic or traditional in that they only repeat the modernist gesture to be different; to Florence, where he finds the Arno and the old bridge that crosses it to its great icon of memory, the museum, an emblem for all art, and then to Rome. In Rome he finds more complex problems, problems that entangle history and tradition and modernism in an uncanny mosaic, "America" being its most inexplicable constituent.

The effort to discover America's history in the laminated text of Rome issues in a strange interpretation that exempts America, which is all future, from the Roman fate while implicating it in the extravagant transactions (the "crossings") that produced the Roman text. In Williams' novel, the effort to "read" the text of Rome, its ruins and artifacts, uncovers a "local" or locus of energies, a chiasmus of oppositions that reveal the true Roman history to be the upsurge of "pagan" or unconscious energies within repressive forms. Rome becomes the psychological model of that desire that animates the American performance of art, its need to begin again, and to be the self-engendering source of its own literature.

Williams' "autobiographical" novel, in its attempt to revise Roman history and therefore expose the enigma it presents to a modern reader, reenacts one of the problems that Freud confronted as a question of "method" in *Civilization and Its Discontents*. That Williams was engaged with the Freudian model of mind when writing *A Voyage to Pagany* is evident from the novel's final scenes, which take place in Vienna rather than Rome and recount the education of an obstetrician who thinks of his work of attending and effectuating birth as analogous to the analyst's task in translating unconscious traces into conscious forms. (Williams' autobiography had affirmed the same analogy.) The critical scene of this transaction is Rome, where, as the main character notes, "Galileo killed" the "geo-centric universe" (151) and where we recognize the signs of "modern destructive" thought. The hero Dev Evans' almost Nietzschean conception of Rome as the *mise en scène* of revolution, of radical changes of paradigm, of repetitions that produce uncanny differences, turns the Roman scene from a spatial model of history into another model that is not yet a model. For "Pagany," as it is called, is a scene of performances, of displacements, that not only reverse but also open up the scene to an unanticipated future and to the possibility of monstrosity. If Rome is, as the novel avers, the "place where the word began," it is not an inscription of logos but the inscription of conflict and of excess, of tropos and not topos. It is not an archive of history but of the language of the unconscious, always already "detached," as Emerson says.

Freud uncovered a similar contradiction while in search of a "method" that would help him account for the transactions between the ego and the external world against which it had shaped itself and been shaped. In his effort to extend psychoanalysis to a study of culture, and hence to the economy that ties the ego to its cultural matrix, Freud marks the uncertainty and variability of anything like a strict demarcation between self and world. It is a question always, he says, of the uncertain "boundary" lines between the two, and therefore of the difficulty in maintaining any strict definition of the one in regard to the other. Most terminologies for dealing with the relation name the ego as something for itself, and the other as something in itself, just as they describe the structure of mind in categories or oppositions. The problem for the analyst is to find a model for dealing with a transaction, between inner and outer, self and world, that can account for the indefinite boundary that separates them and exposes the stability or identity of ego to change. Furthermore, one must account for the "history" of the ego's own development and the changing boundaries effectuated by its own changes: from the "primitive pleasure ego" to a conditioned or civilized ego, which can only be characterized as a network of repressions and for which there is no adequate descriptive language.

What Freud needs, then, is a model to account for the history of this development, a way to reconstruct the continuity of an evolution of ego when all that remains are fragments—ruins, artifacts, monuments, historical traces—of its encounters and exchanges with the external world. At this point Freud, in this discourse on method, turns to a curious but not arbitrary example, the problem of using a historical model that will account for a different kind of history. His example, by some chance, is Rome, or more precisely, a certain history of Rome, but his question is the pertinence of example and model: what is involved, he asks, in "taking an analogy from another field" and applying it as an interpretative system? The topography of Rome, he observes, is a single surface made up of signs, traces, and so on, from widely different times, so that while one can identify some of the different historical periods from their fragments, there is little evidence of the "transformations" from one to the other. Moreover, some evidence is lost altogether, and radical gaps mark what remains as ruins: even the traces may only be restorations and hence interpretative transformations. In a passage reminiscent of *The Marble Faun,* Freud tells us why there can be no "topological map" for this locus: "of the buildings which occupied this ancient area [the *Roma Quadrata*] he [historian or archeologist] will find nothing, or only scanty remains, for they exist no longer. The best information about Rome in the Republican era would only enable him at the most to point out the sites where the temples and public buildings of that period stood. Their place is now taken by ruins, but not by ruins of themselves but of later restorations made after fires or destruction."[7] Rome is therefore not a topos but a text, traces that are traces of traces, a "history" that cannot be understood in spatial terms (nor even in narrative terms). When the analyst thinks of attempting to employ the model of Rome as a "psychical entity" in order to account for the development of the civilized "ego," he is confronted by a methodological contradiction: "If we want to represent historical sequence in spatial terms we can only do it by juxtaposition in space: the same space cannot have two different contents. Our attempt seems to be an idle game. It has only one justification. It shows us how far we are from mastering the characteristics of mental life by representing them in pictorial terms" (17–18).

Freud's critique of representationality is familiar enough, and it stands beyond the problematics of Hawthorne's in the very sense that the modern sciences are beyond the older, yet employ the old language of three-dimensional spatiality. Freud advocates a change of paradigm; yet there is available no adequate substitute. What is available is another form of discourse, but a discourse beyond analogy that cannot provide a metalanguage. It is also a discourse—like Freud's own psychoanalytical language —that had to be developed, even translated, out of an older language of mind, or even from philosophy. It will be a "translative" discourse, yet not in the sense that it will translate that which is not seen into a visible or conceptual language, as depth psychology presupposed in applying Freud's terms as strict concepts. Freud's text must proceed in a language that plays uncannily between narrative history and analytical translation, a strange dialogue of methodical advance and analytical self-questioning, which serves to rework the ruins of history and the ruins of memory into restorations, and restorations of restorations, opening up that analysis terminable and interminable that we have come to know as "French Freud." This dis-

7. Sigmund Freud, *Civilization and Its Discontents,* trans. and ed. James Strachey (New York, 1961), 16–17.

course intervenes and breaches the illusion of strict and regulated boundaries between our discourses—between, say, so-called imaginative and interpretative discourses that work through a genre like the "romance" to produce an excess of genre.

If "autobiography" is inevitably composed in such a doubled language, we will find constructed into it a "reading moment" of the highest exegetical interest, perhaps because that "moment" is also a scene of analysis, of reading, displaced like those we have just observed upon a crossroads like "Rome." If I now turn back to another "American" text, it is not because it is possible to quit what Williams called the "local," by which he meant not a historical place but a point of exchange and resistances in an energy field. Adams in his so-called autobiography offers us such a moment by which to assess the way "American literature" stages its own crisis—in this instance as a question of "education." The *Education* provides us an eccentric overview of what some philosophers have called the "age of analysis," or the break between metaphysics and modern thought. But it does so by revealing that the fracture was already constructed within metaphysics and its vocabulary. For Adams, "education" should be the appropriation or even acquisition of a usable past. It turns out instead to be the acquisition of a usable vocabulary, but one that changes, or even becomes "anasemic," at the very moment it appears to define most precisely a new understanding. It is this changing sense of change that Adams stages as an "autobiography" that can never close upon a realized "self," and as an "education" that can prepare one for nothing but questioning the end toward which education would be directed, or what would be the consequences of arriving there.

"Education," Adams knows, has always implied a metaphysical ideal, the development of an understanding commensurate with the order of things. Yet Adams, in his mid-sixties, heir of a distinguished family whose history parallels the nation's—a successful historian, novelist, and professor in his own right, if not in his own opinion—has to reflect upon the paradox that as he and his country enter the twentieth century, each has been deprived of the myths of continuity and progress, the genealogical and teleological fictions by which an "education" can direct the future out of its understanding of the past. Adams' education has been disturbed periodically by a nineteenth century that everywhere is marked by theoretical deconstructions, so that the century must be described in apocalyptic terms. The *fin de siècle,* the horizon from which Adams is now writing, is only another repetition of increasing discontinuity and dispersal, or entropy. The nineteenth century, the century of historicism, can only be understood as the most radical subversion of the historical sense of advance. The new sciences, the American Civil War, his personal and family tragedies—all have conspired to leave Adams, himself the child of the scions of American history, heirless. He is as much the end of a line as is Poe's Roderick Usher, that fictional figure of the imminent apocalypse waiting within every genealogical fiction of descent or ascent.

Education, as Adams insists in his preface, should be an "economy" of force, the shaping of a young man, who is "a certain form of energy," into an instrument and direction.[8] This demands a theory that can be reproduced in a model that in turn can be applied as a mold. But his century has been a relentless assault on this dream of the paradigm. Its reinvention of historicism has portended an apocalyptic end of history. A child of the eighteenth century, Adams finds himself orphaned in the nineteenth. Each stage of his education, from grammar school through Harvard, disabuses his hope of finding the meaning of the present in some parallel with the past, which is to say, in some past model or paradigm that will account for meaningful repetition. Immediately after his years at Harvard, where the multiplication of disciplines has turned the university into a dynamo, and each discipline in turn into a self-consuming yet self-perpetuating machine, he had set off for Europe to pursue yet more education, ostensibly to study civil law. Stopping briefly in England, bypassing France (whose legendary decadence he will take years to accept), he arrives in Germany for a two-year stay, where he is never able to overcome the obstacle of language, or better, where he discovers that the American, while a translation of Western thought, must think in another dimension. England he finds caught in the eighteenth century; Germany in the late medievalism of the sixteenth. But what he really confronts, in England and in Germany, is what we have come to call the "end of philosophy," or the failure of rationalism and romanticism respectively to account for the paradoxes of the industrial age or the revolution in physics. Everywhere he notes the coexistence of vast energy and the burnt-out ends of progress, the paradox of dynamics for which no theory or existing discipline can account. Everywhere there is an attack on the meta- or the "beyond": "physics stark mad in metaphysics" is Adams' striking

8. Henry Adams, *The Education of Henry Adams* (New York, 1931), xvi.

116

phrase. This failure of the age (which cannot really be an age, since it seems discontinuous with history) to find its theory or theorist, or any paradigm whatever to unite the disciplines, was signified, the old man reflects, by the uncanny (or displaced) force of Karl Marx in the educational canon. At first it seemed no more than the institutional failure to recognize a thought like Marx's at work in the margins of the cultural scene. Just as Marx had no place in the Harvard curriculum and had to write in isolation, if not anonymously, from a London that was intellectually transfixed in the eighteenth century, so Adams senses in Germany, beneath the authority of high romantic thought that was still busy completing the monumental edifice of Western metaphysics, an exclusion of or at least indifference to the revolution in dynamics, the inexorable yet anonymous force unleashed in and by the new sciences of electricity and thermodynamics. Adams will later reflect that he had "long ago reached, with Hegel, the limits of contradiction" (453–54), and as a child of Hegel's century he had never ceased to be a dreamer of unity. Marxian thought, on the other hand, is already at work in the gap opened up by Hegelian contradiction and is busy questioning the dream of unity as certainly as is the new science. But it is not so much that Marx's theory is being verified in the margins as that Marx is simply reading a dynamic at work beneath the surface of the old theories, the old language, for which there is not yet a language, except the one he is providing by turning Hegel upside down. At the time, then, Adams notes, "he had no idea that Karl Marx was standing there writing for him, and that sooner or later the process of education would have to deal with Karl Marx much more than Professor Bowen of Harvard College" (72). Marx is a metonym for all those forces of interpretation that are at work undoing the old paradigms of history, including the old ideal of education.

When German thought—the thought of Goethe and Schiller even more than Hegel—fails him, he moves on to Italy and finally to Rome, where he confronts yet another impasse, historicism. Each stage of his education had been a pursuit of unity, and each was undone when he was brought face to face with contradiction, one seemingly as productive and dynamic as destructive or nihilistic. Thus he formulates a theory of "accidental education," of an understanding that comes not through a rigorous address of a discipline but through a sudden reversal of expectation. In Germany, for example, the student who had long ignored Beethoven undergoes a kind of Joycean epiphany. He discovers beneath the formal structure of the symphonies a "new language" which, though he cannot yet read it, disturbs his aesthetic habits. Beneath the traditional or formal, he discovers a "mechanical repetition of certain sounds" (81) that, as he later recognizes, parallels the revolution in mathematics at large in the century, a repetition that is engendering a monstrous and nameless future.

In Rome, however, he returns to his usual expectancies, seeking the order that historicism has always seemed to promise. Rome should provide his spatial model of history. But instead he finds Rome a "medieval complex" where the forms of high culture are entwined with "anarchy and vice," a Rome that cannot be read: "Medieval Rome was sorcery. Rome was the worst spot on earth to teach nineteenth-century youth what to do with the twentieth-century world" (90). Adams finds himself in the position of Gibbon confronting a "flat contradiction" with his will toward unity, but he can no longer appeal to Gibbon's narrative and dramatistic model, the ontotheological model of "decline and fall" (91). Nor does he have access to the newest nineteenth-century model of evolutionary advance:

Rome was not a beetle to be dissected or dropped; not a bad French novel to be read in a railway train and thrown out of the window after other bad French novels. . . . Rome was actual; it was England; it was going to be America. Rome could not be fitted into an orderly, middle-class, Bostonian, systematic scheme of evolution. No law of progress applied to it. Not even time sequences. . . . The great word Evolution had not yet in 1860, made a new religion of history, but the old religion had preached the same doctrine for a thousand years without finding the entire history of Rome anything but a contradiction. (90–91)

The question that history asks —"Why? why did this and not that occur or recur?"—cannot even be asked of Rome: "No one had answered the question to the satisfaction of anyone else; yet every one who had either head or heart, felt that sooner or later he must make up his mind what answer to accept. Substitute the word America for the word Rome, and the question became personal" (92). Rome, he concludes, "was a bewildering complex of ideas, experiments, ambitions, energies; without her, the Western world was pointless and fragmentary; she gave heart and unity to it all; yet Gibbon might have gone on for the whole century, sitting among the ruins of the Capitol, and no one would have passed capable of telling him what it meant. Perhaps it meant nothing" (93).

The disrelation between Gibbon's story and the unreadable text of

118

Rome—between narrative history and the encrypted ruins upon which Adams gazes—breaks the specular mirror that would allow one to see a future in the past, just as it undoes the dream of "autobiography." We now know what has intervened into the relation between model and repetition: the science of electricity, the new mathematics, thermodynamics, a revolution within physics and chemistry that had once seemed to promise a new paradigm to replace the old (as thermodynamics seemed to displace mechanics) and yet served instead to dismantle the very idea of the paradigm. For his remaining years, Adams commits himself to study this contradiction and thus to continue an "education" that now appears without end, or to end only as entropy ends, in cold death: the search by various theorists for a working model that always detaches and defers the possibility of the model. He sees this dissonance of theory/praxis finally exemplified at the end of the century in what he calls the Curies' "metaphysical bomb," the rediscovery of the sun that throws everything out of orbit. The new sciences not only sweep aside all fictions of continuity but demystify the ideal of systematic closure or eternal return. Gibbon's circular movement that culminates in "decline and fall" is displaced by the unilinear movement of entropic dispersal, just as *telos* is displaced by randomness: the movement from maximum organization (complexity) to maximum disorganization (simplicity and death), from hot to cold, from differentiated to undifferentiated or identical, from class to classless society, inexorable democratic leveling. The relentless acceleration and unilinear direction of thermodynamic motion disrupts not only teleological fictions of education but also the ideal of individual and collective memory on which they depend, since it is impossible to find in the equilibrium of dispersed and undifferentiated things any evidence of their origin, or to read back from the fragment to the whole. If one finds America already in the contradictions of Rome, it is not an America that can be defined as a "nation" or a unity, a repetition of the past, but an America of momentum. America is force or random energy, and therefore it is without identity, like the Rome he cannot read. Everywhere he confronts not reality but a *mise en scène* of tropic and entropic transformations. Just as no road finally connects Saint Mark's and the Forum, the ruins of Rome are fragments that cannot be architecturally or archeologically reconstructed, but signify only an-archy. And when they turn up repeated in America, they cannot be traced back to an origin they never had.

In his preface, Adams had declared that in his search for a model for education he could get no help from "American literature," for American literature in effect did not exist, and what was called American literature appeared in the form of Old World signs. A national literature, after all, is definable only after the moment in which its masterpieces are recognized, when the history of its literature has closed, or when it is in decline: thus Gibbon's belief that he could read Rome, and by reading Rome could understand his own present. But Adams has read a different "Rome," a Rome where thermodynamic was always already at work; so that if America repeats Rome it does so paradoxically in a "repetition without identity." We may go back, then, as a final word, to the conclusion of Emerson's essay on "Art," that "aboriginal Power," as he calls it, which separates and detaches rather than gathers. The last paragraph of that essay associates this power not with an organic nature, as we might expect, but with the power of the new sciences, proceeding as if from the "religious heart" to arise, as he says, in "our commerce, the galvanic battery, the electric jar, the prism, and the chemist's retort" (*CW*, II, 218). Nature is power, and power, "nature." And Emerson's only model for it is language, or literature, which at the same time transports a meaning and tropes or transforms it. Emerson prefigures American art as a "steamboat bridging the Atlantic between Old and New England" and arriving as its "ports with the punctuality of a planet" (218). We might remind ourselves that this is not simply another version of the solar myth, that the motions of planets, as Emerson said of "God's ways," are parabolic and not circular, and that the arrival anticipates no eternal return of the same. But more important, that "steamboat," which has displaced the sailing ship, is a system that transforms matter rather than mechanically channeling natural force. Melville, we might recall, had also represented an America caught in this double bind of contradictory systems—in the figure of the whaling ship that bears in its bowels the fire that transforms animal flesh into a different form of energy. American literature is poised upon that "economy" that Emerson calls the "stream of tendency," of the transformative moment when one language is displacing another, a new literature retracing and rewriting the old. The reader not only becomes but supplants the book, ec-statically opening it to a monstrous future or cold death, the play of tropy and en-tropy.

5

THE "CRYPT" OF EDGAR POE

I

If Poe did not exist, he would have had to be invented. One authoritative critical view holds that he is, after all, a French creation; or even that he invented, by a series of extravagant displacements, French symbolist poetics. T. S. Eliot has provided one account of this curious genealogy: "Poe's influence is . . . puzzling. In France the influence of his poetry and of his poetic theories has become immense. In England and America it seems almost negligible. Can we point to any poet whose style appears to have been formed by a study of Poe? The only one whose name immediately suggests itself is—Edward Lear."[1] In English, Poe is Emerson's jingle man; transcribed into French, he inaugurates the revolution of the word, as in the radical modernism of Borges' Pierre Menard, the "Symbolist from Nimes" who was a "devoté of Poe, who engendered Baudelaire, who engendered Mallarmé, who engendered Valéry, who engendered Edmond Teste."[2] Nearly a quarter of a century before Eliot's short history of this detour from American nonsense to Gallic *nouvelle vague*, Williams plotted another genealogy for Poe in *In the American Grain*. The French, Williams argued, had misread Poe's "scrupulous originality." They failed to understand his "re-awakened genius of *place*," his clearing of the "ground" for the *"beginning"* of a "juvenescent *local* literature" (216–17). Eliot's Poe, who had the mind of a "pre-pubescent adolescent," becomes Williams' forger of a "new" language. The one point of agreement: any in-mixing of Poe and Continental poetics produces an interesting hybrid, a graft and a graph sometimes called by the double name of "modernism."

Eliot's reading of Poeisme, the symbolist quest for a "purity" in which the word is refined of its worldliness, both its referentiality and its materiality, is an attack upon "amoral" modernism, which at the same time he reluctantly praises for its "craft." The fate of modernism, which in Eliot's view

1. T. S. Eliot, *To Criticize the Critic* (New York, 1965), 27.
2. Jorge Luis Borges, "Pierre Menard, Author of the Quixote," in *Labyrinths*, trans. James E. Irby (New York, 1962), 40–41.

led inexorably to the narcissism of Paul Valéry, was to be entrapped in the machinery of its own operations, to exhaust itself in pale fire. The abandonment of "subject matter," of referentiality and at least the illusion of representation (as in a proper symbolist linkage of earth and sky), has produced the twofold vertigo and paralysis of modern poetry. "That Poe had a powerful intellect," Eliot writes, "is undeniable":

but it seems to me the intellect of a highly gifted young person before puberty. The forms which his lively curiosity takes are those in which a pre-adolescent mentality delights: wonders of nature and of mechanics and of the supernatural, cryptograms and cyphers, puzzles and labyrinths, mechanical chess-players and wild flights of speculation. The variety and ardour of his curiosity delight and dazzle; yet in the end the eccentricity and lack of coherence of his interests tire. There is just that lacking which gives dignity to the mature man: a consistent view of life.[3]

Poeisme/modernism marks an "eccentricity" in the order of things; it is aberrational, nonteleological, a stylistic machine. An interest in cryptograms, cyphers, puzzles, labyrinths—they are the obsessions of the child and the pure intellect, and will lead symptomatically to the incoherence of writing.

Poe or Valéry—in Eliot's view both signify the excess and the impasse of a language turned from the world upon itself: "with Poe and Valéry, extremes meet, the immature mind playing with ideas because it had not developed to the point of convictions, and the very adult mind playing with ideas because it was too sceptical to hold convictions" (40). Skepticism, Eliot adds, is a healthy quality of the "mature intellect," but the extreme, as in Valéry, leads to "intellectual narcissism." Poe's "Philosophy of Composition" provided Valéry with "a method and an occupation—that of observing himself write." The "penetration of the poetic by the introspective critical activity," says Eliot, produced the fore-structure and the fore-play of a modernist crisis, a poetics that can neither be rejected nor appropriated, a poetics that dissolves the traditional "ground" of a "real" world (whether subjective or objective) and suggests a recuperation of the barbarously romantic dream of spontaneous, irreflective expression (41). Eliot presents the most recent modernist crisis as an impossible choice between the mutually exclusive illusions of vitalism and formalism, barbarous paganism and civilized restraint, evident in the "extreme awareness of and concern for language which we find in Valéry," a condition "which must ultimately

3. Eliot, *To Criticize the Critic*, 35.

break down, owing to an increasing strain against which the human mind and nerves will rebel" (42).

Williams, to the contrary, claimed that Poe "struck to lay low the *'ni-aiseries'* of form and content with which his world abounded."[4] He called Poe's writing an "attack" on representation or "colonial imitation," an attack *"from the center out"*: "With Poe words were not hung by usage with associations, the pleasing wraiths of former masteries, this is the sentimental trap-door to beginnings. With Poe words were figures; an old language truly, but one from which he carried over only the most elemental qualities to his new purpose. . . . Sometimes he used words so playfully his sentences seem to fly away from sense, the destructive! with the conserving abandon, foreshadowed, of a Gertrude Stein" (219, 221). And Williams describes the method of this "immaculate attack" as a strategic chiasmus: "He has a habit, borrowed perhaps from algebra, of balancing sentences in the middle, or of reversing them in the later clauses, a sense of play, as with objects, or numerals which he *has* in the original, disassociated, that is, from other literary habit; separate words" that do not "'belong properly to books'"(221–22). Poe has little interest in "supernatural mysteries" or the "extraordinary eccentricity of fate," but is preoccupied with "writing": "Method, punctuation, grammar—" (227). Thus, Williams continues, the French mistook a rhetorical inversion for a representation of the "bizarre," when they should have recognized, as in their own avant-garde experiment, the necessity of negative or destructive writing: "On him is FOUNDED A LITERATURE—typical; an anger to sweep out the unoriginal, that became ill-tempered; a monomaniacal driving to destroy, to annihilate the copied, the slavish, the FALSE literature about him" (223). America's imported literary tradition had denied its writers a "natural landscape"; thus Poe could only imitate the "field of cold logic . . . to which his work must still present a natural *appearance*" (228). Language displaces "nature" as the object of language, as the "place" or "local" of the "beginning," its own extraordinary "scene."

Two Poes, two modernisms, at least—Eliot and Williams agree that an abyss has opened up between word and world, and hence in the word itself; but if for Eliot that abyss is the consequence of a skepticism become nihilism, for Williams it is the "desire" for "originality" that compels all writing and marks indelibly the aporia of every modernist strategy to "make

4. William Carlos Williams, *In the American Grain*. (1925; rpr. New York, 1956), 221.

it new" or to "begin again" in a field of language without origin or end. Poe's canon, as Eliot sees it, becomes the fractured mirror of the modern, fore-structuring a literature of moral exhaustion, of purely surface play. In the hollow reverberations of Poesque language the word functions only in an end-less play of displacements that is literature. Every beginning is already a beginning inter-text, in a "field of cold logic" which, we have forgotten, is metaphorical, already always—like Nietzsche's truths that are the vestiges of fictions (figures) whose origins are either forgotten or repressed. The word becomes its own broken reflection, and as in the image of the "House of Usher," the "barely perceptible fissure" disorients even the illusion of a stable if submerged origin/ground. The natural world dissolves in its own im-age, to become the image of nature's absence. There is no accessible point of departure but only a secondary and heterogeneous world, as he describes it in *Eureka,* hence a world or cosmology that can only be revealed as two irreducible plots—God's ideal plot and man's imperfect plot, itself dou-bled, complex, unnatural. Poe abandons nature for the image. His world becomes a text, or a library of multiple texts.

As Eliot and, later, Allen Tate were to see, though they interpreted it as a moral deficiency, the secondary, heterogeneous realm in Poe's theory was nothing other than a world of words, dispersed and materialized into dis-related atoms. In Poe the images of nature are already metonymic substi-tutions for words—or substitutions for substitutions. It is all the more strange that Eliot and Tate, those fathers of New Critical formalism, would be enchanted by the force of his madness, and equally repelled by it. Tate saw Poe as "our cousin," the exemplum of a peculiar variety of American, essentially southern, moral guilt.[5] Yet Tate, like Eliot, was equally attentive to what he called Poe's "angelic imagination" or the obsession with "verbal magic," a belief in the "power of words" (to revert to one of Poe's titles) that char-acterized the extreme thrust of a romantic will to signification. Eliot's con-cern with the impasse of a language turned upon itself reflects Tate's dis-turbance over the romantic displacement of language upon the abyss, upon what Tate called the "zero" of "unity." In either case, Poe is indicted for a poetics which erases that secure zone in which formalist criticism situ-ated language, that uninterrogated margin where a "poetic language" may freely play between its dual obligation to represent the world and trace a

5. See Allen Tate, "Our Cousin, Mr. Poe," in Tate, *Essays of Four Decades* (Chicago, 1969), 385–400. The essay was a lecture delivered in 1949.

shadow of the universal, or mediate between an outside and an inside. For the fathers of New Critical formalism, Poe (and Poeisme) is culpable of removing poetic language from that sanctuary where its power or its impotence need not be questioned.

But it is just this violation of the taboo of literary language to which Williams drew an early attention. It should call our attention, here, to the strategies by which Poe constructed metaphorical puzzles out of metaphorical fragments, or built a house of fiction out of the "crypts" of outmoded structures, those mausoleums of a philosophical (and therefore, if we follow Nietzsche, a metaphorical) history. "The Power of Words," which Tate claims to be the essay most clearly evidencing Poe's drift toward "angelic" madness, dissolves the privileged difference between a discursive and an imaginative text that it seems most intent on confirming. In fact, as a fable, and as a parody of the philosophical dialogue, this "colloquy" tends to erase the margin between a poetic or creative language and an analytical or scientific discourse that seems to be its theme. Rather than displacing language upon the void, as Tate argues, it is a meditation upon the problematics of a reverse displacement, of the abyss that has opened up on the sign, so that the world of words signifies the absence of the world, or signifies absence. Poe's so-called colloquy reflects on a romantic commonplace, the provisional non-presence of language and the possibility of the recuperation of presence in the poetic "void." In the words of one speaker in "The Conversation of Eiros and Charmion": "Let us converse of familiar things, in the old familiar language of the world which has so fearfully perished."[6] The event of the creation is a "fall," as in the dispersal and materialization of the word, leaving the poet with (and within) a medium that only traces, in a "nebulous light," the original and unrepeated creative moment, which is also a destructive moment.

It is a theme familiar in poems like "Israfel" or even "The Bells": the increasing loss of power in words, which are dispersed from the zero degree of unity and also turned from themselves, becoming materialized and leaden. Language is a shadow light, at best, the vestiges of an annihilated universe. The text of the world—for the world has perished and only its language remains—is a non-presence. Yet, a poetic, or should one call it scriptive, hope derives from this negative, for while the poet is deprived of true orig-

---

6. Edgar Allan Poe, *Complete Works,* ed. James A. Harrison (16 vols.; New York, 1902), IV, 2. Hereinafter cited parenthetically in the text by volume and page number.

inality, he may be endowed with an "algebraic" sense, through which his belated representations, which are only "tracing(s)" of "every impulse given
the air" (V, 142), may vibrate across the void. Thus the "power of words"
rests in their original displacement and dispersal, a fall marked by a fissure
in the image. The poet's work, like the angels', is always retrograde and
decadent; the power of words is a physical representation of the metaphysical, and the poet's secondary creative power functions wholly within
a physical ether (language), which he modulates by setting "impulses" in
motion. Poe's colloquy "The Power of Words" concludes with a figure of
fabulous imitation, or fabulist invention, in which the two angels recall
their own imitation of the divine creation as a loss. The angelic Oinos asks
his fellow Agathos why he weeps and his wings droop as they hover over
the "fair-star—which is the greenest and yet most terrible of all we have
encountered in our flight" (V, 143). The star, which Agathos calls a "wild
star," is a figural repetition of the Earth, or the Divine creation that can
never be repeated. It is, therefore, a text, spoken into existence by Agathos'
"impulse," his physical speech. Here are his concluding words: "This wild
star—it is now three centuries since, with clasped hands, and with stream-
ing eyes, at the feet of my beloved, I spoke it, with a few passionate sentences—into birth. Its brilliant flowers *are* the dearest of all unfulfilled
dreams, and its raging volcanoes *are* the passions of the most turbulent and
unhallowed of hearts" (V, 143–44). Agathos' creation is a figure of figure,
a repetition of the original creation and a mocking sign of the absence that
is angelic or poetic repetition. The power of words is no more than a power
to move other words. Words are already secondary, and they repeat only
an original abysm that marks their distance from any "first law." Ironically, their naturalness, or materiality, like the increasing dullness in the
poem "The Bells," signifies at once their "power" and their death. In Poe there
is no natural language, and no nature. Nature is not an origin but a run-
down trope. This is a fable Poe obsessively retells, the wearying struggle to
purify language through language, the poetic repetition of some idea of
"absolute perfection" or some idea of purity that in the same gesture reveals the mark of its own discontinuity with any original form, idea, truth,
reality. The Poesque realm of dream, which is the realm of language, is always a realm of the "unfulfilled." The poetic repetition can never represent "perfection," but only a "difference" of perfection, a turbulence and passion. Poetry is textuality that can only reflect an absence of the ideal.

In what follows, I would like to explore a patchwork of metaphors that nets together much of the Poe canon, weaving discursive and imaginative texts and at the same time erasing the generic margins between the so-called tales of the grotesque and the tales of ratiocination. The metaphors, of course, derive from a double sense of "the power of words" that generates so much of the obscurity and, Eliot might have said, prepubescent melodrama of the tales, and ineffectively conceals the plagiarisms in a quasi-scientific text like *Eureka.* I am referring to the metaphors of "house" and "tomb," of "crypt" and "cryptographer," and therefore the figure of poet-author-analyst whose writing is always an "impulse on the air," a retranscription of some antique manuscript or misplaced letter. The "letter," then, in the double sense of alphabetic character and enveloped message, is related to each of the other figures, each of which, whether library, labyrinth, pyramid, tomb, or house, prefigures the question of the letter's proper location and its eccentric movement, like a manuscript in a bottle or a story within a story. At the same time, however, these metaphors, which have a metaphysical and a literary history, have become displaced from that history and are situated, or rather are floating, in a space between two senses or orders of history, between two notions of literature. In the case of a discursive text like *Eureka,* most of which is openly appropriated from the cosmology of Alexander von Humboldt and Laplace, and hence from the mechanics of Newton, it may be praised by Paul Valéry for anticipating Einstein's law of relativity and the entropic destiny of the second law of thermodynamics. The pseudoscience of *Eureka,* however, is clearly not a proleptic text—not so much prophetic of the new science as it is a critique of the logic that cements the old. It is therefore a critique of the notion of closure (Newtonian and/or poetic); and it perhaps justifies Poe's own claim that it is a poem and is to be judged as a poem after his death, not so much in its curious formulation of an imaginary cosmology as in its marking of the limits of the imaginary. It thus signifies the excess—indeed the literariness — in the enclosed universes of science and the lack or absence in the imaginary and human plots of literature—or what one might call literature's scientificity, referentiality, or naturalness.

Earlier I claimed that what makes American literature extraordinary is that it is a literature without a history, and that its obsession with beginning anew manifests itself in repeated but failing attacks upon the notion of representation. There is another sense in which American literature is exemplary. If we borrow from the French revisionists and not from our own uninterrogated historical periods, we must admit that what we call the beginning of a "native" style or voice is coincidental with what the French consider a break between the "classical" and the "modern," a rupture in the linguistic history of the sign. Charles Feidelson suggested that American literature of the nineteenth century (which he called symbolistic) could finally be read with the advent of modernism, since it was modern in its self-referential preoccupation with being new. The French appropriation of Poe, as against our own history of trying to accommodate him to the literary tradition, is only the most obvious example of his ex-centric displacement into what is called modernism. Poe is in two senses the decadent: the end of a progressively degraded literary history; the sign of some grotesque perturbation in romantic thought, perhaps a doubling and a deconstruction, hence an allegorization of that particularly modern appropriation of romanticism as "natural supernaturalism." Perhaps Poe's "uses of incoherence," as Valéry defined generative style, is only his re-marking of the madness inhabiting the image, a madness aggravated by every poetic attempt to close the play opened up by even the "barely perceptible fissure" traced out in every style.

In the befogged, miasmic atmosphere of Poe's house of fiction, his subject matter is, as Williams suggests, "cold logic." Newton and Laplace's cosmic machine, which represents the universal perfection in its capacity for inexhaustible repetition, is a plot of narrative closure that deprives the poet of originality but not of truth. Criticism as a reversal of this order, as a retelling of its teleology (for example, Poe's critical recounting of the creation of a poem from its completion back toward the unity of conception where it originates), becomes, however, a perturbation that intervenes in this closure. Poe introduces what Schlegel had foreseen as the inevitability for a new literature, a self-critical or self-annihilating textual performance—the poem/story and even the critical essay (as performance) that deconstructs itself. This is Poe's ironic theme in "The Philosophy of Composition" and "The Poetic Principle"—and the thematizing of the poem as the inseparability of Beauty and Death, of the image that re-marks its own absence, thematizes the notion of writing as displacement, supplementation, and radical theft. Beauty as the difference of Truth is neither an image of Truth nor reversible into Truth. The figure of beauty, the dead woman, is the figure of the text in Poe—not of the word that substitutes for truth but of the word that absents itself, or is the material sign of a double absence. Poe introduces a theme that "American" literature obsessively retells—of purloined letters and de-constructed architecture. Like Stevens' lament in "The Rock" that it is an "illusion" we were ever alive and lived in the "houses" of mothers,[7] Poeisme "cures" a "ground" for literature by constructing a deconstruction, by erecting one house upon the remnants of another, like a book, say, made out of the books of some incomplete library, a library never composed except in a fiction. Poe constructs a mausoleum (text) to contain his sign of Beauty/Death.

II

As the narrator approaches the "House of Usher," he feels himself engulfed in its "melancholy" and "insufferable gloom." The natural order of things is inverted: day seems like night, and the house reflects "a wild inconsistency between the still perfect adaptation of parts, and the crumbling condition of the individual stones." The house is a "specious totality," an "extraordinary dilapidation," marked by a "barely perceptible fissure" that runs a "zigzag direction" down its exterior to disappear in the "sullen waters of the tarn." The origin of the fissure is erased in a series of reflections that has no scrutable beginning or end. The narrator is disoriented and overcome with a "melancholy" that is "unrelieved by any of that half-pleasurable, because poetic, sentiment, with which the mind usually receives even the sternest natural images of the desolate or terrible" (III, 273). Everything is a "scene" or "picture" but not a coherent representation. It is like the "after-dream of the reveller upon opium—the bitter lapse into everyday life—the hideous dropping off of the veil." The primary inversion at the beginning of "The Fall of the House of Usher" lies in the beginning of narrative itself, a grotesque "lapse" or fall into a world of images where words and things no longer coincide. The narrator ponders a failure of creative perception, of poetic images, to mediate a scene of vacant nature: "I was forced to fall back upon the unsatisfactory conclusion, that while, beyond doubt, there *are* combinations of very simple natural objects which have the power of thus affecting us, still the analysis of this power lies among considerations beyond our depth. It was possible, I reflected, that a mere

7. Wallace Stevens, *Collected Poems* (New York, 1954), 248.

different arrangement of the particulars of the scene, of the details of the picture, would be sufficient to modify, or perhaps to annihilate its capacity for sorrowful impression" (III, 274). Nature, it seems, is either a text or a chaos. Either or both. Double like an afterdream. As problematic as language.

The narrator first views the "house" as a grotesque reflection in the "lurid tarn," in "remodelled and inverted images." And when he lifts his gaze from the image to the house itself he is almost overwhelmed by the atmosphere or estrangement that, as he puts it, "had no affinity with the air of heaven." Natural order and expectancy is suspended and inverted. Nature and culture, landscape and house, reflect each other without difference. The Usher family, now reduced to twins without "collateral issue," inhabit an estate that bears the "quaint and equivocal appellation of the 'House of Usher'" (III, 275), erasing in the minds of the peasantry any difference between the family and its residence. All differences, natural or cultural, are in a state of collapse or degeneration. But in the narrator's mind, the most ominous disruption in the order of things is signified by a failure of language, of the poetic sentiment to mediate and hence to restore and maintain the priority of spiritual or ideal harmony to natural heterogeneity or randomness. Nature is either in a state of irreparable decay or is a stormy "whirlwind." In either case, it signifies an obliteration of all those hierarchal differences and genealogical fictions upon which the privilege of the Usher family has been founded.

It is little wonder, then, that the narrator's reflections move from the image of the "house," whose architecture reflects a "specious totality" of related differences, to the figure of the "ancient family" that is now without "collateral issue" and is represented by asexual twins who are the last of an "ancient family" that lies in "the direct line of descent and had always, with very trifling and very temporary variation, so lain" (III, 274). This "deficiency," as the narrator twice calls it, signifies the end of both the family and history and reveals that both are problematical metaphors based on a questionable analogy between a biological and a genealogical order. The "quaint and equivocal appellation of the 'House of Usher'" signifies the irreversible direction of exhaustion and decay that predicates a final collapse of the distinctions between nature and culture, or material and spiritual, in the collapse of proper signification itself. It is the idea of the "direct" unbroken "line" of a teleological (and hence a narrational) order that is broken in this incompatible "house." The house of fiction reflects the "malady" in the fiction of the house.

The narrator finds himself directly confronting a "family" that exemplifies a history he cannot understand, but which we, along with Valéry, might suggest to be the entropic history predicated in the "second law of thermodynamics," or in the romantic appropriation of the transnatural law.[8] Poe's own metaphysical preoccupation with energetics, which supplants materialism or naturalism, anticipates this displacement of one notion of history by another. As in *Eureka,* where he plagiarizes and emends the Newtonian cosmos of von Humboldt and Laplace, the end of the creation in material dispersion and extreme heterogeneity must either lead to an inert, stable universe, in which the discrete particulars offer no clue of their origin, or there must be some radical supplementation in the nature of things, an overcoming of this deadly trend toward non-difference by some "different arrangement." Thus Poe will not accept the unidirectional, entropic sense of history that his demystification of the old metaphors reveals to him, but will attempt to reverse them, which means he must allegorize the fiction once again. It is the inevitability of closure, in either Laplace's cosmos or any reversal of it, that aggravates Poe's desire to imagine a new text of the world.

The interior of the Usher house repeats its exterior. It is a clutter of antiquated styles and disrelated objects, a bric-a-brac that can no longer signify the stability of the family's estate in a meaningful order of things or suggest its continuing "line." Like Usher, the narrator is resigned to a desperate hope that by a "mere different arrangement of the particulars" he can overcome the evidence of random distribution and defer the death signified by the collapse of a symbolic system. Yet the narrator, who has been summoned to "Usher" by an agitated "letter" from his boyhood friend, can no more superintend the scene from the outside than he can regenerate it from the inside. The interior disorder of the "house" is as irreversible as the decay of the carefully arranged stones that characterize its archi-texture. When the narrator and Usher turn as a last resort to a hope that through art they may delay, if not reverse, the degeneration, they resort inevitably to the very metaphors or debris in which they are entombed. The hope that

8. See Paul Valéry's essay on *Eureka,* in *Leonardo, Poe, Mallarmé,* trans. Malcolm Cowley and James R. Lawler (Princeton, N.J., 1972), 161–76, Vol. VIII of Valéry, *Collected Works,* 15 vols.

art will restore the spirit, by recuperating a generative origin, can only be prefigured in the metaphors of improvised, or non-representational, art, an art that by analysis restores some sign of an orderly scene, an ideal or centered scene, albeit a scene that unveils the artifice of its instituted center: "We painted or read together, or I listened, as if in a dream, to the wild improvisations of his speaking guitar" (III, 282).

Usher improvises music, paints feverishly, and writes poems, one of which, a so-called ballad, "The Haunted Palace," reduplicates the paintings which in their turn are pure renderings (hence allegories) of "an idea." Usher's allegorical art becomes the phantasmagoria of a desire, an "incoherence —an inconsistency" (like the house) that reflects at the same time an unseen but recoverable unity and the lawlessness of life. Each of his works, however, is inadequate: they render a desire without an object. The "wild fantasias" of his music shatter the norms of harmony but recuperate no sensible structure. His poem repeats the allegory of a green world or happy consciousness, figured in the metaphor of the "stately palace" of "Thought's dominion" situated in a "happy valley" that is suddenly afflicted by motion, time, and decay, the exhaustion of its radiance and the degeneration of its "well-tuned law" into "discordant melody" (III, 284–85). And the one painting that beyond all others entrances the narrator is an abstract or phantasmagorical rendering of a "vault" or a "tunnel," an abyssal structure suggesting some subterranean realm illuminated by a "ghastly" light that is without natural origin, a fictional light inscribed there as a sign that marks the absence of both nature and origin.

Despite the narrator's concern over their perverse and wild air, each of Usher's works represents a rather ordinary desire for a self-sustaining, self-present inside, an inexhaustible presence that can distribute itself effectively through every outside or image. But each can render the idea only by suggesting its opposite, that the artist can only fictionalize this center as a provisional loss; therefore, the images distributed about this center, or dispersed from it, are shadows doubling its absence. In Usher's painting, then, the light becomes the sign of a fiction subject to at least two contrary interpretations, which the narrator indicates in his protests that words describing the picture are inadequate to the "spirit of abstraction," that they render only a "ghostly and inappropriate splendour" (III, 283). In Usher's art, every sign indicates a radical secondariness, a discontinuity between image and imaged. At the circumference of each of his productions there is entropic non-difference—noise, shadow, cold death, random distribution.

Nothing in Usher's house, however, is more inappropriate than his very exclusive library, a bibliography largely made up of an authentic list of pseudoscientific, mystical, and quasi-theological texts, each in one way or another devoted to the idea of "the sentience of all vegetable things" (III, 286). Usher's paintings and writings are repeated by his library, in which each text betokens an animistically centered or unified world, a unity reflected in all the stable differences of a natural world. As the narrator states, Usher's library is another testimony to his faith in the priority of inside to outside, of the one to the many. The collection reduplicates, in Usher's mind, the conception of his "forefathers" in their arranging the "gray stones of the home." The sentience of matter, the orderly distribution of differences in an architecture, would suggest not only the sustaining arche of the family line but would give the material evidence of decay and degeneration an informing myth, a reversed teleology.

Yet rather than alleviating Usher's hypochondria, his art and study aggravate his neurosis. The library, then, is not simply a collection and totalization of books representing and authenticating the family history, thereby situating man securely in the order of nature. The exclusiveness of the library, on the contrary, calls attention to its own arbitrariness. Like the family, the library produces no "collateral issue" or ideas, but reproduces a monomania. Just as it excludes other fictions, it reveals only the "phantasm," the malady and deficiency, of its originator. The obsession of the family with its destiny has generated a sterile fiction, of which the library with its single idea is the primary metaphor. The library reduplicates the "specious totality" and "wild inconsistency" of the "house"—an outside of disrelated stones repeated in an inside that is a specious totality of texts. Moreover, the library is not only a central room, but another closure that stands outside or over the central tomb. The texts that stand for one idea signify its absence. They are signs of death.

Of all its listed books, only one, the romantic melodrama "Mad Trist," which the narrator chooses to read to Usher during the time of his most extreme hysteria, is purely fictional—except, of course, Usher's own works of art. But this produces yet another exception, since "The Haunted Palace" is Poe's own poem, previously published. House and library repeat the *mise en abîme* of fiction-within-fiction: like Don Quixote's library, which contains one of Cervantes' books. The narrator condemns "Mad Trist" for its "uncouth and unimaginative prolixity" (III, 292), but it of all the texts in Usher's library is a simulacrum of a master book, the central image. "Mad Trist," according to the narrator, was "the only book immediately at hand," and though it is unworthy of Usher's "lofty and spiritual ideality," the narrator uses it as a distraction for his friend's increasing incoherence. The romance narrates a knightly quest that includes the slaying of a dragon and the winning of a "shield." It is read against the background of a "whirlwind" that swirls up around the house coincidentally with Usher's hysteria, while both he and the narrator listen to the "muffled reverberations" from the sister's crypt. Again, inside and outside collapse, and nature (whether vegetable or human) is signified as unnameable force, an in-coherence.

"Mad Trist" is employed by the narrator to defer both his and Usher's sense of the torment, the question, encrypted at the center of the house. Yet it can only amplify the question of the tomb. Ultimately, the story's own fictional center, the "brazen shield" of enchantment that attracts the Knight, must be approached, the last sign at the interior of a receding tunnel of fictions, an image that doubles all the rest. But as soon as it is won, and the dragon dispatched, the shield falls to the ground, metal ringing against metal with a dissonance that repeats every other center in the house/tale. The narrative within the narrative reduplicates the fictional labyrinth of the house; the "romance" reflects the fictional center of all the other texts of the library, the shield of enchantment that forever defers any direct look into the abyss. Usher's desperate repression of the question, his dispatching of his sister to the tomb, is a last futile gesture to maintain the structure of "house" and "family," a last will to signification, a final attempt to preserve presence or life by a reinstallation of some sign of presence there where the center is absented. The body remanded to the tomb is alive; yet like a body or sign that stands for life, it is dead. For Usher, his repression of death conceals the absence of life in the house, but in the same gesture reveals the death or nothingness that has always inhabited the "house"/"family"/"direct line." The house's crypt, like Usher's art, conceals the secret of the center, that it is neither a presence nor an absence but a place constructed to install a sign of presence or absence.

Everything in "The Fall of the House of Usher" is a metaphorical detour, a delay in the course of a narrative that pushes toward its own tautological conclusion. For the thrust of every narrative reduplicates Usher's madness: the need to sustain differences yet the desire to realize the ideal of some final, ultimate unity. The double fault of the house of fiction must inevitably fall inward upon itself. Still, every narrative is at the same time a deferral of the center, of that "enshrouded figure" (Usher's sister) or "brazen shield" that is only another sign of the sense of an ending. As the narrator retreats from the house, he passes along the "old causeway" by which he entered, amid a storm that obscures and shadows every detail. His last view is of some "wild light" that has its source in a "blood-red moon" radiating through the "barely perceptible fissure" of the house. As the fissure widens, the house collapses inward upon itself, reduplicating the collapse of the twins upon one another. The airing of the crypt exposes the secret that sustains all such structures of difference, including narratives: "While I gazed, this fissure rapidly widened—there came a fierce breath of the whirlwind—the entire orb of the satellite burst at once upon my sight—my brain reeled as I saw the mighty walls rushing asunder—there was a long tumultuous shouting sound like the voice of a thousand waters—and the deep and dank tarn at my feet closed sullenly and silently over the fragments of the 'House of Usher'" (III, 297). The fragments of the narrative collapse upon themselves and are enclosed in a final metaphor that contains the figure of the house, the family, and the story itself—an infinitely refracted series of fictions without origin or end, without the sustaining center of the crypt. The metaphors of "family," "house," and "library," or of art as the rendering or expression of "idea," are all figures concealing a tomb at the center. Poe's renowned aesthetic ideal of a "unity of effect" is itself a metaphor, of an architecture elaborately constructed upon the zero metaphor, the arche that is neither present nor absent. The "House of Usher" is built out of old books, the fragments of legends, romances, superstitions, and quasi-scientific metaphors, all erected upon a "hollow coffin" that must be protected even as it is ultimately opened and revealed as the place of just another missing body, another simulacrum of a simulacrum.

III

On the other hand, in a text like *Eureka* Poe begins, as Valéry points out, with the notion of God and the concept of original unity. The created universe, according to Poe, is a "plot of God," and therefore an inimitable perfection, to which the "plots of man" are secondary metaphors, discontinuous and indeed inadequate to the only original. The "plot of God" is already a metaphysical or aesthetic concept, a kind of primary metaphor that is already an order of language, of logic. What lies behind or before the "plot"—either God, unity, or nothingness—turns out itself to be a figural name for the non-figural. The "plot of God" would be a kind of poem; the "plots" of men, interpretations. Poe's strategy is to forget the origin—even the "creation," which could only have occurred once in all its completeness, and can never be repeated—and hence the "fall" implied in God's plot; then to conceive of man's plots, in all their imperfections, as a metaphoric play evoking, by repetition, a God-like supplement to his machine. Cosmology is only a history of interpretations that proves the limits of a representational or empirical system. Since the creation is completed, no image of it survives. Only the created is an image, to which every other image is belated. The dualistic notions of time and space and their accompanying laws of deduction and induction are examples of plots of man, images not of the logos but of some imperfect image, some logocentric interpretation. The cosmos, which is projected as a system of dispersed material entities reciprocally functioning according to the laws of attraction and repulsion, is already a text, a secondary and heterogeneous structure of signs that can only be plotted regionally. Man's plots move only in one of at least two directions, while the ideal plot would move in two directions simultaneously. Every one of man's plots is a shorthand cypher, a figuration of the whole that also images its own fissure. To repeat, even God's plot, the created cosmos, is already a text or a map. Like Josiah Royce's ideal map of England, which Borges calls the fantastic paradox of philosophical invention, God's plot would have to include as one of its elements a plot of God's plot.

What, then, if one begins with the text as poem, as the excess that is literature, including the obvious discordance of any text that comments on its own imperfection and makes of that commentary an image that is itself the belated "original" image that the text represents? *Eureka* is a diacritical text in which the criticism is the primary and the imaginative is the secondary or representational dimension. Of course, neither the imaginative nor the critical is primary. Nature has long since disappeared in several removes of the image. A cosmology, which presumes to be a systematic description or representation, turns out in Poe's rhetorical maneuvers to be a succession of interpretations at different removes from the primordial order it must presume. The privileged or authoritative text is primordially a poem: Kepler's poetic intuition of the laws of gravitation serves as the beginning of Newton's mathematical deductions. This last is not stated as historical or scientific fact, but is recorded in that fabulous letter that Poe's philosopher/poet claims to have "found corked in a bottle and floating on the *Mare Tenebrarum*" (XVI, 187), that is, in a geography that exists only in some philosophical myth. The "letter," which the present writer claims to have transcribed, not translated, comes dated from the year 2848 A.D., or a millennium after the present writing. In this compression of time all possible texts are already always present, including the possibility of a master text that can only be mapped in invented texts; that is, the created system, like a language, is complete, and thus contains all texts, past and present, or all possible maps. The letter from the future includes all past systematic explanations of the cosmos, including those that are now obscure vestiges of once great poems. The originality of an intuition lies in its deviance from, its discontinuity with, all previous interpretations. It represents discontinuity.

Poe's hoax, which includes a juvenile parody of the systems of Aristotle ("Aries Tottle" or "Ram") and Bacon ("Hog"), or deduction and induction, presents the cosmos as a palimpsest of texts. Every intuitive leap displaces or overwrites a previous one, relegating scientific fact to the status of mythic sign. The philosopher's accidentally discovered text looks forward (or backward) to Borges', for while it holds that no "catalogue of catalogues" has ever been discovered in the universe (or the library), the fact that such a book is possible is enough for it to exist. Thus for Poe, or for the writer of that futurist letter found in a bottle on the *"Mare Tenebrarum"* of poetic invention, there are no "degrees" of "impossibility"—"one impossibility cannot be greater than another" (XVI, 201)—and thus no one "impossible conception" can be more peculiarly impossible than another "impossible conception." Poe's cosmos, like Borges' library, includes "all verbal structures," and the true scientist is a theorist, like Kepler, but also a cryptographer, like Champollion, who "guided mankind to those important and innumerable truths which, for so many centuries, have lain entombed amid the phonetical hieroglyphics of Egypt" (XVI, 196).

The attraction of Egyptology to the nineteenth-century imagination is extraordinary. For Poe, in particular, it is the revolutionary thrust of decipherment, more even than any truth uncovered or secret revealed, that aligns interpretation and intuition. Cryptology puts old cyphers back into circulation, invents a semiology by a semioclastic displacement. Champollion's "solution" of the Egyptian "cyphers" is a recuperation of "sacred fury." It is as if the writer of the letter had declared, "In the beginning was interpretation" (and what else could Valéry have meant by fable?)—but not interpretation as a restoration of the sun. On the contrary, interpretation recovers the old signs whose "fury" had been directed against the death that inhabits them. Poe may not share Melville's theme, except by indirect address, but *Eureka* moves among the old in the way that *Pierre* will later explore the blank at the center of all monuments, whether the authoritative old texts (folios) or the pyramids of Egypt. For Pierre, at least, writing implicated the writer in re-writing, in "federat[ing]" in his "fancy," the old texts. This probing of the funerary signs had its analogy with grave robbing:

The old mummy lies buried in cloth on cloth, it takes time to unwrap the Egyptian king. Yet now, forsooth, because Pierre began to see through the superficiality of the world, he fondly weens he has come to the unlayered substance. But, far as any geologist has yet gone down into the world, it is found to consist of nothing but surface stratified on surface. To its axis, it is found to consist of nothing but superinduced superficies. By vast pains we mine into the pyramid; by horrible gropings we come to the central room; with joy we spy the sarcophagus; but we lift the lid—and no body is there!— . . .

For the more and the more that he wrote, and the deeper and the deeper that he dived, Pierre saw the everlasting elusiveness of Truth; the universal lurking insincerity of even the greatest and purest written thoughts. Like knavish cards, the leaves of all great books were covertly packed. He was but packing one set the more; and that a very poor jaded set and pack indeed. . . . So beforehand he felt the pyramidal scorn of the genuine loftiness for the whole infinite company of infinitesimal critics.[9]

Poe's account of the "imperfection" of writing differs from Melville's only in the radical possibilities for the new interpretation/intuition to agitate or move other signs. Thus the "sacred fury" of cryptology is a double notion of recuperation. The nothingness at the center (unity) of Poe's cosmos is at once like and unlike the nothing at the center of Melville's pyramid. It permits or demands interpretation/intuition, which is a kind of radical sub-

9. Herman Melville, *Pierre: or, The Ambiguities*, ed. Harrison Hayford, Hershel Parker, and G. Thomas Tanselle (Evanston, 1971), 284–85, 339.

stitution. And in Poe's text this substitution is commanded by the notion of "irradiation" (or a double movement of attraction and repulsion that refuses either priority), which supplements the tendency to think of a dualistic balance between gravitation (or the tendency toward unity, the one) and repulsion (or the tendency toward dispersal, the many) that is implied in the law of difference, the law interpreted in the complementary disciplines of deduction and induction. Poe has not stolen, by radical plagiarism, the Newtonian cosmology of von Humboldt and Laplace, only to add to it suggestions of an emerging new science (though notions of electricity as a displacement of mechanics abound in his text, and as Valéry has shown, there may be an anticipation of thermodynamics in the ironic treatment of Newtonian physics). He has, indeed, stolen from the cryptology of the Egyptians. He has stolen the myth of Ra, or the myth of Thoth as writing, stolen the metaphor of the crypt, of the crypt as metaphor. Hence the narrator's hasty espousal and renunciation of the proleptic "letter" he has found and transcribed so that he can get on with a present writing of a new, intuitive cosmology that will revise the authoritative texts of his day, thereby repeating Kepler's intuitive break with the old science and his launching of an entirely new science on the basis of a poetic rupture. There is no "direct line of descent" in Kepler's productive intuition. The place of the futurist "letter" in *Eureka* must be explained, then, not as a future summary of a unitary history of science, but as the very sign that science (as an order of interpretations) progresses by discontinuities and radical alterations, like Thomas Kuhn's changes of paradigms.

Poe's introjection of "irradiation" (perhaps also thermodynamics, as an idea of linear discontinuity) into the metaphor of electricity is nothing less than a myth of theft, or rewriting, of the legend of Thoth as intermediary, as secretary, of the sun, of Ra. *Eureka* is an ir-Ra, and not an ur-Ra, a deviant text and not an original text, as if a text could be original and not always already a letter found floating on the *"Mare Tenebrarum."* Poe's argument for the text's status as a poem can be accepted if one resists the literalism of his obsessive argument for the synonymous definition of poem and originality. Poetry (Poeism)—and this is perhaps the "originality" that Williams claimed for him—is decipherment, in the double sense of protecting and revealing, and in particular of protecting some secret, except that in Poe the secreted is already that which has been stolen. Poetry is radical theft, a substitution of a letter not for some more original letter but for the fissure that is signified by some other letter. This fable—as in Valéry's formulation that for Poe the beginning is "fable"—Poe retells in the form of the detective fiction, or the fiction of detection.

IV

The so-called tales of ratiocination may be said, then, to be fables of the will to intuition/interpretation/power. Derrida even suggests this when, in his deconstruction of the Lacanian Seminar, he reveals that a fiction which is made into a model of a metaphysical truth (in this case, the recuperation of a lost or provisionally misplaced truth) must inevitably reveal the fictionality of its own structure. In *Eureka,* Champollion and Kepler, as historical exemplars of the analyst/poet, must think they have seized a "sacred fury," whether of the Egyptians or the universe, but in either case they have only appropriated an old text. The philosopher of *Eureka* plagiarizes old texts, and thus transcribes and displaces them, revealing in his extension or supplementation of them not only their limits or imperfection but that all interpretation is situated in the textual crypt. *Eureka* repeats the revolution of the narrator in "The Pit and the Pendulum," who awakes to find himself sentenced to death by mute lips. In his entrapment, he can resort only to the cautionary wisdom of "antique narratives" or to the principles of interpretation available to him from the classical sciences, empiricism and deduction. Yet the abyss rules the center of his universe, the prison, and no amount of reason will free him from his sentence to a dualism that is composed over a void. His only escape is a perfect plagiarism, the appropriation (or intuition) of the deus ex machina of romance, as a machine of discontinuity/substitution. "The Pit and the Pendulum" is an allegory of fiction's resistance to its own closure, or its resort to the machinery of artificial closure.

The stories of ratiocination would seem to be only formal variations on this thematics: a revolution that restores some temporarily disturbed order. The narrator's theory that Dupin represents the "Bi-Part Soul," that there is a "double Dupin—the creative and the resolvent" (IV, 152), transcribes a venerable old philosophy into a poetics of interpretation. Dupin's theory of the mathematician whose analytics must be supplemented by poetic intuition repeats the argument for creation as radical appropriation in

Eureka. The will of a "double Dupin," of the creative and the resolvant, irrupts in a labyrinth of excessive and contradictory signs, the disarray of evidence that marks the beginning of every game. He is the double of every game, the doubled center that Poe recognizes when he employs the analogy of literature to the game. The theory of the game, between two equally powerful wills, is not a moral or a psychological representation, but a theory of poetic overdetermination, of a game that must always have, in Derrida's terms, a remainder or remnant. Dupin is the name of the author; his stories are Poe's deconstruction of the author.

We should emphasize the problematics of beginning in the Dupin stories, of a beginning that in every way refuses a proper notion of beginning: the beginning of "The Murders in the Rue Morgue" in a preface that disclaims it is a treatise, and then the second beginning of an exemplary narrative, which, if it represents a history, must suggest that the history exemplifies an idea; and the beginning of both stories in a "library," the one in the Rue Montmartre where the narrator and Dupin meet accidentally while "in search of the same very rare and very remarkable volume" (IV, 150), and then the internalized library of the lodgings that the two establish, the rooms provided by the narrator and the books presumably by Dupin, since they are the "sole luxuries" left to him from an exhausted "patrimony." This beginning in a "scene of writing," or in a maze of reference to other writing, other texts, marks the whole problematic of fictional framing. At the inner interior of this beginning scene there is a library where accidental crossings take place and out of which a new home and family, a simulated center, is constructed. The city is a labyrinth whose chance center is a library; the library is reduplicated in the narrator and Dupin's accidentally endowed home, only in the reconstruction the library is now centrally placed: a scene of "dreams—reading, writing, and conversing," as the narrative clearly records, a secure refuge for "madmen" (IV, 151).

The centralizing of the library has extensive ramifications. It situates a world without external reference, a center that can refer only to itself; it is a "book-closet," indeed, a crypt. It virtually denies what Dupin later notes, in his act of deciphering the incoherent clues of the murderer in the "Rue Morgue," that "madmen are of some nation, and their language, however incoherent in its words, has always the coherence of syllabification" (IV, 181). In the "Rue Morgue," Dupin learns to identify with the unreasonable clues of the "murderer" just as in "The Purloined Letter" he identifies with the radical or doubled thinking of Monsieur D——, a kind of identity signified by their common cipher but no less by an exchange of signatures carried off by the distractions of a "madman." The library, then, is a pure house of fiction, hermetic yet multi-centered. It represents the "madness" of a will to truth, the obsessive search for the "same rare and remarkable volume" that is at the same time a search for a maximum luxury and security, a doubling of death. In his crypt (whether in the library or walking the dark streets of Paris), Dupin marks the aberration of all texts. Valéry, in his own marginalia upon Poe's *Marginalia,* refers to the uses of incoherence in literature and to the romantic notion of the criminal and the madman as poets who have had an immense role in history: "They raised the Pyramids," he notes.[10] They buried the king and raised the monument of difference, as both Vico and Hegel concluded.

Like the madman whose language is necessarily that of some nation, even if an incoherent rather than a coherent repetition, Dupin's interiorized library is a place of "madmen" that reflects the structure of all libraries. It is a crypt of differences, of writing. The structure of the library undoes what it presumably represents, a closed and centered world. As in Borges' tale, no "Central Hexagon" or master book is located. Dupin, like Usher and Arthur Gordon Pym, has been all but deprived of his patrimony and his family. But the chance meeting between him and the narrator leads to a "closer communion" and a surrogate family, only this time a family founded upon a fraternal and not a filial relationship. The metaphorics of the double displaces the metaphorics of father-son; the library as representation is displaced by the library as repetition, as a scene of writing, of an endlessly repeated decipherment/encipherment. At the center of the library-universe, as if at the center of a pyramid, is the author as analyst, the doubles who have displaced the father, the double of the king who is not there.

A similar shift in the metaphors of the game, the contest of wills as decipherment, interrupts the two narratives. The "preface" that introduces "The Murders in the Rue Morgue" literally proposes a game played within the rules of Hoyle that is won only by going beyond the conventions of the book. The writer prefers the model of "whist" or "draughts" to a game of chess, because chess is a game played within the restraints of fixed values and the rules of logic. Moreover, chess begins with an artificial balance of power, while games of chance are inaugurated by an uneven distribution

10. Valéry, "Poe's 'Marginalia,'" in *Leonardo, Poe, Mallarmé,* 192.

of power. Therefore, "draughts" is a game of will and wit, never ruled by the place of the king, a game that cannot be played by "the book," a game determined by the dropping of false clues and distracting gestures. The "preface" to "The Murders in the Rue Morgue" suspends the authority of the "book" and opens the game of writing, of "draughts" in both its senses. The metaphor of "puzzles" in "The Purloined Letter" puts in question the notion of representation, of the proper relation of inside and outside, that governs the classical idea of detection or unconcealment (*aletheia*). What is concealed in writing, the metaphor of "puzzles" seems to inform us, is the fiction of concealment/unconcealment itself, upon which all theories of representation are based. In "The Purloined Letter," detection is repetitious thievery of animated substitutions and displacements that indicate the letter is never at the center, is never representational, except as a sign that it is always elsewhere. In the game of "puzzles" it is the commonsensical notion that every place has a proper name, and that the name and place are identical, which Dupin metaphorically disrupts. There is no signified, but only a play of signifiers. The illusory depth is produced not by what is hidden but by the signifier that names all the other signifiers, yet locates them only in their random distribution. In the game of "puzzles," there is never any reference to that reference for which the map and its name stand; the name spread across the map names the other names on the map. Therefore it is hidden from the logical mind who thinks that names are proper, or have a proper location. The field of games and fictions closes off the outside in order to prevent the closure of its own play.

From the beginning—which, as Derrida has shown, is a pseudo-beginning—of "The Purloined Letter," the very idea of authority is in question. The author of the letter is already out of the game. The letter is already two times (at least) removed from its origin, since the queen from whom it was stolen was only its recipient. Yet it is the curious sign of her power, that which signifies the royal presence and power. Both Dupin and D—— implicitly question this metaphor and reveal its arbitrariness; yet in generating a contrary metaphor, based upon the "will" to power, both simulate the old fiction. Dupin as a "partisan" would restore the letter to its proper place; and D—— would appropriate it to himself, thus simulating the place of the king. The prefect likewise is out of the game. For him concealment demands only an "ordinary search," an empirical probing and penetrating of appearances for what they conceal. A stolen letter that contains the signature of authority would itself be concealed in its appropriation. Presence remains at the remotest interior, or at the illusion of an interior.

"The Purloined Letter" signifies, albeit indirectly and ambivalently, a radical displacement of one fiction-of-fiction by another. The elaborate twist of Dupin's overcoming or displacing D——, of doubling his double, is itself a cunning metaphor of repetition. It projects the illusion of a stable order that is threatened but ultimately preserved (thus Lacan's reading), yet at the same time indicates the fissure in this metaphor that literature repeatedly calls into question by revealing its own artifice (Derrida's reading). Both Dupin and D—— manipulate the fiction of the proper word, of a patrilineal authority, rather than attempt to overthrow it, since it is as inescapable as the city-library-language in which their game has long since begun. Yet Dupin and D—— each becomes a supplement of the game. The double displaces the queen. The analyst displaces or doubles the author. The analyst— creative/resolvant—doubles as a thief.

The place of authority no longer engenders and governs a biological, genealogical, or teleological history. The origin is no longer filial but fraternal, double rather than simple. The will to power is played out between enemy twins, for whom the queen (whose authority is other, is in the letter) is that figure of presence and power that makes the protracted game of substitutions and appropriations so rewarding. It is necessary to maintain the fiction of authority if meanings are to be produced, if the game of signification is to be repeated, if a simulation of "truth" is to be either revealed or rendered. The game of detection, then, produces a representational model for the fictional production of presence, authority, power.

Much has been written about the strategy of Dupin's ruse: his discovery of the letter, concealed yet unconcealed in D——'s apartment, but turned in a way so that its outside dissimulates a difference from the "original" letter, a letter whose physical condition suggested a simple, proper relationship between outside and inside. In its circulation, the property of the letter (both whose property it is and what properties certify its propriety) will be confounded. Dupin produces a facsimile of the appropriate letter, now marked by the D—— cipher, which had been "once folded and pressed with a folder" and is now "refolded in a reversed direction, in the same creases or edges which had formed the original fold." "It was clear to me," he continues, "that the letter had been turned, as a glove, inside out, re-directed, and re-sealed" (VI, 49–50). Yet, its inside (message) is not outside, except insofar as we must now accept the always provisional absence of an inside, a signified. Having planned his move, Dupin turns up with his facsimile at D——'s rooms, where he pretends to recover a snuffbox. At a planned time, some paid agent acting the role of a madman, thus reduplicating the role Dupin has assumed in withdrawing from the logic of a daylight world, causes a distracting commotion, allowing Dupin to exchange the facsimile for the "proper" (physical) letter. In such a fictional scene of writing, where the "pretended lunatic" introduces a disruptive style that appears authentic just to the degree that it disguises its representation, the original theft is repeated, the tautology of fiction is played out. The notion of a "proper" letter is obscured. The place of authority is multiplied, the more so by a doubling of the theft, which seems to restore the letter to proper hands.

When Dupin first detects the stolen letter, torn and smudged and thrown almost carelessly in D——'s "card rack," he notes that the "only point of correspondence" between it and the original is size. The tear, however, seems "as if by design," and the cipher of the original is absolutely reversed, so that the letter once addressed from a ducal family (whose seal is a small red *S*) is now addressed to D—— (in large black letters, written in a feminine hand). Dupin's discovery turns, as he says, on observing the "*radicalness* of these differences," which are "excessive," like the "excessively obvious" letters stretched across the full surface of the map that the adept at "puzzles" selects to deceive his opponent (VI, 49). (The treatise on "puzzles" precedes the description of reading the clues, thus posing a question of the example. Does the game explain the *real* event, or is the event a game?) Dupin's search, which doubles the minister's theft, turns on the identification of "radical" differences. Both thefts multiply the production of differences. Decipherment produces excessive reencipherments. Both Dupin and D—— exploit the "excess" of a system of signification. Their interpretations engender a play of signifiers that can only be closed by artifice. They return a letter rather than uncovering what it conceals or contains. (The play or reversals of masculine and feminine signatures is crucial to this production.) But it is precisely this production of differences that restores the letter, or produces the illusion of the letter restored. The restoration of the signifier reveals the fiction of the signified. What is restored, even as its artifice is revealed, is the fiction of the author; Dupin, the "partisan" of the queen, and her surrogate, reveals himself in the place of the author, the double, the creative/resolvant thief who closes the game with his stolen signature.

A narrative that began in a "library" and a system of references to other texts can never reclaim an authority it never had. Dupin's curious (and cursive) signature, inscribed in a tunnel of quotation marks, has by its very excess produced a library of commentary or supplementary texts that will not allow the story its ending. At the very interior of his signature within a signature, which is the vengeful turn of the screw against the minister, he inscribes a clue appropriated from literature, from the library, and indelibly marked as stolen. That is, he inscribes his own pseudo-signature and then interprets it in the same gesture, refusing the minister any further role in the game. But a signature that inscribes another text reveals, as Derrida says, that there is an excess or remnant left over, and that the present narrative has its origin in literature and nowhere else. Dupin appropriates his pseudo-signature from Crebillon's *Atreus* and dutifully cites it, like a good critic, so that we are aware of Crebillon, the thief whose play (or text) originates in the excess of yet another literature, a myth about origins the origin of which is unlocatable. The myth of the house of Atreus, after all, is a patrilineal myth that, like Dupin's signature, is a *mise en abîme*. The myth, in fact, weaves together both a filial and a fraternal order, and marks the flaw in each metaphor. The fraternal crimes of Atreus and Thyestes repeat the sins of the father—of Tantalus, who fed his son Pelops to the gods, who in their horror restored the son and reengendered the family lines; hence Atreus' repetition of his grandfather's crime. He "originates" an ancient transgression, an excess of violence that attends a generative history or histories. The myth also involves Hermes: patron of poets and mathematicians, of gamblers and games of chance, and of rhetoric—Hermes the thief, as he is called, a surrogate of Thoth, who restored Pelops and thus the author (and surrogate father) of the repetition of original violence. This violence has no beginning or end. At the remotest interior of a series of references without bottom is the name of a king and a crime, a father displaced, yet a royal line arbitrarily restored, a history that is a violently mixed metaphor. The inaugural crime is barely covered up by the layers of different interpretations (thefts) it has produced. May we say, then, that Dupin's signature can only tantalize us? Where we think we see the proper authority of the king/queen, we see only the double signature of son/brother, or Hermes/Thoth, the creative/resolvant who is the "excess" of every metaphor.

The final signature of "The Purloined Letter" is the signature of writing, a perfect, and not a prefect's, plagiarism.

Does Poe, then, provide us with an allegory of the transition from a classical to a modern writing, from "readerly" to "writerly" texts? In one study of the drift of modernism, Edward Said has argued that the change of paradigm between classical and modern, or as he calls them, "dynastic" texts and "productive" or "intentional" texts, may be formulated in the antithetical metaphors of a filial and a fraternal series, like those I have indicated in Poe's writing. If classical narrative follows a biological and genetic analogy, the modern is a deviation and displacement of nature, Said argues. The one is representational, the other based on repetition: "The series being replaced is the set of relationships linked together by familial analogy: father and son, the image, the process of genesis, a story. In their place stands: the brother, discontinuous concepts, paragenesis, construction."[11] For Said, this displacement of authority from the notion of origin to that of beginning constitutes a break with the tyrannous legacy of the past, a legacy that is more textual than substantive; modern writing is a will to power over "dynastic" texts, and it produces a radical shift from the gloomy nihilism that traditionalists find in so much modern writing. The productive force of modern writing, as Said interprets it, fulfills Nietzsche's will to truth. It is a productive, dynamic nihilism, inaugurating a new writing.

Poe, of course, offers us some signs of this transition, though trapped in the gloom of his nihilism and in the poverty of his decadence. In *Eureka* he celebrates the poetic will, which can overthrow the old, exhausted fictions of logic; and in the tales of ratiocination, decipherment produces differences that break up the prison house of "antique narratives." Yet Poe may have another lesson for us. In the signature of the modern, of the analyst who displaces the author, of the repetition that disorients representation, we see that nothing has really changed after all. If the modern analyst mines into the tomb to expose the absence of the king, it is only in order to situate himself there, as de-constructor; but his decipherment/encipherment, his exposure of the fiction of the origin, exposes his own doubleness, the fissure of this "will" that is the invention of fiction and not its source after all. What is called "modern" narrative exposes the fiction of the origin by

11. Edward Said, *Beginnings: Intention and Method* (New York, 1975), 66. This distinction governs Said's "history" of the change of paradigm in narrative, most fully elaborated in the long chapter "The Novel as Beginning Intention."

exploiting the fissure in the mausoleum, library or pyramid, which has concealed this absence; but it performs this operation only by laboriously constructing a house upon the flawed structure of the old house. Its deconstructions produce an allegory of construction, an always doubled creative/resolvant text. This does not lead to an open text that is the reversal and displacement of the closed text, but instead produces a play between those two metaphors. The modern text is no more open than closed, but is always interpreted as one or the other, as tending toward one or the other. Poe's decentering of the author, his multiplying or doubling of the place of the author, is what the French seem to have misread into the productive Edgar Poe, into Poeisme or Poetics—the author as thief who is always already double, and distributed among the two texts or the many texts that make up the textual library. Thus Poe authors his interpreters, as in Mallarmé's remarkable line: "Such as into himself eternity has changed him." Some critics have interpreted this to suggest that Poe in death has become the permanence of his texts. Poe died, as it were, in-text-ate. Mallarmé's poem is itself an inscription upon Poe's tomb, his text, which rewrites and radically disseminates Poe's texts. But if we were to mine into that (which?) tomb, we would find neither the presence or absence of the author, but the cryptic writing on the crypt—a sign like a "barely perceptible fissure," the sign of "double Dupin."

6

POE'S FABLE OF CRITICISM

I

Among the several things Poe is credited with inventing or fabricating—
and "original" poetry is certainly not one of them—are at least two sub-
genres, the detective story and science fiction, and perhaps a third,
Symboliste poetics. This ignores the "hoax," which appropriately enough
he stole, or appropriated. But the "hoax" is, at best, not a genre or sub-
genre; it is a mimickry of genre and thus a doubled modality or performative parody. The "hoax" accentuates its secondary and parasitic function,
in contrast, say, to satire, but in the same gesture puts all notions of "firstness," to borrow Peirce's term, into question, marking every representation as at the same time an interpretation. The "hoax," that is, is a critical
genre, problematizing both the ideal of literature as "original representation" (an oxymoron) and criticism as reflective and self-reflexive overcoming. The "hoax" doubles its double, to anticipate Borges' and Nabokov's
brilliant expropriations of Poe, and exposes the very tenuous category of
genre proper to question. The notions of originality and invention are made
to tremble, reverberate; and the law or laws of genre are violated. "Hoax"
acts—that is, mimicks, parodies, repeats, transposes—by a kind of theft,
thus inaugurating again a kind of writing before the letter; it "acts" in gestures of quotation and translation, a fabulistic supplementation of fable,
one might say, that points one way out of the modernist's dilemma, his
conscription by the rule of mimesis and the authority of tradition. Poe was
certainly one of those engaged in the invention of American literature, if
only in the sense that the one singular characteristic of "American literature" seems to be its claim to be singular and thus to have no such identity
or characteristic. To be a "song of itself," it would have to re- and con-fab-
ulate the idea of invention as beginning again, and turn interpretation or

criticism, as Emerson foresaw, into a creative event—performing, even by quotation, its own originality as auto-insemination.

The "hoax," that is to say, is a generic hybrid. And just as a hybrid is produced by a combination or a graft that in effect suspends the genealogy or identity of a singular entity, a generic hybrid puts the discrete notion of genre into question. It names a heterogeneous rather than a homogeneous structure and context, an open rather than a closed and autonomous form, and a self-analytical rather than self-reflexive work. It is performative rather than representational, and turns the very ideal of art, the "poetic principle" of "unity" that Poe celebrated and hypostatized in his theo-critical essays, into its parodic double—a closed circle into a parabola, to employ a formal figuration. Reading poems like "The Raven" in conjunction with essays like "The Philosophy of Composition," which putatively describes their origin and realization, one is hard put to determine which is the "work" and which the commentary or criticism. For "The Raven" is as surely a hoax-poem or parody of the "poetic principle" as "The Philosophy of Composition" and "The Poetic Principle" are theoretical tales or critical fables: narratives of the genetic fiction, allegories of the origin. The "hoax" for Poe is not simply a sub-genre that classifies a number of marginal tales, like "Some Words with a Mummy" or "The Facts in the Case of M. Valdemar," but a trans-generic intervention that undoes the hierarchical opposition of philosophy and literature, poetry and criticism. For Poe as for Emerson, with whom he shares little else, the "American" gesture of originality demanded that one clear the ground of all determinable and determining concepts, the old, inherited ideas, if one were to perform originally. It meant, among other things, not simply resituating an ideal of poetry as "principle" in opposition to philosophy, and thus substituting one Platonism or formalism for another, but re-fashioning the very idea of "unity," the "unity of effect," within an entirely different configuration—a kind of trans-figuration.[1] That is, Poe needed to reinscribe the old ideal of art as "unity," "oneness," a transumption of temporality (even as Pound would prefigure it, as an Image encompassing an "instant of time") within an entirely new and proleptic configuration, a "possibility" as he would call it in his greatest "hoax," *Eureka*.

It is perhaps not too extreme a generalization to argue that all of Poe's writ-

1. See Edgar Allan Poe, *Complete Works*, ed. James A. Harrison (16 vols.; New York, 1902), xiv, 196. Hereinafter cited parenthetically in the text by volume and page number.

ing, including his "theory" of writing, reenacts the structure of the "hoax" and is thus performative. That is also to say that it stages, by a kind of remarking of itself, a scene of self- or auto-analysis, not simply as the detective fiction thematizes analysis and the analysis of analysis, but also in the manner of the so-called tales of the grotesque and arabesque, which, to take "Ligeia" and "Usher" as examples, inscribe the therapy-resistance of narration within a general scene of neurosis. For the latter as for the former, reason functioning as recounting and accounting is woven together with a language or rhetoric of effects, a kind of utterance that uncannily repeats the onomatopoeis of the poetry, so as to "effect" a sense of unity and harmony (a homogeneity) that can only be apprehended in signs of disintegration (heterogeneity). Everywhere language bore its double, even in the echo of the poetic refrain, and doubled itself to infinity. Recall the "chain" of associations Dupin recounts or recalls early in "The Murders in the Rue Morgue," which are articulated as "loose fragments" of "paving-stones" of a "causeway [that] is undergoing repair," or by a "sterotomy" of words, which at once evoke a great "nebula" or constellation and a sense of unity that can be known only as hypothesis, or by a satirist's "disgraceful allusions" (IV, 154–55). Just as the double structure of "hoax" remarks its artifice of construction, that the unity is the unity of story or tale and not some unity the story represents, it recounts the game by which such constellations are achieved. The narrative path, the reconstructed "causeway" and repaved road, represents only the performance or "gait" of the teller-analyst, in this case the double Dupin, who in rerouting himself by a chain of associations through such landmarks, signs, and by-ways as the "little alley called Lamartine," manages by a kind of reappropriation to repeat originally, that is, with a difference, the "larger links of the chain" or all the old "theories." For the old theories and hypotheses have also been at once units and performances of reconstruction, repaving, in a generalized scene of analysis that Dupin associates with the *Theatre des Varietes.*

The structure of the "hoax," therefore, represents a scene of writing as at once a scene of acting (repeating, as in Stevens' "Of Modern Poetry," "what was in the script") and of analysis, as a performance that deconstructs the scene of repetition and reveals its uncanniness. But in the gesture of displacing representation with performance, it re-marks the inscription of the one within the other, for the logic of analysis is exposed as a "game" being played by certain arbitrary rules that it serves to reinforce and remotivate. Displaced by the game, exposed as the game, the story or tale returns as a fable of criticism. The interpretation transfigures the scene of interpretation, producing an activity without beginning and end and without borders, but not without "effects"—effects without efficient causes, which are capable of signifying, but not specifying, future effects. Like the folds of quotation that conclude "The Purloined Letter," literature inscribes philosophy as a future and ever-deferred end of writing and the beginning of the book. But that also means this "modern" tale—the structure of the "hoax"—writes an end to the era of the "book" as surely as does Hegel, and allegorizes the "beginning again" of writing. Poetry (poeisis, and poeetics) is always already before philosophy, that is, *avant la lettre: before,* as evidence, and as prior to the case at hand.

It might be useful to note that the "hoax" as structure, as sub- and transgeneric form, is neither a form nor a genre at all but a certain gainsaying of structure. A joke. And as with Freud's structure of the joke, it irrupts or arrives belatedly in the tradition of literature like an explanation of the dream to the dream—that is, as a parody of its supposed form or grammar. The structure of the joke, to appeal to Freud's poststructuralist interpreters like Samuel Weber, falls somewhere between telling and interpretation and cancels the decisive margin between the two, between fiction or dream narrative and analysis.[2] Just as Freud's theory of the *Witz* is less an explanatory account of a kind of social exercise than an indirect exploration of theory itself, Poe's theory of poetry is an allegory of the allegory of genesis, and of genre, a theoretical problematics of theory. Thus Poe from the beginning, whatever that might mean, was engaged in a problematics of alterity. Freud's structure of the joke, and this is why I would relate it to Poe's notion of genre (or genre-cide), opens the question of what he calls in his own, putatively scientific theory of psychoanalysis, deformation, and what poststructuralist theory deals with on the level of supplementary reflect/effect.

Freud's theory of wit, of the *Witz* as a distortion of the classical sense of wit as reasonable play, invades the whole notion of the aesthetic formulated by the Kantian critique of play and judgment, that supposedly middle term and bridge (hence metaphor) between the practical and the

2. See Sigmund Freud, *Jokes and Their Relation to the Unconscious,* trans. James Strachey (New York, 1963); and Samuel Weber, *The Legend of Freud* (Minneapolis, Minn., 1982).

pure, experience and idea, fact and theory, or any other of the possible binary and hierarchical oppositions that complicate philosophical advance. That criticism, as a form of play, opinion, and hence judgment, inhabits this mis- and dis-placed middle, indicates the crux of the issue. It is the crux itself. Freud's gaming *Witz* undoes wit, just as in de Man's theory of allegory rhetoric undoes grammar and logic. Just as we cannot read Freud's theory of the joke as a straightforward reading of a social event, the telling of a story which in itself exploits the laws of logic, grammar, and even genre, but must instead "read" it as a "case" and thus an objective and exemplary part of that which it theoretically has been developed to examine —so that it is at once the whole and a part of the whole it would explain or represent—the theory of the joke necessarily aggrandizes the joke.

The joke, for Freud, was not essentially a case, an example, despite the number of examples he tried to provide, but a condensation. It thus belonged to the activity of telling and hence to the order of language—but to the orderly disorder of language at play. As Weber, in the most sophisticated and discerning analysis of Freud's "theory," has observed, Freud in the act of theorizing can only complicate and implicate himself, that is, re-infold his own scientific desires to produce a theory. His theory of the joke involves the problem of a third person—and in this, as Weber shows, Freud mounts his theory on the model of language, of a grammar in its uneasy relations with logic—who in his/her response or effective return, laughter, is necessary for the completion of the joke. That is, the effect is necessary to validate the "subject" of the teller, making the effect an efficient cause. But the effect is not necessarily efficient; or certainly not in any classical sense. The effect as cause is not only supplementary or diffusive; it is at once gainful and gaming. And it predicates only an activity. Freud's notion of the laughter-effect, the explosion of response that cannot be accounted by any rational economical means, which is necessary for the teller of the joke, the subject, to become the subject, but also for the respondent of the joke to become a subject—this complication, as Weber's book makes clear, is the truest theory and allegory of theory. Out of this kind of consequence, Poe fashions a theory of how one can receive but emit originally. His theory of "effects" is not to be read in terms of recent reader-response aesthetics so much as it is a reflection of the impasse Kantianism and romanticism brought to aesthetics by reinscribing the problematic of the subject as performer and thus problematizing the supposed resolution of the aesthetic.

Poetry, or poeisis, can no more return as the ground of philosophy than philosophy (and aesthetics) can reclaim its priority as idea and inspiration. The subject had become activity, or even force, and electromagnetism had displaced simple mechanics in Poe's world. But already the modern question, of how this active subject could define or reflect itself, could both be active and identify itself by position in a universe (to be called Heisenbergian) marked by alterity, becomes self-evident to any poet who would engage, who had to engage, the apocalyptic claims of the "new age" and the entropic ones of those who had written so many ends—the end of history, the end of philosophy, the closed circle of narrative, along with the "ends" of the theory of ends. And so, Poe had to set about setting about, reclaiming by a kind of appropriative theft the old dream of origination or originary power. A theory or hypothesis of "effects," of an effect at once voluntary and involuntary, at once distributes the idea of the author/subject into an uneasy relation of writer to reader, creation and recreative response, but it usurps the priority and hierarchy that defined the literary tradition and the American's belated and fated place in it.

It is as if Poe were forced to survey his own uncertain position in terms of that pro-positional uncertainty that would attend the developments of science for the next century plus and regulate the ever-widening gulf between science and logic as certainly as between literature and philosophy. This is what Valéry finds in Poe when he ascribes to him the anticipation of the "laws" of relativity and finally indeterminacy, as well as the laws of thermodynamics: not Poe the logician, nor less the prophet, but Poe the poet/philosopher, who in making logic attend to itself begins to perform that questioning of language by language. This Poe is not, however, the inventor of new genre, or laws of genre—including, in the literal sense, the detective story or science fiction—but a performer of language and thus one bound to the uncanniness of its logic and its play, its cogent deceptiveness. To note even generally some analogy between Poe's "hoaxes" and Freud's structure of the joke is to remark nothing more than the linguistic matrix in which they are inscribed, including the necessary place of a third subject or agency that suspends and disturbs the binary formations of cause and effect. Whether we analogize, in the most general sense, Poe's notion of "effect" to Freud's theory of "laughter," to Peirce's notion of the interpretant, or even to a Husserlian notion of return-response (*Rücksfrage*), the position of the "effect" is more than a position of the effected; and certainly not that of reader to text or author. Poe hypothesizes a feedback of effects and in turn often inscribes it in thematic and scenic reenactments; so that the tunneling structure, say a scene of interpretation, as in "The Purloined Letter," or a scene of reading, as in "The Fall of the House of Usher," or scene of writing and reading, voyaging and drifting, as in *Pym*, produces at once object-scenes to be interpreted and resistances to interpretation. Just as Freud's laughter-effect is necessary for the completion of the joke, and thus is necessary for the subjectivity of teller, but is itself resistant to interpretation, Poe's staging of the hermeneutical circle renders both scenes and effects that represent performance and resist that interpretative act: for example, the ape's language in "Murders," or Dupin's fold of quotation-thefts in "Letter," but also the uncanny language of the tomb in "Usher" and "Ligeia," of the raven in the poem that uncovers everywhere the coinscription of logic and raving, and of the ever-deferred silence of "Ululume." It is this resistance, dramatized as the power of a negative that is not simply nothing and thus as effects and effectuating, which signifies for Poe the possibility for the new-world writer to escape the impasse of his belatedness, the pathos of inwardness or of the self that finds no identity in the past.

Freud's joke, as Weber reads it, is a form of non-knowledge that nevertheless holds open, by a "diversion of consciousness," the possibility of meanings to come; but not necessarily lost or old meanings that have temporally and provisionally been repressed and might be systematically disinterred. The joke invests meaning or the idea of meaning with a new sense, implicates it with curiosity and surprise: it yokes inhibition and play, desire and deferral. It produces by condensation something on the order of an oxymoron. Above all, it is performative or, more precisely, perlocutionary; and therefore it entails a new structure of communication which, by definition, cannot be described by the old structural laws. This is why Freud was bound, says Weber, to theorize indirectly (by narrative or tale, or by the joke that is a narrative gone awry, though deliberately it seems) and thus in a form that would forever preclude the systematic closure of his theory. Within the structure, praxis and theory are never separable, nor ever reducible to a unity. The same may be said for Poe's performance upon genre, and for his obsession with re-writing, albeit in a Nietzschean sense, an American genealogy.

II

The hoax, like the joke, cannot be reduced to generic or sub-generic definition, and it serves to point up the problematics of the category-concept genre itself. The assumption of a closed field, of self-contained enabling laws, of totalization and self-reflexivity, reveals that the taxonomic and descriptive authority claimed by criticism also has a performative, interventionary force. The mastery of poetry by philosophy, or its reverse, the claims of priority of poetry to philosophy, is replicated in the critical performance, since criticism seems always to assume a self-contradictory stance—to explain, clarify, evaluate, and master, yet to efface itself before the essence of the "work." Poe called that essence Beauty, and he debated the question in terms of the familiar opposition between *Dichtung* and *Wahrheit,* but what his criticism and fiction alike reveal is at once the uncertain difference of the categories and the performative force of both. Poe's theory of "effects," then, can never be purely theoretical, and the performative effects of literature function not simply to reproduce or represent sense (whether as feeling or meaning), but to produce reactive gestures that are in themselves effective. We have seen this in the thematics of the letter, dramatized as the scene of writing-interpretation in "The Purloined Letter" and as reading in "Usher," but it is no less present in the reverse narratives of his critical discourse, as noted earlier. The relation of cause and effect, therefore, not only defies logic but supplements it. Every generic entity is doubled within itself, and the illusion of self-reflexive coherence—the *work* as unity, the unity as work—by the equivocal opposition that marks the double function. Thus Poe can thematize the performance of criticism as a creative act, and theorize the created work, poem, or tale, as a critical or interpretative form.

Interpretation as critical performance, however, cannot in itself be theorized, nor its effects be predicated with absolute authority. Like Freud's laughter (after) effects, that which is produced assumes in its alterity a certain priority, as if in a feedback loop. What poststructuralism has projected as the performative force of iteration, and hence of quotation, in a certain sense, the American writer had to meditate from his position of belatedness. Poe, like Emerson, as we have and will see, had to consider his place in literature as an imitative, representational activity—that is, from a post-position—and to repeat, as it were, the crisis of quoting originally and originarily quoting. The American writers' "complex fate" of performing always already within and against the grain had to be, in the modernist formulation, a posthumous existence. How to write a "book" that would, indeed, transform the idea of the book, the universe, quoting it originally and turning it into that which could not be repeated, imitated, or even worse, represented—that is the modernist question of poe-tics. Poe knew that the fate of the American writing was a question of the after—as well as a question of the "beyond"—of after as copy, imitation, and as a variation that had transformative and displacing effects. The eerie Borgesian joke of perfect quotation. Of theft. Thoth-ing. The "beyond" and "after," as Poe conjectured, or threw forward, was like that text which would issue from the drift of Pym's boat into the blank figure at the end of all narrative, the erasure of an anthropomorphic language that could never, after all, occur. *After* what, since the "after" was before in being beyond?

The question of genre and structure, then, is inscribed at the core of any Poetic, and of poetics in general, as is the question of quotation and originality; and this applies whether we refer to the poet as philosopher, or the critic as poet. The impasse of the modern involves the pun that Poe employed so unshapelessly in *Eureka,* between Kant and cant, the homophonic pun that displaces man the authorial subject from the language that speaks him. Or her. Though he is the least humorous of writers, Poe must laugh. His writing is a kind of laughter after the fact—an effect intended as a cause of effects. Where does one begin and end in this circuit? And how could Poe have understood, and even less intended, where he stood in this line? As Williams discovered in writing *In the American Grain,* Poe's crisis of genealogy was the representative American crisis, the democratic crisis of representation and individuality, of self and anonymity, or original naming and misnaming. Of posthumous origins.

The performative effect of quotation, of theft, of reappropriation, functions like that of laughter to the joke. For just as the laughter of the other is necessary to complete the subjectivity of the teller, it also displaces the subject and produces, as Weber argues, a quite other form of knowledge. In a sense, then, effects are genetic in being defractive, and the reader-interpreter creative-resolvant, as Poe thematized the reflexive-effects of detection. This also undoes the circular thrust of narrative and introduces that kind of "disconnection" that Gertrude Stein defined as the character of modern writing, and thus of American writing in general. Thus Poe's compulsion to engender new genre, to produce hybrids, and thus to repeat a kind of family romance, had at the same time the effect of deconstructing the very myth of origins and the genetic laws that defined the literary tradition. He produced, as it were, the oxymoron of the joke, a deconstructive genre.

In a longish essay that examines once again the "place" of Poe in the Franco-American transaction, especially the most recent chapter focusing on the Lacanian-Derridean interventions, John Irwin begins by asking what distinguishes the mystery or detective story, or any tale that produces a single effect or resolution that, once read or experienced, does not repay rereading or critical study, from a work of art that not only rewards but demands reflective scrutiny.[3] "The Purloined Letter," he concludes, is certainly a prototype if not archetype of detective fiction, but it is not exhausted by the resolution it dramatizes. Its thematization of analysis induces or summons further analysis, just as it has become—almost because of the very kind of self-quotation it practices—a *mise en oeuvre* of the problematics of analysis: for example, Lacan's model for a "true" Freudianism or scientific practice. Furthermore, its effect as the provocation to appropriation, its instigation of readings of its scene of reading, and thus its problematic role as model or exemplum, even as a certain genre or sub-genre, has had the effect of undoing that genre or sub-genre of analysis we understand as critical discourse. Hence, it has put all the assumed "laws of genre" at jeopardy, but with the startling result of inducing, instigating, or provoking a surplus of discourse-analysis, which dismantles the strict distinction between the creative and the critical and, moreover, between theory and practice. In the Lacan-Derrida counter-deictic, as it were, we have an instance of such an instigation, to emphasize Pound's term for a kind of provocative, yet productive, discourse, for which the Poesque tale is at once a model and a force.

Irwin's essay re-composes another instance of this instantiation, of the critical essay as story of a story, interpretation of an interpretation; for it stands itself in the position of a strange and estranging effect. Reading Poe not against but within the readings of Poe that irrupt from the Lacan-Derrida exchange—themselves readings entwined with the history of a French appropriation of Poe from Baudelaire through Mallarmé and Valéry, and ex-

3. See John T. Irwin, "Mysteries We Reread, Mysteries of Rereading: Poe, Borges, and the Analytic Detective Story: Also Lacan, Derrida, and Johnson," *Modern Language Notes* CI (1986), 1168–1215.

tending in rhizomatic threads to the discourse of and about psychoanalysis, through Marie Bonaparte back (?) to Freud and forward (?) to Lacan—Irwin narrates the return of Poe's own analytic to the question of literary criticism and creative writing from which it had seemingly originated. Thus Borges, like some "collateral issue" of the Poesque imagination, arrives to re-write the tale of the double analyst, poet, the creative-resolvant who at once precedes and undermines the desire of criticism, and science, to divide and rehierarchize the creative and the critical. Borges, then, can only repeat Poe's already doubled and equivocal origin or pre-origin, itself always already a generic hybrid that instigates but does not and cannot regulate what it uncannily engenders—reading effects. Irwin attempts to account for this chain of readings according to a model of the game already inscribed in Poe's detective fiction, the game of "odds and evens," which in its way introduces a mathematical set repeatedly beset and supplemented by an irrational number. The apparently orderly game, however, inscribes the disorderly as a productive force, an effect that assures a surplus reading and resists any closure of the game, although every reading aspires to such a totalization. The defraction of effects that are themselves instigatory cannot, then, be contained within the mathematical model that is also a puzzle, like those philosophical puzzles of Lewis Carroll or Josiah Royce, says Irwin; or even like, though "like" now inscribes a dissemblance, a Gödelian undecidable.

It has become commonplace for poststructural criticism to stress this dissemination of discourse that irrupts from the force of a kind of originary writing, or pre-original *difference*. But it is also the responsibility of criticism to account for the unaccountable or surplus, the economy of defraction that is not simply an entropy, even though it follows the very rules of irreversibility or of repetition with a difference. What Derrida calls the "uncanny logic of repetition" is a change and transformation for which there is no adequate systematic accounting. Or in other words, there is no enduring, universal language, no stable conceptual language, to which one can return in order to measure the deviation and derivation. One must account for this slippage or defraction, but even the accounting must be made in the language of what it is trying to count and account for. The slippage is always already at work in the in-discrete margins of narrative accounting, and thus also of criticism, even that criticism which would account for narrative or would be the narrative of narrative.

The very inscription of the mathematical or paralogical game that Irwin cites as the model for the Poesque story marks, therefore, the limits of understanding the potentially infinite game that is narrated. It becomes another version of the abyssal structure, like that of the poem within the narrative or, better, the narrative within narrative, like "Mad Trist" in "Usher." Is the game-model a part of the narrative or a form of it? or an interpretation of it, and thus of itself? The illusion of fictional and interpretative specularity, of that self-reflexive model that became the defining characteristic of a modernist (symbolist) literature, is submitted to the risk of the game, of the model. Modality is put at play, "gamed," as it were, and in a kind of "just gaming" that makes Poe the marker of a post-Kantian disruption as surely as that phrase has become a *jeu de sens* for speculations on the postmodern. A so-called literary discourse, in its ideal form of poetry or its essence as *poesis,* necessitates a double or allotropic writing. Poeisme is one—Franco-American, as it were—of the names for this geneo-transitive performance.

III

When the time came demanding, at last and at length, the ultimately original work—after all the echoes and purloinings, those quotations that proclaimed their originality—Poe would inevitabily discover, right up front, that the original was a hybrid. After insisting on the privilege and priority of literature over philosophy, and even poetry over fiction, he would arrive, by a kind of parabolic logic, at the conclusion that he could marry "Poem" and "Romance," could write the original and even perlocutionary work, the "philosophical poem," not something in imitation of the great, albeit etiolated, poems, but some kind of pre-original if not primordial performing of the word. Poe's tale of the "spoken" creation, as we have seen, does not simply repeat the ontotheological romance of the "logos," but recommits that act as a performative moment, subject to all the conditions we now understand as limiting the notion of the performative. The creation of the universe as, in a word, a "word," and an inimitable or unrepeatable word at that, inscribes the very problematics of the originary act that haunts the literary desire to create originally. Poe's *Eureka,* mixing memory and desire, proposes the "act" that undoes all individual and even transcendental "subjects," and makes the literary, that is, repeated and etiolated, act the very possibility of a new "literature."

What Poe discovered, as exclamation ("Eureka"), is the problematics of the act, the performance. He invents, as it were, postmodernism, not in the sense of some historical or periodic moment of going beyond, nor in the sense of re-turning to and into the moment of irrational game, but in all the senses of advancing, procedural steps or methods, and yet negative or resistive interventions, asides, deflections. That is, he broaches the sense of messages sent, put out, launched, as if for the first time, which nevertheless bear all the marks of having been merely transferred—received perhaps, perhaps happened upon, maybe stolen, inarguably delayed as much as relayed—from one place (post, position) to another. These messages are sent by the universe to itself, but this communication constitutes not so much a circle as a parabola.

The monumental, yet incomplete, text of *Eureka*, then, could not have possibly named itself, either as "poem" or as "philosophy," and no less as "philosophical poem," but only as an act of breaching or delegitimizing such "genre." We might claim that *Eureka*, as an *act* of *genre*, or postmodern "piece," is the foreplay of the postmodern, and its deferral—that is, a declaration that the being of the postmodern can and may not ever "be." We have to meditate, and mediate, this problematic today as the problematics of the "margin," or of the surplus, and thus of the question of that which at once stands between, beyond, and behind the classical demarcations of philosophy and literature. It comes down in "American" literature to a question of "How to Read" or *How to Write,* of the instructional letter before the letter, and even to a certain pragmatics that will insistently divert itself.

And so—what does it mean to discover, to declare, to say, after the fact as it were, "Eureka," since the fact would be what was discovered, the fact before the act that was determined by the act? This "complex fate" of the American writer could in itself produce strange and estranged effects, not predictable by the analysis of Freudianism, or simply explained as sexual repression, transference, compensation, and so on. Could Poe not have, as Mallarmé intuited, invented by etiolation the game? Prolonged it by restaging it? And thus made possible and impossible (the idea of) "American litererature"? He would thus have produced, in the sense that a commentary makes a product of its object and of itself, a beyond of genre, a lawless hybrid, an interpretative orphan. A postmodern text, one that performs in that it produces the effects it narrates but is unable to narrate its own act. Poe's poem engages the impasse of the "philosophical fable," for it cannot account for its own construction. But in producing the "effects" of what are a kind of saturnalia, the poem that plays irresistibly through the "philosophical" re-counting, the allegory of poetry's belated originality is fully and exhaustively narrated.

As philosophy, its Truth would lie in its logic or consistency, as the poet-narrator of *Eureka* argues; as poem, or romance, its effectiveness can only be the result of its power to persuade, what the narrator calls "suggestiveness." The same problematic inheres in Poe's theories (they are never singular) of poetry; for while, as he argues, a poem must be consistent, it is more important that it appear consistent, or seamless, and this requires not only careful, technical construction but an effort of erasing the artifice of the seams. It is the poem's iterative, mesmeric power, its tintinnabulating rhetoric, which must serve to efface the marks that remain after covering over the logical inconsistencies. Thus the argument of Poe's poetics, that a poem must be both "consistent" and "satisfying," uniting Truth and Beauty, reintroduces perturbation and eccentricity into the very form, the symmetry that his poetics has assumed *a priori*.

Eureka is the story of that poetics; one might say, the *aporia* of that *a priori*—but with an added twist. If Poe's effort throughout his metaphysical criticism is a common attempt to reverse the metaphysical tradition that gives privilege and priority to philosophy over poetry, the reversal cannot take the simple form of uncovering a still earlier poetics, a primeval poetic that is closer to Being and Nature than the dualistic thought that subsequently divided it (a story with a Heideggerean aura about it). Nevertheless, a certain reversal was necessary, but one that would double and overcome, and thus produce a hyper-logic to which all previous logics would be mere cant. As in the fiction of ratiocination, then, one good turn demands as well as deserves another, and the doubling of the double begins to reveal the cracks and gaps of the old notion of reason displacing it in the same way that the new sciences of electricity, mathematics, geometry, and thermodynamics were beginning to produce distortion and eccentricity in the forms and ratios of the old science they were displacing. This distortion is even more evident when we recognize that the new science had to express itself in the old language, effecting a transformation of language by language. In *Eureka*, poetry and philosophy remained poised in opposition, each vying for its authority and privilege. But more important, Poe chooses to conduct the dialogue in yet another scientific language or borrowed terminology, the language of cosmology, that science which seeks both to describe and account for the physical universe but must rely on the language of metaphysics, of the One and the Many, as well as the language of mechanics. Thus by exploiting the Enlightenment's developing split between philosophy and science or metaphysics and physics, he can reveal that the split between philosophy and poetry is not a simple, albeit primary, one. This split, or double split, turns up in every atom, every concept, every word. Poe grasps the opportunity of exploiting the ever diffusive or self-dividing tendency of the *logos* to redefine the notion of creative volition, not only by way of resisting the deistic argument for a closed word, but in order to preempt the romantic reification of the autonomous self. Poe redefines *logos* and *logocentrism* by introducing into language a notion of the performative, the notion that language itself is creative or engendering, and that the poet is the embodiment of the word.

Poe's project, then, has a curious double trajectory. On the one hand, he seems to be repeating a romantic critique of the Enlightenment, therefore reversing the mechanism and associationism of Newton and Locke. On the other, he seems to return to a pre-romantic deism in order to counter a romantic atomism and an alogic he finds in Kant and, especially, Coleridge. One might argue that his theory of creation as original coalescence, which we recognize in Newtonian gravitation or the combinatorial tendency governing matter, reverts to a Lockean emphasis upon fancy set against any idealization of the synthetic imagination—a plausible enough conclusion if one remains within the discrete history of ideas that requires such choices. But it is precisely the impossibility of such a choice that has led to the impasses of philosophy; and even the Hegelian resolution, the dialectical movement of sublation, in which the negated is resurrected and carried on in the new unity, cannot escape the question of negative creation or negative theology. Hegel is conspicuously absent from *Eureka*, whether out of Poe's ignorance or by determination is of no matter. But certainly any totalized system projects a utopian and apocalyptic closure that Poe sought to resist or defer in the name of some vague sort of continuous and open creation. His own proclamations of consistency, symmetry, and eternal return, then, come with built-in resistances or strategic deferrals, to what end we do not know, except the need to deny the end, the death and non-identity implied in the notion of spirit's self-presence. Death, we will find in Poe, is not a conclusion of a process called Life, and the universe is without beginning and end. But the stories we tell of it all retell that ontotheological narrative of spirit's double deaths, the fall into history, the return of end upon beginning, the resurrection and the life. One thinks of Eliot's *Quartets,* a story Poe would have loathed. To tell any other tale demands an intervention of telling, that is, writing, and thus a strategy of narration with built-in resistances or self-interferences that resists the end or conclusion.

Eureka turns upon the premise that the idea of the One is unthinkable, that God is unknowable, yet this idea is the cause of all thinking, and all secondary cause. But what caused the idea of the First Cause? What act of thinking produced this thesis of original unity that subsequently determines all thinking about it to be a degraded, fallen, oppositional thinking? Where, he asks in effect, do we begin to think origins, except by a kind of circular process that determines circular thinking? How, indeed, do we enter the hermeneutical circle except by breaking the circle, by an intuitive leap. Hypotheses, which are the product of human thinking, albeit the "intuitive" thought of geniuses, scientists, philosophers, and above all poets—and better, combinations of the aforementioned, like Kepler or Dupin, poet-mathematicians—are therefore "leaps" in a process or narrative already begun; though secondary and provisional, hypothesis is a beginning even when it is a "leap" beyond accepted theses, even when it introduces eccentricity into the old concepts, the old language. If the universe, as *Eureka*'s narrator puts it, is a "plot of God," then its *telos* is but a certain limited reading by man, and most cosmologies simply repeat the old narrative circle of beginning and end. Yet in offering his reading of the "plot," the playwright, unlike Stephen Dedalus, may either repeat other plots, reverse them—which would leave them, in effect, the same—or deflect or intervene, introduce an anomaly or change their direction. Kepler's intuitive leap may have found a truer plot of the universe than what preceded him, but like Kuhn's "change of paradigm" it followed the old notion of plot in name only, producing in the old form and language an entirely new sense of the universe. It introduced a quantum indetermination, a deflection. The question for Poe, as for a postmodern writer, is how to regulate the quantum of his own addition, or write a law of the non-law, without being dragged back into the old plot or repeating the old formula. How can one produce a new sense of the universe that still bears the same name—and implies the unity of time? An impossible question, we know; the problem of indeterminacy theory, of how to determine the measurer's role in the results he acquires; but not an impossible problem for human desire, which always plots its satisfactions and resists them. *Eureka* is the allegory of desire, and the fable of criticism as desire, "man's plot," a "possible attempt at an impossible conception" (XVI, 200).

But this plot never quite gets going. Or at least the plot proper is deferred, if by that we mean the narrator's text, which would be the proof of his thesis. First there is the epigraphic announcement in the form of a "preface," that the text is a "Romance," a "philosophical poem," which stands between the title *Eureka, A Prose Poem,* and the second title, "Eureka, An Essay on the Material and Spiritual Universe." Then we have an opening sentence inscribing an author, perhaps "E.A.P.," who signs the "preface." And the author introduces himself in the immediate act of writing: "It is with humility really assumed—it is with a sentiment even of awe—that I pen the opening sentence of this work" (IV, 185). The story of creation is being performed, not described, and the performance is writing, interpretation. We are later to learn that the narrator's real text is not the one he begins in the first sentence, but the development of a "thesis" that begins later, after he has stated his "hypothesis" and then proceeded to write a condensed history of the failure of Western philosophy, from "Aries Tottle" (Aristotle) to "Hog" (Bacon) and "Cant" (Kant). That history is then doubly denounced by a "letter" this poet-narrator has received from the future, exactly two millennia hence—well, not exactly received but "found," a message in a bottle floating upon the *Mare Tenebrarum* or philosophical ocean. From myth we come to myth returnest, the structure indicates, passing through philosophy.

Despite the hoax, the letter has a certain order. It dutifully recounts a certain history of Western thought leading from the Renaissance to romanticism and, more precisely, from an old science to a new, a story told in terms of certain of those who merely repeat Aristotle's story and those who interdict it. The most important of the latter metonymic figures are Kepler and Champollion, two cryptographers (and translators), as it were, who found their way from one universe to another, or out of one hermeneutical circle into another, by reading the gaps in such systems and introducing a perturbation. The "letter" from the future, curiously enough, seems to be nothing more, and nothing less, than a message from language itself, telling the narrator that it already contains all the possibilities for such substitutions and interventions, and thus for new theses of origin and end. The message prophesies an endless created system that is also an endlessly revised system, and thus makes it clear that a new notion of origins, of creation, will always be needed. It is reasonable, therefore, to think that we can quote the future, as reasonable as to think we are all, as Emerson said, "Quotation and Originality," quotations of the past. Quotation has no beginning and no end. And this is what Poe's narrator-poet discovers of all cosmologies, despite the imperative that cosmology by definition give us a closed universe, a circle rather than an ellipse. All that we will ever know of the universe, including the death of the supernova that happened yesterday and will be perceived tomorrow, is already contained in the bottle, in the letter. It is an infinite limit, an alpha without an omega, an alphabet. And we are cryptographers already entombed or encrypted in the bottle, uncertain of whether we are inside or outside and forced to recognize that neither position, like that of beginning or end, really provides a *point d'appui*. Thus our own interpretations or decodings, while limited, are nevertheless provocative and productive. A thesis is a condensed interpretation that provokes further investigation.

Well into *Eureka,* the narrator-poet announces that he has quit quoting and will offer his thesis and its proof. The proof that follows, a kind of story, a kind of argument, a grammatical verification of a logical truth, turns out to be a claim of prophecy, of what will be even beyond the revelations of the "letter" or message language sends from the future. So that even the narrative, the immediate penning of thesis and proof, must promise a sequel, a self-overcoming. It plots against its own desire for proof, for closure. The thesis suggests and provokes the writer to tell stories about it, which will in turn provoke other narratives of this narrative. The beauty of the argument supplants the cold and passionless truth of its conclusion, like an arabesque design that undoes di Vinci's model of the human universe and projects us into the human parabola whose curve does not quite return into itself. The structure of *Eureka* has already announced its theme. It is before us, like that letter from the future, but we cannot read it because we are implicated in its message. We are Champollions in the interstices of the hieroglyph, whose breakthrough was a new method or thesis of interpretation, not the message or secret presumably contained in the hieroglyph he decoded.

Concluding his long quotation from the letter in the bottle, the narra-tor-poet of *Eureka* declares that he will thenceforth cease quoting and of-fer his own thesis. What follows as the body of his own argument is in a sense quotation, in the form of description and summation of old partial theories his will reverse and complete. It is the manner and not the matter of the reversal, however, that constitutes his claim of originality, a strat-egy of argument that indicates the performative and translative effects of quotation. In fact, the last quotation from the letter, which is a quotation of a quotation, is a kind of free translation of Kepler's declaration that his work will await its true interpreters and thus indeed create future inter-preters: *"I have stolen the golden secret of the Egyptians. I will indulge my sacred fury"* (IV, 198). Kepler was a "theorist," the writer of the letter asserts, who like Champollion had "stolen the golden secret." The theo-rist, though belated, an interpreter or cryptographer, does not simply uncover or recuperate ancient truths or messages from the past. In his acts of deci-pherment he steals the sun or that central and originary energy. That is, he steals a mode of writing and hence thinking about the idea of origins and order. And his new method is itself genetic or creative. He is a kind of Thoth, deity of physicians, thieves, liars, and writers, a figure of intrigue, who in stealing for the sun-god Ra steals from him. And Thoth rather than Ra, the substitute and amanuensis rather than the deity of self-presence, is truly the *logos* or word. Language is already stolen and is therefore not original but originating (originary). A stolen thesis is, as it were, pre-original. It is writing that produces further writing, interpretation motivating further in-terpretations, more plot.

As noted previously, Valéry claims that Poe's cosmic Poem in effect steals Carnot's first law of thermodynamics and yet anticipates Einstein's general law of relativity. If so, he does it by an intervention into Carnot's principle of conservation that unveils the contradiction that will become the second law. The intervention is produced by an interpretative act that proceeds like a logical argument, only to reverse itself or curve back into itself like a self-interfering structure. This sudden reversal-intervention is already built into the logic of a closed system. Thus when the narrator-poet introduces his own "legitimate thesis" of the universe, he is condemned to repeat the structure of every such thesis, even by reversing accepted ones, unless the act of reversal, the troping, the writing can effect some deviation or eccentricity in the hermeneutical circle of thesis and proof (deduction), or of proof and thesis (induction). The effort of every theorist, to be consistent, to complete the circle, is an act of covering over the gaps, of closing the circle. A reversal, if done quickly enough, if it becomes a reversal of a reversal, might serve like an ultra-violet light to highlight the gaps and cracks, or accentuate the ellipses and discontinuities—not, however, to reveal the nothingness or meaninglessness beneath every structure but to reveal the possibility within the impossibility of creating again, of making a different as well as a better plot. Thus the doubling argument of *Eureka,* which does not give us a tale of regressive interpretation, leading backwards or downwards to the interpretation behind every interpretation. On the contrary, *Eureka* opens the play of interpretation to the future, to possibility and desire.

The narrator-poet's account of his thesis, as is well known, is little more than a summation of Newton's physics as it was repeated in Laplace's cosmology, the so-called nebular hypothesis. It is a rather dry, straightforward summary, a kind of quotation to which can be added some eccentric twists. The twists or tropes, however, are provided by the quotation, as in a Borges tale. *Eureka* performs a kind of "stolentelling," to recall Joyce's word, through a series of preste-digital substitutions, to coin one myself. Hence, the act of stealing is never fully covered up, and that which is stolen remains disguised in full view, like the purloined letter in Monsieur D——'s lodgings. For whatever the narrator's *thesis,* Poe's is not one that can be served by proof. Like the poet, who can only reveal his creativity in the poem and who yet must recognize that his creation is only a shadow of the pure idea of Creation, the writer must justify "secondary creation." But he must not only justify it: he must give it privilege over primary creation. And secondary creation is interpretation, an act of the mind, story-telling, plotting. He must therefore offer as found what he has meticulously produced or manufactured out of the shards of some other thesis and their illusionary completeness. *Eureka* proclaims "I have found it," but what is found is really what has been left, a game Poe's text acknowledges and does not confuse with the cognition of a "truth." The game becomes productive, creative, and the game is critical.

The universe is "God's plot," but within it, we know that plot only through a number of subplots or laws, the most authoritative one for Poe's narrator being Newton's theory of gravitational reaction, or attraction. Gravity, therefore, manifests within matter all we know of the creative act, the combinatory tendency or desire of the Many to return to the One. Yet since God was this self-created One in the first place, Newton's plot of this tendency, which remains now manifested in a dispersed and divided matter, can only be a shadow of the true and unimaginable oneness, which is also a nothingness, in that it was never divided like matter. The physical universe, the divided universe, is "God's plot," not God. "But gravitation *has* taken place," the poet writes in summing up the deist plot; "therefore the act of Creation has ceased; and gravitation has long ago taken place; therefore the act of Creation has long ago ceased. We can no more expect, then, to observe *the primary processes* of Creation; and to these primary processes the condition of nebulosity has already been explained to belong" (IV, 264). Though we see the material universe, it is only a shadow of the One creation that has been. And Laplace's nebular hypothesis, which in effect translates Newton's law into a cosmology, implies an action within the action that cannot be fully expounded by logic or mathematical language. Yet it is this nebulous and sublime element in the hypothesis that summons us to know it, rewrite it, improve on it, complete it. If gravity is reactive, and yet associated with the original gathering of "Creation" into God's oneness, there had to follow a secondary creation or dispersal to get things to the present point where the primary creation can take place again, or is taking place again. Only this secondary reaction does not exactly repeat the first, which can have no imitation. "God's plot," the manifest universe, must have been created by a slightly different principle than gravitation, therefore, or must have included an opposing force, which the narrator calls "Repulsion," identifying it with radiation or irradiation, and even electricity. Like the world of matter, "God's plot" is already doubled, and in opposition to itself, and Newton's law takes account of only one of its directions. Some kind of activity is still going on that confutes the deistic law, an activity that the narrator finds nearer to the idea of creation than unity. It is the will or tendency toward unity, he concludes, a volition which, unlike the divine volition, includes an antithetical principle, a resistance to catastrophe.

Thus, while "Attraction" and "Repulsion" appear at first to operate like binary oppositions, and the universe to function by "reciprocity of adaptation," the narrator discovers that their reciprocity functions by a strange ratio or economy, "Repulsion" belonging to a tendency toward the "abnormal condition of the Many" (IV, 207), and "Attraction" tending toward a return to the normal One, and nothingness. If they seem, then, to be equal and related forces, or to function like logical oppositions, they nevertheless do not constitute a stable system. While Poe can talk of them in analogy with body and soul and good and evil, their relation cannot be thought, whether hierarchically or horizontally, in terms of a fixed value for each. The more one contemplates the system, the more uncanny it appears, for man's contemplation begins already within the "abnormal," the divided or many. Yet this divided plot radiates an energy; it is a productive and even independent force, a negative that produces positive if uncanny effects by refusing to follow the path of the dominant law and submit to ultimate non-identity.

Their relation is equivocal, not stable, so that the universe can only be thought, from the inside, as a new form of interrelation for which there is as yet no language, only the only word, *universe*. The old stability of grammar and logic, with its circular understanding or eternal return, is no longer accountable for this new sense of energy as transformative. What the narrator requires is a new mode of description, a new mode of narrative, for while man's plots are always flawed in relation to the ideal of "God's plot," and every writer works to efface these flaws and produce some simulation of perfection, that is, narrative unity, it so happens that the harder he works at perfection the more he brings out the gaps and ellipses of artifice, imperfection, abnormality. The more one works at construction, the more traces of artifice emerge. But, strangely enough, by another reversal, the more evidence of artifice and imperfection, the more one can claim some contribution by the artisan. In the language of indeterminacy, the more the measurer can be factored into the measurement; or in the language of present-day criticism, the more evident becomes the supplementary play of rhetoric within the logic and grammar of disciplined thought.

Creation, as the narrator reflects, always has an element of the catastrophic in it, as in the collapse of the Many back into the One. Catastrophe, then, inhabits every strophic movement and is not simply its opposite. As in Freud, pleasure is unthinkable without pain; indeed, pure pleasure is death, but so is pain unthinkable as an absolute negative of a pure pleasure. Attraction and Repulsion, naming respectively the old and the new sciences, are interdependent and equivocal—two laws in one, neither with absolute authority, each relative to and interdependent with the other. One can never fully displace the other. In fact, it is the reinscription of the one within the other, the encrypting of one within the other, the intertextuality of the two plots, that the narrator imagines as the new creative ratio. So, just as he cannot displace Newton's law, but only amend it, re-write it, translate it into a new law but in much the same terms, he can only write a new narrative by doubling the laws of the old. He must, therefore, offer in the name of God and creativity an anomalous plot, a nebulous plot or theory against the old God. He calls the new counternarrative a "blasphemous idea of special interposition": "We have to suppose that, in the particular instances of these 'nebulae', an unerring God found it necessary to introduce certain supplementary regulations—certain improvements of the general law—certain retouchings and emendations, in a word, which had the effect of deferring the completion of these individual stars for centuries of centuries beyond the era during which all the other stellar bodies had time, not only to be fully constituted, but to grow hoary with an unspeakable old age" (IV, 264). Creation, at least secondary creation, is a deferral by supplementation, a notion strikingly consonant with what we now call postmodern intervention, or even "interposition." But also we can recognize Poe's own tropology, of the universe as a text of interwoven plots and the author an editor, translator. In other words, to emphasize Poe's rhetorical turning of an aside into a diacritical statement, the creator is here his own critic whose "retouchings and emendations" produce a Universe of multiple times, of births and deaths, goings and comings, that are never in absolute harmony. Poe has, to echo Mallarmé, touched narrative. And if these "retouchings and emendations," this critical self-reflection or redoubling, is a blasphemy, then the negative has strange positive effects, produced by this resistance to things collapsing or dying back into their normative condition.

From the beginning of his essay, the narrator's problem has been one of beginning, or of finding a position from which one can survey the "sublimity of . . . *oneness*" (IV, 186); and he posits a kind of Zarathustrian perspective in which an observer atop Mount Aetna might by "whirling on his heel" at the rate of the earth's revolution take in the whole "prospect." He returns to the question of beginning and totalization after his report on the letter from the future, only to discover that the man who is already a part and particle of the created universe can assume no fixed or transcendent position. The problem of the "centre," as he puts it, and thus of the position from which to launch any "legitimate thesis" of the universe, is always split between two alternative and discontinuous possibilities. But more important, it oscillates between "two modes of discussion" that he calls "ascent" or "descent," or, respectively, the movement from part to whole and from whole to part (IV, 198). He chooses the latter, to begin with Earth, or the "habitation of Man," and move "indefinitely outwards" through a sequence of centers, to the Sun, then to the galaxy, and on toward an eventual totality. The emphasis here, however, is on the movement of thought, and not its arrival or conclusion. The problem is compounded because the starting point, like all beginnings, is at least arbitrary, whether the "centre" be Earth or the Man who inhabits it. In short, neither micro- nor macro-center can be determined as absolute, and thus the very notions of beginning and end are already problematical. Thought, the essay, writing, and so on, begin always already *in medias res,* which is to say, in language, or in a textual field for which there is no certain center, but a multiple of centers. Just as *Eureka* has demonstrated the deferral inscribed in all beginnings and beginnings again, and thus in the performative or tropological force of quotation, translation, and the like, the narrator is aware that he must begin by repetition, and that his mode is *"iteration in detail"* (IV, 199). Repetition, like the play of the refrain in "The Raven," or the strange reversal of beginning and end of the voyage in *Pym,* is already at work in language, most forcefully in concepts like "Infinity," "God," and "spirit," all words, according to the narrator, that do not so much express an idea as motivate the act of thinking, of writing. Such word-concepts, then, inscribing the equivocal oppositions of Attraction and Repulsion, provoke an "effort at" ideas and point out the "direction of this effort." To revert to the metaphor of electricity as the form of Repulsion, every word-center is like a transformer, a direction pointing toward or beyond the limited but, by the same token, marking the impossibility of ever fully representing that sublime and sublimated "beyond." Infinity, therefore, names the "tendency of the human intellect," not its essence. "Infinity," which must be put in quotation marks, can only represent the *"thought of a thought"* (IV, 200), a self-reflexive but infinitely open series.

It is clear from other of Poe's texts, like "The Power of Words," that he thinks of language as a universe made up of individual atoms, thus created particles. But these are atoms themselves constituted by opposing forces that deconstitute them and demand their interdependence with other atoms. They also affect other atoms, as particles of matter inscribe oppositional forces that at the same time affect and are affected by other, different and differential quantities of matter. This "tendency" of words, like the tendency of thought, rules out a writing and thinking on the order of "analogy." The narrator's prolix discourse on man's instinct for "analogy," that is, his faith in grammatico-logical forms of analogical representation, determines that a true language functions to point up the limits of analogy, to point beyond analogy. This is what poetry adds, by supplementation, to mathematics or logic: the power of suggestiveness and thus of "tendency." Thus the narrator explains his need to be prolix, in contrast to Poe's economical theory of a poem's "unity of effect," his need to recombine and repeat the opposing plots of "ascent" and "descent" in an *iteration in detail.*" Repetition is not repetition of the same, but a retouching and amendment.

Into man's conservative instincts, his desire for symmetry and consistency and analogy, poetic intervention introduces a certain eccentricity and perversity. Just as the Newtonian circle is an idea that does not fully account for the elliptical orbits and parabola of nebular motion, a narrative will be truer to things by going beyond analogy and representation, by suggesting the tendency toward a new concept, by revealing the "eccentricity of orbit." It tells the story of an "orbit" or circle that does not return to its proper starting point, reuniting end with beginning, but rather inscribes the perturbation observed in all logic when it is submitted to close scrutiny, to a logical analysis of logic. To use the example of language, if one tries to take a full account of language through language, or invent a metalanguage, he will have to confront the paradox of his instrument of study being a part of what is being studied. Language and the narrative mode of iteration, far from accounting fully for itself and a Truth, breaches itself, returns into itself, parabolically. So-called postmodern meta-narratives, we might observe, mock the idea of a fully accountable or self-explanatory narrative, but they do produce the strange effects of a Möbius strip or an "ocean of story."

This is the allegory propounded by the narrator when he adds to and amends, retouches and reverses, Newton's limited plot. By adding the reverse tendency of diffusion or "Repulsion" to Newton's, and thus introducing a resistance to satisfaction into the structure of desire or tendency toward satisfaction and death, which gravity or "Attraction" signifies, the narrator has done something more than reverse and recapitulate the old system. For the diffusive is also a tendency, associated with the will; and this "diffusive Volition" or will toward difference is always already inscribed in its opposite, the Creative impulse, and, as it were, in the *word,* and in words like *infinity, God,* or even *universe.* By proposing the equal attractiveness of Repulsion, the narrator indicates that the Newtonian law had always demanded its contrary but had worked logically to efface all contradiction. Thus, by narratizing the Newtonian law, by indicating that it involved a double movement rather than a single Attractive impulse, the narrator "amends" and "retouches." Volition as a force and a limit as a resistance or critical opposition, is reinscribed in the creative in a way to displace the Creative—just as Dupin's creativity derives from his cryptic, interpretative power. Thus the creative is indeed the critical.

Poe's cosmological allegory is a fabulistic poetics of interpretation, that is, of decentering, the effects of which emanate from his reinscribing a supposedly stable concept like Infinity or God into a set of relations which in turn produce effects not comprehensible within any single concept. It is this destabilization that poetry effects by its reinscription of philosophical terms. Thus poetry can only work its will toward symmetry, consistency, unity per-versely; just as in "The Philosophy of Composition," Beauty is Truth only when it upsets the desire for stability, or reveals the death drive of such a will. The opposing Volition, the repulsive, re-emerges like the return of the repressed.

This is the indirect moral of that sequence of passages in *Eureka* that rehearse the tendency of Newton's law of collapse or catastrophe in terms of the desire to return to the "centre" and, specifically, to reveal the "brotherhood among the atoms" by showing their desire to rejoin their "lost parents." In "The Poetic Principle," Poe had associated Truth (with a capital *T*) with "homeliness," that is, canniness or familiarity, and Beauty with *unheimlichkeit,* the uncanny (see XIV, 271–76). The genealogical metaphors, the family romance, haunt his *oeuvre,* as all the psychoanalytical criticism from Bonaparte to Lacan underscores. But we need not conclude, with the analysts, that this is the anxiety or paranoia of the American orphan; for Poe recognized clearly the ironic structure of this desire, the son's will for an identity that could only be a non-identity, for a name that would be another. Into Newton's law of reactive return, therefore, the narrator introduces a reversal that includes a certain resistance. If all things desire, normal by the compact of brotherhood, to return to the condition of the One, this cannot be read as simply a *"tendency . . . to a general centre"* (XVI,

221). For the one idea of Creation has long since occurred, and is over. God's secondary creation of Himself, as "plot," which issued in the Universe, was ironically creation by diffusion or Repulsion. Now, gravitation, which is in effect over, is evident everywhere in the physical universe that Newton has observed. But Newton, obviously, had only observed a figuration, albeit an empirical world, or the original gravitation. Thus the gravitation he describes as a tendency of all things to return to the "centre" can be stated only as a general "law" that never exactly coincides with things as observed, like a circle to an ellipse. The symmetrical law of tendency toward the center cannot be represented in particular cases, since atoms tend toward different masses, different centers. And while they may tend toward the "centre *as such*," this center cannot be any particular particle or position: "they seek this point not in its character of point" but because it lies in the direction of a "greater number of atoms than along any other straight line" (XVI, 235). The nebular galaxies are multi-centered, and no one point or location is the "centre *as such*." The original parent *as such*, and the genealogical line of descent, is only another story of metaphyics. But for Poe, as for poststructuralism, creativity or engendering is that which does not "return to the father." It is what Derrida calls "dissemination."

All the surrogate or simulated centers, which are figures of the general principle of a tendency toward Unity, nevertheless signify a resistance to the return. According to the narrator, if gravitation is a general principle, the tendency of all atoms to return to origin after they have been dispersed to the edges of non-identity indicates a volition that resists following the same path back that it originally took in falling from One into Many. While Newton's observed law of gravitation is only a repetition of the original Creation, any localized interpretation of it will record that the path of the return cannot have repeated the path of the original dispersal. Ingress does not repeat egress. Repetition, then, involves certain deviations, a certain randomness and redundancy. To steal, retell, quote, translate, amend, retouch —in effect, to imitate Thoth, to write—all manifest a kind of secondary Volition, a secondary creation, in which the smaller and belated force, the secondary, becomes primary, if in name only.

I am tempted here to conclude with a broad generalization, but not a law. Poe's deconstruction of the genealogical fable, his particular reinscription of the family romance as a reverse model of the myth of origins, of creation, is a fable of the origins of American literature—an attempt at a fabulous displacement. He foresaw what de Tocqueville was to describe in more dispassionate prose—the paradoxical situation of the writer in a democracy who had not only to confront his belatedness but to recognize that if all minds were equal, then out of non-identity would come nothing unique, nothing new. Poe needed to conserve the last iota of a self, a volition, and not simply the self as outsider, as the negative. But the language he was given, the language of oppositions, of the either/or, was all he had. The American had to begin somewhere. Why not, as Pound wrote decades later, not "indulge the American habit of quotation"?

INDEX